The Mastery of Reason

P9-BJA-399

Critical Psychology

Series editors

John Broughton
Columbia University

David Ingleby
Vakgroep Ontwikkeling en Socialisatie, Utrecht

Valerie Walkerdine
Birmingham Polytechnic

Since the 1960s there has been widespread disaffection with traditional approaches in psychology, and talk of a 'crisis' has been endemic. At the same time, psychology has encountered influential contemporary movements such as feminism, neo-marxism, post-structuralism, and post-modernism. In this climate, various forms of 'critical psychology' have developed vigorously.

Unfortunately, such work — drawing as it does on unfamiliar intellectual traditions — is often difficult to assimilate. The aim of the Critical Psychology series is to make this exciting new body of work readily accessible to students and teachers of psychology, as well as presenting the more psychological aspects of this work to a wider social scientific audience. Specially commissioned works from leading critical writers will demonstrate the relevance of their new approaches to a wide range of current social issues.

Titles in the series include

The Crisis in Modern Social Psychology
Ian Parker

The Psychology of the Female Body
Jane M. Ussher

Significant Differences: feminism in psychology
Corinne Squire

AUGUSTANA LIBRARY
UNIVERSITY OF ALBERTA

VALERIE WALKERDINE

The Mastery of Reason

COGNITIVE DEVELOPMENT AND THE PRODUCTION OF RATIONALITY

London and New York

First published 1988 by Routledge
Reprinted in paperback in 1990
by Routledge,
11 New Fetter Lane, London EC4P 4EE

Simultaneously published in the USA and Canada by Routledge
a division of Routledge, Chapman and Hall, Inc.
29 West 35th Street, New York, NY 10001

© 1988 Valerie Walkerdine

Printed and bound in Great Britain by
Mackays of Chatham PLC, Chatham, Kent

All rights reserved. No part of this book may be reprinted or
reproduced or utilized in any form or by any electronic, mechanical, or
other means, now known or hereafter invented, including photocopying
and recording, or in any information storage or retrieval system,
without permission in writing from the publishers.

British Library Cataloguing in Publication Data

Walkerdine, Valerie
   The mastery of reason: cognitive development and
   the production of rationality.
   1. Mathematical ability in children
   I. Title
   510'.1'9   BF723.M3/

Library of Congress Cataloging in Publication Data

Walkerdine, Valerie.
   The mastery of reason.

   Bibliography: p.
   Includes index.
   1. Mathematics – Study and teaching (Primary).
   2. Cognition in children. 3. Learning, Psychology of.
   4. Number concept in children. I. Title.
   QA135.5.W25   1987   372.7'2   87-34840
   ISBN 0-415-05233-5

Contents

Acknowledgements

The work described in this volume was carried out largely under the auspices of a Social Science Research Council Fellowship in Early Childhood Education and a grant from the Leverhulme Trust. I am extremely grateful both to the SSRC (now ESRC) and the Leverhulme Trust for their support for this and subsequent research. Professor Barbara Tizard of the Thomas Coram Research Unit also generously allowed me access to the recordings and transcripts from her study of thirty 4-year-old girls, without which this analysis would have been impossible. Graham Corran carried out a considerable amount of work in the infant school study and his ideas and fieldwork were extremely important. My colleagues in the Girls and Mathematics Unit have been important in helping develop these ideas and in offering unfailing support. I would particularly like to thank Helen Lucey, Diana Watson, and Rosie Walden.

Valerie Walkerdine, 1988

'Modern man likes to pretend that his thinking is wide-awake. But this wide-awake thinking has led us into the mazes of a nightmare in which the torture chambers are endlessly repeated in the mirrors of reason. When we emerge, perhaps we will realize that we have been dreaming with our eyes open, and that the dreams of reason are intolerable. And then, perhaps, we will begin to dream once more with our eyes closed.'

(Paz 1985: 199)

1 Introduction

In the last twelve years or so developmental psychologists have been concerned with 'the social' and its relation to the production in children of language and reasoning. The term 'context' has often been used to understand and explain the way in which children's thinking has a social dimension. In this book I shall be concerned with these issues. What I set out to demonstrate is a way in which we might approach the social production of language and thinking.

Perhaps the greatest body of work on the matter of children's thinking is the genetic epistemology of Jean Piaget. The task in the early to mid-1970s seemed to be how to graft 'context' onto the fundamental insights that Piaget offered. Empirically many hours were spent demonstrating that Piaget was wrong here or there, that children were faster, slower, cleverer, or whatever than he had suggested, that he neglected this, that, or the other. I shall not now rehearse the exhaustive list of such work. What I want to write about in this book is, rather, how a different account and theoretical framework might be possible to account for and interpret data on children's linguistic and cognitive development.

While British developmental psychology struggled with 'context' in the mid-1970s, European social theory was taking a different turn. In the wake of the events of May 1968 much work had gone into developing theories of ideology and subjectivity which extended and critiqued basic Marxist notions of ideology. Why should this be relevant for developmental psychology? Piaget's work is part of a 'realism' which treats the material world as knowable. Marx's classic theory of ideology, too, treated the material world as knowable, but as distorted, seen as in a 'camera obscura' because of the effects of ideology, or through a 'false consciousness'. Piaget, like Marx, built upon a scientific realism, linking back to the rise of science from the seventeenth century and to the nineteenth-century work of Darwin.

What later work began to question was the relation of the material to the social – was the latter simply a layer distorting, or was it productive, in Louis Althusser's (1971) terms, 'relatively autonomous', it could be scrutinized as productive in its own right. Thus, complex and detailed analyses of 'representations', of cultural and ideological practices, of the media, of texts, began to be produced. This is important in several ways.

This work drew upon psychoanalysis, linguistics, and semiotics to examine how texts and cultural and ideological practices operated. Ultimately it depended on the formative linguistics of Saussure (1974) but with, as we shall see, many important modifications.

Saussure took for granted that people must engage in the production of signs. His interest was, of course, not to analyse this process, but theoretically to formulate the object of linguistics as part of an envisaged science of signs in general. Accordingly, he consigned investigation of the process to the province of the psychologist, even though many of his explanations of linguistic phenomena rely upon assertions about psychology. Saussure's work has left its mark on the whole of semiotics and much of linguistics. But the fundamental problems which might have been posed by his remarks on the psychological aspects of the sign have not been addressed directly, at least not by developmental psychology. Those in the field of language acquisition have tended to devote their interest to the investigation of the linguistic sign system: to the acquisition of grammar or semantics, while the semiologists for their purposes have taken for granted that a sign system can be 'read' and that people's facility to do this can be assumed. For Saussure the sign is constituted by the unifying of the signifier and the signified. This is commonly presented schematically as a 'fraction':

$$\frac{\text{signified}}{\text{signifier}}$$

Or more specifically, and in relation to phonological signifiers:

$$\frac{\text{concept}}{\text{sound image}}$$

Saussure is credited with recognizing the importance of the fact that the relationship between the signifier and the signified is arbitrary; that is to say, conventional rather than necessary. If this is so, what unites the signifier and the signified to produce the sign? And what guarantees that they will be united to produce the sign? And what guarantees that they will be united to produce signs in accordance with convention? To answer the last question Saussure invoked the 'collective mind'. For the first he assumed that in the production of the sign the signifier and the signified were united by a simple association in the mind:

> Both terms involved in the linguistic sign are psychological and are united in the brain by an associative bond.
>
> (Saussure 1974:75)

Saussure was writing seventy years ago, but we may presume that in our time none of these questions has been satisfactorily answered. Yet the questions, in essence, remain and may be fruitful for developmental psychology. For example, how do children come to read the myriad of arbitrary signifiers – the words, gestures, objects, etc. – with which they are surrounded, such that their arbitrariness is banished and they appear to have that meaning which is conventional?

Posing the question in this way potentially avoids the dichotomizing 'cognition' and the 'social context'. Rather than constituting cognition and context as two phenomena, the relations between which must be analysed, even if they are not conceived of, discretely, it becomes in principle possible to ask how what is described as 'thought' is constituted in terms of and in relation to a system of signs, which by definition are social.

Piaget's formative influence upon developmental psychology may have pre-empted the raising of this question in relation to intellectual development. His reading of Saussure – and Pierce – in his presentation of the semiotic function rules the question out of court. For Piaget the relationship of signifier to signified is one of representation; the semiotic function:

> consists in the ability to represent something (a signified something: object, event, conceptual scheme, etc.) by means of a signifier which is differentiated and which serves only a representative purpose.
>
> (Piaget, quoted in Gruber and Voneche 1977:489)

Although this view grants to the semiotic function a major role in raising thought to a representational level, it sees the signified as arising extra-discursively, from the general co-ordination of actions which form operational structures which themselves arise outside of any relationship to systems of signs. Within this view it must, for example, be the case that mathematical signifiers (e.g. 1, 2, 3 . . ., +, −, etc.) represent schemata (signifieds) whose origin lies *not* in the subject's relation to a system of signs as a social phenomenon, *but* ultimately in the coordination of actions whose function is successively to equilibrate the subject (as a biological entity) and its environment. The picture is clouded by Piaget's idiosyncratic use of semiotic terms. For example, he gives the name 'sign' to what Saussure would call an unmotivated signifier:

> Broadly speaking, the semiotic function gives rise to two kinds of instruments: *symbols*, which are 'motivated' – that is, although they are differentiated signifiers, they do present some resemblance to the things signified; and signs, which are arbitrary or conventional.
>
> (Piaget, quoted in Gruber and Voneche 1977:492)

It is clear, at least, that although Piaget shares Saussure's terminology, he does not share his ideas.

The problematic relation of *signifier* and *signified* to produce a sign is central; that is, if sign systems are social phenomena, might their systematic nature be 'relatively autonomous' from the objects they are taken to represent? Within European Marxism this questioning led to a split in the kinds of work being undertaken – that analysing sign *systems* (texts, media, etc.) and that working on more classic approaches to the 'people's experience' (see, for example, Samuel 1983). Is everything after all ideology? Are we only in the realm of the signifier or is there a determining materiality? It has been amply asserted that the post-modern era is one in which 'reality' ever eludes us, in which 'real objects' which never exist can be created in all their perfect detail on the screen of a computer.

The French psychoanalyst, Jacques Lacan, asserted the primacy of the signifier over the signified, transposing Saussure's fraction. Others (for example Hirst 1976) argued that since we could not know the material world except through discourse then it was the arena of the discursive which was to be studied. All of this suggests important ways in which we might utilize such insights to go beyond the initial formulations of Piaget and the attempts to graft on context.

But there is more. This introduction glosses over a whole other body of work and developments from the 1970s. The aim here is simply to introduce the kinds of concepts which will be utilized in the analysis of the empirical work. This is not intended to be a theoretical presentation. The latter is contained elsewhere (for example, Adlam *et al.* 1977; Henriques *et al.* 1984). However, it is important to mention post-structuralism, particularly the work of Michel Foucault, as his insights are evident in the kind of analysis which I attempt.

To introduce this, let me return to Piaget. His work developed in the context of evolutionary biology and a concept of nature which presents an object world as an environment to which the organism successively adapts itself. Piaget was deeply politically committed to the eradication of war and, like many of his contemporaries, found in the popularization of Darwinism a determinism about the inevitability of war, of competition, which he abhorred. His project concerned the possibility of the triumph of reason over emotion through stressing the naturally adaptive processes of organisms; Piaget felt that the animal passions would be left behind to found a better world in reason. This view was shared by many liberal and progressive thinkers who envisaged the possibility of a rational and democratic society, operating upon free will and reason. The stress on natural reasoning and its importance today must be understood in those terms.

Piaget founded his work on the idea of a set of universal, basic structures. Others, like Saussure and Lévi-Strauss, also used structural notions. The 1970s work on ideology, particularly that utilizing the work of Althusser and Lacan, was structuralist too. The post-structuralist work of Foucault allows us to engage with the production of sign systems, but not as universal, trans-historical systems, but as specific historically generated bodies of knowledge. Not only that, but modern scientific accounts, like Piaget's, can be understood as implicated in the production of our modern form of government – the democratic government of reason. Foucault goes beyond the idea of ideologies as relatively autonomous, as sign systems, to discourses which produce a truth, which claim to be an account of 'the real'. Thus the remnants of the idea of a potentially truthful science and a distorting ideology, still present in Althusser, are moved beyond in Foucault. For me, the importance of this work lies in the way in which actual social practices may be discursively regulated by the production of 'truths', 'knowledges' about children, for example, which claim to tell the truth about child development. These produce the possibility of certain behaviours and then read them back as 'true', creating a normalizing vision of the 'natural child'. Here, the sense of materiality is vital, but it is never comprehensible outside bodies of knowledge, which claim to tell a truth. For Foucault this 'truth' is powerful because it is precisely what regulates citizens in the democratic order. The scientific truth about children's reasoning has become a very powerful tool indeed in pedagogic practices, especially in early education. By producing 'natural reason', it is felt that the government by reason, of reasonable people, is assured. But if the 'natural reasoning' is itself a 'reading', a 'truth' produced in the regulation of actual children, the place of Piaget's vision, his work, and the take-up of his ideas, take on a quite different complexion (Walkerdine 1984, 1986a; Walkerdine and Lucey, in press).

In calling this book *The Mastery of Reason*, I am questioning the confident assurance of mastery over the physical world, the idea of independent autonomy, of rational government, and all that goes with it. I have chosen to examine children's reasoning by focusing upon the production of pre-school and early school mathematics. For Piaget, and for many in early education, mathematics *is* reasoning. Logico-mathematical structures are the structures of rational thought. To develop 'mathematical concepts' in children carries the supreme task of creating reasoners and all that that entails. By focusing on mathematics, then, I am able to prise apart both the current psychological and pedagogic 'truths' about children's learning and to suggest other possible 'readings'. I will argue that mastery is a fiction shakily and scarcely achieved, and then only at great cost. The easy assertion of the government of reason covers over both its sociality and the unconscious lurking beneath.

Mathematics as reason

> Professor Whitehead said 'Every child should experience the joy of discovery'. We can say, with complete assurance, every teacher who embarks on a programme which will enable children to make their own discoveries will share to the utmost their children's enjoyment of mathematics and their increasing confidence in their powers.
>
> (Schools Council 1965:124)

Joy in discovery, pleasure in order; not pleasure in other less rational matters, but love and pleasure in ideas. The rational dream sought to produce children who would become adults without perverse pleasures. These are the hopes invested in the power of reason and in mathematics teaching.

Current practices of mathematics education depend heavily on their inscription in the wider body of discursive practices which can be described as child-centred. I began the basis of a genealogy of child-centred practices in an earlier publication (Walkerdine 1984), to which the reader is referred for more detail. Central to my analysis was the examination of a shift in practices from an overt form of regulation of the population to a covert form. That is, at the end of the nineteenth century it was overt and obvious surveillance which was felt important to produce correct 'habits' and thus a population freed from criminality and pauperism, the twin problems in the social body. These became surmounted by a new set of practices which counterposed covert to overt regulation. The new practices were premised upon a set of discourses concerning the 'nature of children'. Although the centrepoint of such discourses was the pro-duction of a 'freedom' premised upon enabling the possibility of a natural sequence of development, I attempted to demonstrate that such practices themselves produced the regulation of what natural child development meant, that is, they created a regime of truth within which readings were made and therefore what counted as correct was both made possible and validated. This took place within a specific set of historical conditions when the concern about producing a self-regulated citizen was paramount within the tech-nologies and apparatuses which made up the practices of government and administration (Walkerdine 1986a; Foucault 1979b). I shall not elaborate on that here. Rather, I want to examine child-centredness as it was established within mathematics education and the regulative practices which were therefore established, and how certain figures, namely 'the child', and certain steps, such as 'stages of cognitive development', figured as signs within the relations of the regulation of the practices themselves.

An overview of changes in mathematics education since the late 1950s, of the aims of the changes and how far these aims have been realized, has been provided by Howson (1978). Like most com-mentators, Howson sees the Mathematical Association's Report, *The Teaching of Mathematics in Primary Schools*, published in 1956, as a catalyst in initiating far-reaching changes in early mathematics edu-cation. He says:

> It was a remarkable forward-looking document which expressed
> very clearly the point of view which was to dominate national
> thinking on primary education during the next twenty years.
>
> (1956:24)

This point of view is encapsulated in this often quoted extract from the Report:

Children, developing at their own individual rates learn through
their active response to the experiences that come to them; through
constructive play, experiment and discussion children become
aware of relationships and develop mental structures which are
mathematical in form and are in fact the only sound basis of
mathematical techniques. The aim of primary teaching, it is
argued, is the laying of this foundation of mathematical thinking
about the numerical and spatial aspects of the objects and activities
which children of this age encounter.

(1956:v, vi)

As a guiding principle in mathematics education this view was
quite new. Indeed, it represented a complete change of emphasis
from the original intentions of a committee which would have produced a report in the 1940s had not the Second World War inter-
vened. That committee would have drawn up a curriculum and
specified which mathematics should be taught to children of different ages. Instead, the Report which finally emerged advocated
treating children as individuals, guiding their responses to everyday
experiences and constructive play, and fostering the development of
appropriate mental structures.

In primary education as a whole, however, this view was not
entirely novel. Many of the ideas it expresses, particularly the notion
that children learn best through activity and experience, had been
developed and put into practice in the so-called 'progressive' schools
which had been established, mainly in the private sector of education, between the two World Wars. Other areas of the curriculum
were already treated as 'activities' and the Mathematical Association's Report should be seen in the context of a more general incorporation into the state educational sector of many of the ideas which
had been developed earlier by the 'progressive' movement.

The Report evoked a good deal of national interest and, following
its publication, considerable efforts were made to ensure that its
message was heard. Various methods were used and had the effect of
disseminating the Report's recommendations and encouraging the
teaching profession to put them into practice. A most notable advo-
cate was Miss Edith Biggs, an HMI who directed numerous courses
for teachers, and produced the first Schools Council Curriculum
Bulletin, *Mathematics in Primary Schools* (1965). The provision of
new materials and in-service training for teachers on a large scale was

undertaken by the Nuffield Mathematics Project, through the production of a multitude of teachers' guides, and the setting up of courses at what have now become local authority teachers' centres. The Nuffield project limited itself to the provision of ideas for practice which the teacher developed and modified for her own classroom use. The curriculum scheme, *Mathematics for Schools*, later developed by Harold Fletcher and produced on a commercial basis, provided not only teachers' guides but also a series of graded workbooks for classroom use. These are only two of numerous books published directed at teachers of young children. Not all these schemes, projects, and publications were formally tied to the Mathematical Association's Report, but they followed from it historically and all embodied its spirit: they shared what Howson called its 'forward-looking point of view'.

I shall argue that the 'truth' about children's 'mathematical development' is produced in classrooms, and that all learning can be understood as taking place within social practices in which the relation between signifier and signified is constantly problematic.

The analysis opens, in Chapter 2, with an examination of the production of certain 'mathematical' relational terms in spontaneous speech data, recorded in the homes of young children. It attempts to move away from the idea of 'universals' of semantic development, towards a view of meanings generated in the regulation of practices. Chapter 3 goes on to explore the production of 'size' and 'family' terms in classrooms and in an experiment, analysing both in relation to discursive practices. Chapter 4 explores these issues further by examining their production in home practices. Chapter 5 examines out-of-school practices in which so-called 'mathematical signifiers' are produced, but argues that these are not the same signs as those in school mathematics. The analysis is extended in Chapter 6, where the transformation of non-mathematical into mathematical discourse is explored. In Chapter 7 more home and classroom examples are analysed to demonstrate the problems with notions of 'experience' and simple transfer from one context to another. The achievement of reasoned mastery is explored in Chapter 8. Chapter 9 explores further the idea of that mastery as both pleasurable and as suppressive, while some further, concluding points are drawn together in Chapter 10.

2 Relational terms in everyday social practices: more or less reconsidered

Introduction

Terms such as 'same' and 'different', 'more' and 'less', are considered a central part of children's acquisition of a 'mathematical' lexicon. Classically, from the 1970s, studies of semantic development in children utilized notions of universals, derived from the work of Bierwisch (1970) who argued that 'all semantic structures might finally be reduced to components representing the basic dispositions of the cognitive and perceptual structure of the human organism' (181–2). Bierswisch's version of structuralism owes more to Chomsky than Piaget, but his work was extremely influential in the approach to semantic development. Based on a notion of 'primitives', the theory proposed a feature-approach, which understood the lexicon as composed of a tree-branching structure, such that words containing fewer features were considered more 'primitive' and therefore acquired first by children. This led to a rigid hierarchy of acquisition when it came to the 'mathematical' terms, so it was assumed that the perceptual and semantic primitives of a pair would be acquired first, for example 'more' before 'less', 'same' before 'different'. Furthermore, Eve Clark (1973) proposed that children would 'over-extend' the meaning 'less' as though it meant 'more'. Clearly the implications of this work for mathematics learning were, taken together with work on cognition, that children would have trouble with some mathematical concepts and not others, and that the acquisition of word meanings was a universal phenomenon, ultimately relying upon perception.

From that time much of the work, including my own (Walkerdine 1975), used the idea of 'context' to demonstrate the specificity of children's comprehension and production of word-meanings. But, as I have remarked in Chapter 1, this move, important as it was, was not enough to counter the universalism of the theory which underlay the work, because it maintained the individual/social dualism. In this chapter I shall examine more recent empirical work on the 'mathematical' signifiers and go on to argue for an understanding of the production of meaning in discursive practices, based on an analysis of two sets of recordings of spontaneous speech.

The discussion will relate to more recent contributions to that debate around the terms *same/different* and *more/less* (Estes 1976; Glucksberg, Hay, and Danks 1976; Grieve, Hoogenrad, and Murray 1977; Holland and Palermo 1975; Karmiloff-Smith 1977; Kavanaugh 1976; Trehub and Abramovitch 1978). I shall also consider Sinha and Carabine's (1980) study which replicated and extended work on the mastery of conservation of discontinuous quantities and the interpretation of the terms *lot* and *little* begun by Sinha and Walkerdine (1978) and Walkerdine (1975). In their discussion of the results of their experiments on variants of the lot/little test (Sinha and Walkerdine) and the more/less experiments (Donaldson and Wales 1970), Sinha and Carabine remark:

> The child's perception of the task demands is determined by extremely complex and sensitive rules for relating words to particular aspects of the situation within an overall social and communicative context: the rules for governing reference in this context are not *specific* to particular lexical items, but the likelihood of one complex of rules being selected or activated rather than another is modulated by lexical choice, and that some lexical items are more strongly associated with or integrated into particular rule complexes than others.
>
> (Sinha and Carabine 1980:125–6)

I want to explore further the notion of 'rules for relating words to particular aspects of the situation'. The argument to be developed is that reference is not a universal, but rather an aspect of the regulation of social practices which form the daily life of young children.

It is now well known that the phenomenon loosely described as 'context' is important to the comprehension and production of lexical items and to children's solution of cognitive tasks. Many experimental studies have shown that minimal changes in procedure can make huge changes in performance. However, experimental studies, while they are an important source of data on the controlled study of shifts in task-demand, reveal relatively little about how non-experimental contexts operate.

That context is not simply a 'given', background feature, but is actually constructed and created is well documented by studies of mother–infant communication, particularly those dealing with 'Motherese' (Snow 1977; Lieven 1978; Howe 1981, for example). Although several studies of early communication have tended to understand meaning as created inter-subjectively (Bruner 1975; Lock 1978), in producing the meaningful context, the participants themselves do not operate in a social vacuum. Communication takes place within and about those everyday practices which make up family life (feeding, playing, shopping, bedtime, and so on). By examining how reference is not a fixed attribute of a lexical item, or a fixed mode, or representing a particular action-pattern, we can begin to explore how that reference might relate to the regulation of specific relations in specific practices, thus helping to understand what it means to say that context is created. Since it is social practices which are the focus, we would expect the relation between lexical item and practice to be related to how particular actions form part of a relational dynamic within practices themselves. These relational dynamics are not created inter-subjectively in any simple sense, but are produced in relation to aspects of social practices which are culturally and historically specific. Thus it is argued that conversations are not simply organized on the basis of turn-taking, for example, but also on the basis of the particular relationship between the participants: who is in a position, allowed, and permitted to say what to whom and with what effects. In addition, it will be argued later that such relationships are also strongly emotive and that the concept of the unconscious is necessary to understand that dynamic. Generalizations about children's comprehension or not of lexical items as though it were a phenomenon *tout court* is not necessarily justified. If reference is variable then comprehension itself varies and is not an all-or-nothing phenomenon.

In their conclusion, Sinha and Carabine suggested that the relation of children's lexical comprehension to their success in conservation-type tests should be understood in terms of the insertion of a variety of lexical terms into particular discourse formats which are produced as the frameworks of everyday practices. To take that assumption further requires the analysis of the spontaneous comprehension and production of relational terms in relation to the practices in which they are produced. In what practical problems do relational terms arise? How are the practical and material relations under discussion in the situation understood and what is the relation between them? The attempt to answer these questions draws on an analysis of spontaneous speech data from two sources. The first source is a corpus of mother–daughter conversations, each lasting approximately two hours, of fifteen middle-class and fifteen working-class girls, with an average age of 3.9. These data were collected by Barbara Tizard at the Thomas Coram Research Unit for the project, *Language at Home and at School*, to which she has kindly allowed me access. The second source of data is a corpus of recordings collected by the author of six pre-school children, three girls and three boys, aged between 2.5 and 3.5, in their own homes. Each extract from the Tizard corpus is identified by a code referring to the transcript name, page, and line number.

Previous studies

In the recent studies of children's comprehension of the relational terms *more/less* and *same/different* (mentioned above), the original studies demonstrating that children over-extend the meaning of *more* to include *less* and *same* to include *different*, and that children respond to *less* and *different* items as though they were *more* and *same* items, have been both generally replicated and qualified. It has been suggested that the responses are to some extent an artefact of the experimental presentation, and indeed, Sinha and Carabine took this interpretation further when they demonstrated that children responded correctly to *more* and *less* when they were given additional cues to reinforce their judgement. They replicated the Sinha and Walkerdine (1978) *lot* and *little* test and produced evidence to suggest that children could successfully respond to a task of conservation of inequality which involved giving a small dog 'a little to drink' and a big horse 'a lot to drink', even when the drinks were transferred to beakers which produced perceptually incongruous data. Three-year-old children were successful at this task as well as a variant which used *more* and *less*; however, at four years children's performance declined. Successful conversation was achieved with this age group when the drinks were colour-coded to match the animals. These results, taken together with the doubts cast by other studies, suggest the importance of looking to the practical contexts of the presentation of such tasks to children. It is usually assumed that if children appear to treat marked terms as though they were unmarked ones their comprehension is at fault, and that, if those terms are included in cognitive tasks, their thought has not achieved the requisite stage of development. I have argued elsewhere (Walkerdine 1982, 1984) that in examining practices it is unnecessary to invest children with capacities or abilities which unfold. Rather, an examination of the relations involved in the practices themselves provides points for understanding the creation of subjectivity.

What the above studies suggest is the necessity of looking more carefully at the way in which material, practical, and linguistic relations are produced. Grieve, Hoogenrad, and Murray (1977), in attempting to explain their data (which supported data from other studies) that the term *under* was more difficult than *on* and *in*, discussed the *under* items on which errors were made. These were relationships such as *table under chair/cup, bath under baby*. They conclude that errors on these items could not be the result of any failure to understand the term *under per se*, because the same children did not make errors on other *under* items: *chair/cup under table, baby under bath*. They conclude that, in order to understand these data it is necessary to assume that children's comprehension of such terms 'does not arise simply from the physical characteristics of the objects, or from the child's knowledge of the customary relationships of objects. Rather we must look to an interaction between such factors and the way the objects concerned are referred to in the instructions' (p. 147). They are therefore making a point of departure from the simply perceptual or simply functional approaches of earlier explanations. If we take a closer look at those *under* items which the children found difficult, it is noticeable that they refer to relationships between objects which are a commonplace part of the everyday social practices in which children are brought up. Cups certainly relate to tables and chairs, as do babies to baths. However, what is important, and Grieve, Hoogenrad, and Murray stress this, is the way in which those objects relate and *those relationships are talked about in everyday practices*. Although the physical relation is likely to be spoken: babies are commonly spoken as being *in* baths. Similarly with the relation of cups and tables: we would normally speak of the cup as being *on* the table to mark that *same material relation*. Thus the children must learn such relational terms as part of appropriate social practices, in which similar material relations are linguistically marked in a variety of different ways, depending not only on the functional relationship of the objects, but also the practices on which those objects are inserted at any one moment.

It is not so surprising, therefore, that the children did not so readily make errors on such items as *baby under bath*. Since the practical relations would signify as *baby in bath* the children are less likely to be confused as in items in which a familiar relationship is called up by the relational term, such as *table under chair* in which the relation of chairs going under tables is likely to be most salient. Where the relational term does not call up a familiar practical relation, then, there may be less likely to be so much confusion, and the children may indeed find such items amusing, or at any rate little connected with everyday practices.

Sinha (1980:13) argued that language comprehension and production should be seen as 'processes of production oriented to the encoding of messages-in-context'. In a similar vein, Cole and others at the Laboratory for Comparative Human Cognition (Cole 1981; LCHC 1980) have argued for the specific relation of cognitive skills to actual social practices, arguing against a 'central processor model', such as that used in both language and cognitive development in favour of an account which understands learning as specific to the practices in which it is produced. They suggest that the transfer of cognitive and linguistic operations across contexts is not as frequent as the literature in general would lead one to believe.

I argued earlier that an examination of the mode in which certain material relations are made to signify in discourse as part of particular social practices might throw a light on children's response patterns in the kind of experimental approaches discussed above. How are relational terms habitually presented to young children: as part of which practices and how are particular material relations presented? The focus will be on the terms *same/different, more/less*, but other terms which relate to size and quantity relations will also be examined. With reference to the spontaneous utterances contained in the corpuses described earlier, both the frequency of production by parent and child of the terms will be explored. I will discuss the way in which those terms are used and the relationship of one term to another.

If we examine how the relationship between object, action, and word is produced as a relation within any particular practice, it might be possible to explore children's acquisition of such relations of signification in terms of their own insertion into a relational dynamic within the practice itself. I use the term 'relations of signification' to attempt to understand the phenomenon of word/object/action, not as a relation of representation of an object by a word, a signified by a signifier, but as a complex, a relation of signification within a practice itself. If a word does not simply represent physical relation, but rather provides the basis whereby any particular physical relation is inscribed as a relation within the organization of a practice, then we are not justified in speaking simply of 'representation'. If children only learn such relations through their own insertion into a relational dynamic within such practices, we can argue that they become a subject as, and in, those relations. Such relations are multiple. How far, then, is this the same as talking of the acquisition of concepts or of meanings as though it were a function of an object world, a physical world, a physical environment, or a structure or process *applied* to the social world. Previously, I have used the term 'always-already social' (Henriques *et al.* 1984) to imply that there is no physical relation for any infant which is not always and already a social relation.

Size and quantity relations

Table 2.1 below gives the terms used to denote size relations in the Tizard corpus, together with their frequency of occurrence. The terms were coded once only if they occurred several times within the same exchange and were also coded according to whether the term was introduced into the exchange by mother or child.

Although *big* and *little* predominate there is a wide variety of terms which are used to denote the same or similar relations. The terms are almost always used relationally, that is, they are used to make comparisons as in *big flies*, for example. It is not the case that only those objects which have high quantitative measure are called *big* or vice versa. If we compare the frequency of particular contrastive pairs we can see that some pairs appear in both marked and unmarked forms, but others do not. Taking the *big/little* pair, it becomes clear that there is a problem in deciding what to count as the polar opposite of *big*, since, although *little* is the most frequent, *small, tiny, weeny* would also count. Indeed, if we add together the frequencies for these terms they come to 41 mother and 27 child utterances: more than for the unmarked term, *big*. We can assert that at the age of 3.9 children can easily comprehend and produce these relational terms and that there is no basis here for concluding that the marked term is more difficult than the unmarked.

The comparison of *tall* and *short* is also interesting. While *tall* appears, *short* does not but *shorter* does, as well as *as tall as*. An examination of the utterances themselves will help to reveal why. *Tall* is used to refer to the height of the children as in:

c: Look, nearly reach up there. Watch mamma. Nearly reach up – I've reached.
m: You're very tall now, aren't you.

(RP21)

In the extract on p. 18, *shorter* is used contrastively, not with *taller*, but with *bigger*. Here, the size being spoken of is the child's, as is most

Table 2.1 *Size and quantity relations*

Term	Frequency: mother	Frequency: child
Big	30	13
Bigger	8	9
Biggest	1	1
Bit big	3	2
Very big	1	2
As big as	1	
Not big enough		1
Not big	1	
Bit bigger	1	
Too big	4	1
Little	25	18
Littlest		1
Small	9	3
Smaller	3	1
Bit small		2
Too small	5	1
Tiny	7	5
Teeniest		1
Weeny		1
Long	1	2
Longer		1
Too long	3	
Bit shorter	1	
Much shorter	1	
Tall	1	
Thin	1	
Large	1	
Heavy	3	6
Too heavy	1	
Same size	2	
Right size	1	
Your size	1	
Enough for you	1	1

Note:
lot and *a lot* are contained in a separate analysis.

usually the case, but the same relations of child size are represented using *big* and *small/little* as well as *short* and *tall*. *Big* and *small/little* also have the advantage of being multi-dimensional and in the context do more work than the more specific terms. That is, they signify increased age, and overall growth, as in the terms *big girl/little boy*. Thus their signification is multiple – they are polysemic – and this multiplicity and ambiguity is often deliberately evoked:

c: Mummy, I shall grow up before Anna won't I?
m: Not much darling, she's about the same age as you.
c: Oh, 'cos I'm bigger than her.
m: Yes, but Anna will probably always be a bit shorter than you, 'cos Anna's Mummy and Daddy are much shorter than Mummy and Daddy, so Anna will probably never be as tall as you even when she's grown up.
c: Why?
m: It doesn't mean to say she won't be as grown up as you, she just won't be as tall as you.

(ED4)

Tall therefore appears only to be used when height and not overall size/age needs to be invoked, as in the example of reaching a shelf above. The point is that the same or similar material relationships are represented differently with different relational terms. The relation of the lexical item, practical purpose, and material relation is clearly important. It is also possible to speculate why *short* does not appear in these transcripts. We have seen that height is referred to in a variety of ways and that *tall* is used only in specific circumstances. In each case the height being referred to is that of the child or other children. Because, for children, the salient characteristic is that they grow *taller*, it is unlikely that they would be referred to as *short*, it would be more likely to be *not tall enough* or some such phrase. It is equally possible, of course, that in other contexts with other topics *short* may be appropriate and would be used. In relation to time, for example, the term *short* does appear, in which case its polar opposite is *long*. It appears that the terms do not have *fixed* opposites: they change and shift depending on the domain of practice which is the field of reference. In the following example *long* and *short* are used contrastively:

(m *and* c *are talking about going on a cross-channel ferry.*)
m: Well, we're only going to be on the um, in the boat for quite a short time.

c: But it's quite a long way.

m: It's not very far really to go from here to France.

(KSB18)

Notice that, in this example, *long* is also used to refer to distance, and the child appears to have no difficulty in understanding that the same terms can operate differently in different discursive practices.

Taking another example from Table 2.1, the term *heavy* is used by adults and children, though *light* does not appear once. We might be led to conclude, therefore, that *light* is a marked term which is more difficult because it contains more semantic features and is therefore conceptually more difficult for children. However, if we pause again to examine the practices in which it is used it seems that the term *light* is simply not relevant or appropriate. Every single utterance refers to objects which are *heavy* for the child to carry: it is that heaviness and the child's lack of strength, being small, which merits attention; but in these instances lightness is not an appropriate feature unless child or adult were to remark that something was lighter than expected. For children, however, most things are too heavy rather than light. Again, the relation of being able to carry something is likely to be linguistically marked in terms of 'being able to carry' something, rather than re-marking on the lightness of an object. For here the comparison is *not* between *heavy* and *light* in an absolute and quantitative sense, as in school mathematical discourse, but between what children can and cannot carry; in other words the comparison is between the object's weight and the child's strength.

Lot and little, more and less

When Sinha and Carabine (1980) replicated Sinha and Walkerdine's (1978) conservation of inequality task, described as the *lot/little* test, they found the same response patterns as those in the earlier experiment. However, they were able to produce equal performance with the terms *more/less* when they colour-coded the drinks to match the colours of the toy animals used in the test. In a post-experimental comprehension test of the pairs of relational terms, though, children still produced more correct responses to the *lot/little* pair than the *more/less* pair.

Clearly, these results do not support a simple version of a semantic features or non-linguistic rules hypothesis. In order to examine further how the relational terms are produced within actual social practices, the Tizard corpus was examined for instances of utterances using the terms *more, less, lot,* and *little.* We have already observed that the term *little* is in very common usage with respect to size relations. It is also used contrastively to refer to quantity. I have included for analysis all those utterances in which either of the terms *lot* or *little* is used contrastively to refer to quantity. These are recorded in Table 2.2.

Table 2.2   *Lot and little in spontaneous speech*

Lot/little
M: Do you want some more dressing?
C: (*Nods*)
M: A little?
C: Yeah – *quite* a lot.
M: No, just a little.

(SN8)

C: Can you give me a little bit more butter?
M: Shall we try to get that bit out of the dip, because, look . . . there's really quite a lot in there that's got stuck you see . . . there's that bit round . . . there, it's really enough, isn't it?

(LB27)

M: You can't have too much rose-hip syrup.
C: Why?
M: Because rose-hip costs a lot of money.
C: Is Megan going to drink it all?
M: Megan only drinks a little weeny bit, as it lasts a long time, but if you drink it you drink it you drink about a whole bottle a day.

(MJ32)

Little bit/big bit
M: Just a little bit.
C: That's not a big bit.

(MS26)

M: I think I've eaten all my mushroom.
C: Here's a, there's a bit.
M: Oh there's a bit . . . there, you're right.
C: I've got a big bit.
M: I'll eat my little bit and you eat your big bit.

(JB21)

Table 2.2 *(Cont.)*

Lots/number
(M *has cut up an apple into pieces.*)
M: How many have you got there?
C: One, two, three.
M: Mm.
C: That isn't a lot is it?
M: Not really.
C: Well it is a bit.

(MJ13)

M: You've got lots of holes in your tights, Claire.
C: Where?
M: Three now. Where you fell over.
C: Oh.
M: Mm.
C: I got three.

(CW30)

M: You've got three pairs of jeans upstairs . . .
M: I got lots of pairs.
C: Have I?
M: What?
C: Got lots of jeans?
M: You've got three.
C: Hm.

(MJ13)

(M *and* C *are talking about a caterpillar.*)
M: They've got lots and lots of legs. Ever such a lot of legs.
C: (*Paints several legs: number unclear*) Is that a lot?
M: Yeah.

(MJ49)

There are also four instances of the use of *lots/a lot of* referring to discontinuous and continuous quantity:

> A lot of water.
> Lots of money.
> Lots of pennies.
> Lots and lots and lots of teddies.

In these exchanges *lot* and *little* are apparently used in the way in which they are articulated in the *lot/little* test. They are used to refer to amounts of food and drink to be consumed and centre around parents' attempts at portion control. In that sense the *lot/little* test taps precisely the same practice. However, other terms such as *a lot*, *a bit*, *a big/little bit* are also used as alternatives within the same practice. When discontinuous quantities are referred to, *lot* can be contrasted with a number, in which case the practice also opens up into an opportunity for pedagogy and signals the use of specifically pedagogic discourse (Walkerdine 1982; Corran and Walkerdine 1981). What is perhaps most important for the argument here is that *lot* and *little* do form a contrastive oppositional pair, used in relation to practices involving the *regulation of consumption* of food and drink. Turning now to *more* and *less*, it is possible to examine whether these terms articulate the same relation and are used in the same practices.

Table 2.3   *More and less in spontaneous speech*

Child initiated

c: I need some more mashed potato.
m: Only a little, Stephanie.

(SN2)

c: I need a little bit more cabbage.

(ED23)

c: Can you give me a little bit more butter?
m: Shall we try to get that bit out of the dip, because, look . . . there's really quite a lot in there that's got stuck you see . . . there's that bit round . . . there, it's really enough isn't it? . . . OK?

(LB27) (also included in Table 2.2)

c: Could you get some more knives out?
m: You can only use one at a time.
c: No! I need a few more.
m: What for?
c: A . . . 'cause we're all going to have dinner at the same time.
m: Oh, you can't have one, two, three . . . you can't have five because I don't think I've got five. You've got one already, haven't you? You can get four now.

(EG8–9)

Table 2.3 *(Cont.)*

c: What are you doing? Getting some do . . . some spoons out?
m: Only one.
c: Get a bit more spoons out!
m: A *bit* more?
c: Yeah.
m: A few more.
c: Yes.

(EG6)

c: I want some more.
m: No, you can't have any more, Em.
c: Yes! Only one biscuit.
m: No.
c: Half a biscuit?
m: No.
c: A little of a biscuit?
m: No.
c: A whole biscuit?
m: No.

(EG59)

c: I'm not going to eat any more.
m: Ahh, let's make a nice clean plate.
c: No, I won't.
m: Just two more mouthfuls, mm?

(RS5)

c: Is there any more empty jars?
m: No.
c: Let me see!
m: Oh, there's one . . . there aren't any more.

(SO'T)

c: Can I have some more Mummy? (*Vanilla essence to put in a cake.*)
m: No.
c: I need more. (*Milk.*)
m: Oh no you don't.

(JS3)

c: Who gave you that? (*Cleaning fluid for sink.*)
m: Granny gave me that little bit 'cause I ran out.

Table 2.3   *(Cont.)*

c: Has you still got some more?
m: Hm?
c: Have you still got some more?
m: Just enough for today and get some more tomorrow.

(TD10)

c: That's mine. I think I'd better have some more. (*Paper to draw on.*)
m: Some more what?
c: Paper.
m: You've got one there.
c: There's something on there.
m: There's one. It's only got little things on it. There's one with none on it.

(AC21)

Mother initiated

---

c: Am I allowed to have a cherry on it? (*Pudding.*)
m: I haven't got any more cherries. I've finished my cherries.

(RS6)

(*m and c are putting a canvas cover on a Wendy House frame.*)
m: Oh, you're pulling my side, give me some more.

(JO'K14)

(*c is making cakes: there is a small amount of mixture left.*)
m: That's better, now do one more.

(JS6)

(*m, c, and d are playing picture dominoes.*)
c: You've only got two (*cards*) left.
m: I know – well, you snatched all the cards and got more than anybody else.

(LA84)

(*c has made little cakes and some mixture remains.*)
m: I'll give you a few more. (*Cake cases.*)
c: Yes, give me a few more, those, those must be enough.

(SO'T)

(*m is making pastry.*)
m: No, I don't want any more flour.
c: Ooh! Have some of this bit. Have this bit.
m: Mm, I don't want any more, don't throw it.

(SO'T)

Table 2.3 *(Cont.)*

c: I can't roll it out enough.
m: Well, come on bring it over here a bit more.
   (m *pulls table out so* c *can get behind.*)

(SO'T)

(c *is making pies.*)
m: Only a little drop. (*Of water.*)
c: No, a big drop.
m: You're not to have a lot, Dawn.
c: Litt . . . a little bit heavy.
m: That is all, no more, absolutely no more.

(DH49)

m: Do you want me to make some holes? (*In a mask* c *is making.*)

(RP57)

m: After lunch I'm going to put some more paint on the outside of the doll's house.

(KSB8)

(m *and* c *are doing a number jigsaw.*)
m: Is there anything with five . . . anything with five things on there?
c: No.
m: They've all got more haven't they?
c: Mm, that. (*Finds one with six.*)
m: Well, count, I think there may be more.

(LA59)

What is immediately striking about these examples is that although they all contain *more*, *less* does not appear once. Since this corresponds with previous hypotheses about the complexity of *less*, are we therefore to assume that this provides more evidence in support of those hypotheses? There are several reasons why caution is advised before coming to that conclusion. First, the practices of which these examples form a part are of two kinds: there are examples from the regulation of food consumption, like those from *lot/little* in Table 2.2. The other kind is similarly part of regulative discourse in which a child's access to discontinuous quantities of objects is quite different from those of the original Donaldson and Wales (1970) task. In that task, the judgements were not made for an explicit practical purpose, but simply to test the children. While such instances of pedagogic discourse do exist in these and other home recordings (Corran and Walkerdine 1981), they do not refer to the judgement of relative quantity in these examples at least. Judgements of relative quantity are certainly made in terms of the regulation of amounts of food, but here the discussion centres around what does or does not constitute a lot of food. The dimension of *less* is simply not relevant and does not form part of that practice. The opposite of *more* in food regulative practices is something like *no more*, *not as much*, and so on. *More* and *less* only form a contrastive opposi-tional pair with respect to certain practices and these practices are pedagogic. Thus it is not surprising that young children find the *lot*/*little* test easier than *more*/*less*; it taps that relation within familiar practices: *more* and *less* does not.

Nor should it be surprising that children find *more*/*less* easier with colour-coding, since they have been provided with an extra mode of signification which suggests that the two tasks are the same. We might indeed be justified in concluding that children do not understand *less* as well as *more*, not because of any general linguistic or cognitive deficit but, rather, because *less* does not form part of the contrastive opposi-tions presented to the children or part of practices with which they are familiar: they are therefore not conversant with it. However, we cannot conclude that because they are less familiar with *less* that they are cognitively incapable of making judgements of relative quantities: those judgements clearly take place but as part of clear discursive practices using different relations of signification rather than *more*/*less*. We can predict that this is because quantity relations do not form the object of pedagogic practices, in these excerpts at least.

It is striking that almost all the examples of *more* from this corpus form part of practices where the regulation of consumption is the object. In every case initiated by the child, she either wants more precious commodities, of which the mother sees it her duty to limit consumption, or the child does not want to finish food which the mother sees it her duty to make the child eat. The differential position of the mother and child is made salient by the mother-initiated episodes in which the mother can stop the child giving her more, and can announce that she is going to do more of something. It is important that the child is not in that position. This, therefore, presents a relational dynamic or a position within the practices relating to power, rather than a simple view of turn-taking in those practices.

In terms of consumption within our culture it is *more* which is valued: that is what consumption is about. The discourse thus has to take the form of the regulation by the mother of the child's consumption of 'more'. In this sense we can certainly propose that in *this set of practices* (rather than in a universal set of linguistic contrasts) *more is the positive term*, though its value does not come from the internal relations of the linguistic system or a set of perceptual universals: it comes from the regulation of the social practices which make up our culture. Again, it must be emphasized that in these practices the opposite of *more* is not *less*: given the position of children (that is, that they are to be regulated) the rules of the practices are first of all to eat up the portion of food dished up and then to ask for a second helping. Because of their position, children are less likely to be allowed to say what an adult might: 'less than that please'. It is not that the term simply does not enter the practice, but that the children's position within that practice ensures that a position which is possible for an adult is not as open to them. Similarly with the consumption of commodities in other examples: it is the mother's task to ensure that not too much of valuable and expensive items is consumed; it does not matter, therefore, if children do not use very much. This means that again the term *less* is not likely to be an appropriate term within that practice.

Same and different

In the same vein, to understand the marking of similarity and difference it seems important to examine how those markings are produced within specific practices. In the Tizard corpus there are seventeen instances of the word *same*; only one refers to identity, the rest to equivalence. There are seven instances of *different*, all about equivalence. We might therefore, on first sight, be led to conclude that since *same* is more frequent than *different*, and equivalence than identity, the standard feature theory and conceptual approaches (i.e. equivalence being conceptually prior to identity) are validated. However, it will be argued that the reasons for these differences lie neither in the linguistic system *per se*, nor in the conceptual apparatus of the children, but concern the relative importance of the marking of similarity versus difference in the practices presented in the corpus, and therefore those practices most familiar to young children.

As with *more* and *less*, *same* and *different* are not always used as a contrastive pair. In seven instances, although similarity and difference are linguistically marked, difference is asserted using a dimensional term, depending on the dimension referred to, for example, *same* versus *bigger than, smaller than*. Similarly, *same* is also sometimes replaced by other terms such as mentioned in the previous section. In these cases, although *same* and *different* may not always be used as a contrastive pair, there is no reason to assume that children have any difficulty in understanding difference, at least in relation to equivalence and as a relation within these specific practices. However, in other examples, difference is not marked because it is difference that is expected and similarity is itself 'the difference which makes the difference' (Wilden 1980). Even here, *same* is not often used to mark the equivalence of cards, since the discourse of Snap dictates that the term 'Snap' be used. All the other examples conform to this pattern. That is, it is similarity which is unusual and therefore noted, the term *different* therefore not being relevant. Examples of these are as follows:

(M *and* C *are playing in a Wendy house: fantasy about a doll.*)
M: How old is this little baby?
C: Five. . . . Just had her birthday.
M: Has she?
C: Two months. Do you know when her birthday was?
M: No.
C: September 16th, that's when my birthday is.
M: Oh, on the same date is it?

(AL76)

C: I can see the word 'at' on my Fuzzy Felt.
M: Not quite. It's a 't', a 't' at the end of 'felt'. Haven't got a word like 'at' though have you?
C: Well, the last letter's the same.

(RS7)

Equally, where difference is expected rather than similarity it is the term *different* which appears alone:

(M *and* C *are playing Snap.*)
M: They're two pink ones but they're different.

(LA67')

(M *and* C *are playing a card game in a simple version, the more complex of which involves swapping cards.*)
M: You don't swap in this game.

c: You don't?
m: Take another card out.
c: Why do you swap it when you buy things?
m: That's different then.

(SO'T)

(m *and* c *are eating sausages;* c *has three ends of sausage left, while* m *doesn't.*)
m: They must be three ends of sausages I suppose.
c: And you haven't got any ends.
m: I cut mine differently.

(SO'T5)

What implications can be drawn from this analysis? I have argued that the very complexity and multiplicity of the connection between relational terms, actions, and objects suggest a more complex explanation than those currently put forward. The Semantic Features Hypothesis assumes a linguistic system in which meaning is created in relation to a set of universal features, and that complexity is established by a step-wise progression of features. Here we have perceptual universals and an object world. Although critiques of this approach stressed the importance of the social function of objects, the later works such as those of Grieve, Hoogenrad, and Murray (1977) and Sinha and Carabine (1980) stress the positioning of the objects within a regulated social world. It is in this respect that it is important to point to a set of problems in assuming that an object world exists. Yet those approaches stressing universals have continually focused upon human development as a matter of an individual interacting with her/his physical environment. Of course, the most notable exponent of this approach is Piaget, but it is considerably more ubiquitous than that. This has certain effects, as we shall see later, particularly with respect to schooling practices in which the metaphor 'environment' is used to reduce a classroom to a physical environment. Clearly, there have been attempts to move beyond such a position; and indeed, Vygotsky's work (1962; 1978) makes an important attempt to produce a social account, as does the work of the Russian linguist, Volosinov (1973).

However, Vygotsky's work, coming as it did in the wake of the Russian Revolution, stressed the role of language as *representation* of the material world. In that sense, following the classic Marxist work on ideology (*The German Ideology*), representation is seen as a true or distorted reflection of materiality or the real. The problem with such an approach to ideology is discussed elsewhere (Henriques *et al.* 1984, Section 2). More recent work in the field of ideology and semiotics has stressed the *productive* power of signification; that is, it is the very social production of relations of signification which provides the possibility of subjectivity. This distinction is crucial for a number of reasons.

If material phenomena are only encountered within their insertion into, and signified within, a practice, this articulation is not fixed and immutable, but slippery and mobile. That is, signifiers do not cover fixed 'meanings' any more than objects have only one set of physical properties or function. It is the very multiplicity which allows us to speak of a 'play' of signifier and signified, and of the production of different dynamic relations within different practices. It is for this reason that I used the terms 'signify' and 'produce' rather than represent. If social practices are points of creation of specific signs then semiotic activity is productive, not a distortion or reflection of a material reality elsewhere. Moreover such practices, and therefore such signs, are not fixed, but multiple. Different words do not have fixed meanings but enter as relations within the practices themselves. If such signifiers have multiple meanings, articulated within different, and sometimes contradictory, practices, might not the creation of subject-positions within them be multiple too? If we move away from a unitary relation, then can we not move from a unitary subject? The individual human being who interacts with an object world develops along a fixed path determined by 'nature'. In this view, language and the social come to build upon this singular path. But if there is no action which takes place outside the framework of social practices, and if the object world is only understood in terms of its meaningful insertion within particular discursive practices, then why should we assume a unique and singular developmental path, a unique and singular subject? Clearly, central to this analysis of the social is also a critique of the idea of a unified social domain (see Henriques *et al.* 1984, Section 2), suggesting that the social is not a fixed and singular totality, but a contradictory series of discursive practices. Thus a position such as that adopted by theories of 'social cognition', or by Donaldson (1978), for example, which graft the social as 'context' onto the edifice of development left intact, fails to engage fully with the implication of the point made here.

If signs are produced as the dynamic intersection of action, object, and word within a practice, and if the sign functions as a relation within the practice, signification is not reducible to representation, or to a singular developmental pathway. It follows that any conceptual apparatus is created within social practices, which themselves position the participants as relations. Since the practices are multiple, the sites for the creation of such relations are multiple and shifting. Thus subjectivity is multiple not singular and we should expect that the relation between different 'meanings' or relations within and between signifiers might have a particular effect for the subject who lives those relations. It is Jacques Lacan's (1977) use of semiotics which has crucially tapped this domain, as I shall examine later (see also, Corran and Walkerdine 1981; Urwin 1984).

However, with respect to the examples discussed in this chapter, let us draw out some points of the relational dynamics created within the practices. First, the relations between mother and daughter cannot be described simply by a discourse analysis based on turn-taking. A central feature of the production of terms such as *more* was their relation with a practice of regulation of consumption. The relation between the participants is marked by the *positioning* of the girls within particular practices. Centrally implicated, therefore, is an analysis of power: there are not two equal participants. Furthermore, the meanings created within such practices relate to the power and relationships inscribed within them.

I shall develop the theme of the dynamic later, but let me here raise some concluding points. The practices, for example those regulating consumption, are specific. They relate to other material aspects, such as the amount of money available to the family, and so forth (see Chapter 7), and we cannot therefore expect the inscription of such signifiers as *more* to be equivalent across class and culture, for example. That is, *more* as a relation within these practices, is *lived*. Additionally, there are public discourses and practices in which the participants are inserted. I shall use here two terms from semiotics and post-structuralism: 'regime of meaning' and 'regime of truth'. The former refers to those sets of meaning relations inscribed within particular practices and therefore which specifically position the participants. Foucault (1979a; see Henriques *et al.* 1984) delineates a sub-section of these, particularly the discursive practices of the human and social sciences, in which the meanings inscribed within them have particular effects. They claim to describe the 'real' or 'tell the truth' of what is happening. I shall examine the effectivity of this within school mathematics practices.

In Chapter 3, I shall examine some specific aspects of the insertion of certain relational terms within practice of home, school, and psychological experiments, in order to show the regime of meanings produced, but also the powerful and productive effects of claims to truth within those practices.

3 The insertion of size and family terms in school and experimental practices

This chapter falls into two parts, which together form an examination of some practices in which size and family terms are produced. It allows us to examine not only the assumptions which are made about performance, but also to explore the relationship between the impressions gained of performance within each practice. This provides a basis for examining further the discussion of multiplicity set out in the previous chapter, particularly when all such examples are usually taken to provide information about a basic stage of development.

'Readiness' is an important concept within early schooling practices, because as a sign within such practices it has the 'truth effects' described earlier. That is, within the discursive practices, a regime of truth is created in which it is considered harmful to conceptual development to introduce children to a new topic before they have reached the appropriate 'stage'. This means that not only are opportunities provided for the production of 'readiness', but that readiness forms a sign for teachers: an intersection, of performance and their reading of that performance, a reading of 'evidence'. This has powerful and productive effects. Children are not taught until they display what signifies for the teachers as 'readiness': their behaviour, and her regime of truth, together produce the sign. This is not a view of 'labelling'. The behaviours are produced because that is what the practice is set up to do. I shall explore this in more detail in Chapter 10.

For the purpose of this examination, however, it is necessary to understand how the children's behaviour signifies for the teacher as a nexus of signs within the practice. It is also possible, then, to prise apart signifier and signified and to read this production in terms of another discourse. It is the effect of the reading which I shall explore in the context of other possible readings. Here then I am not talking about the teachers' misinterpretation, or a distorted representation of the 'real capabilities' of the children (i.e. that they are capable of more than she sees) but rather the positive effects of her readings in terms of what happens to the children – how they are positioned within that practice. I shall look in particular at their multiple positioning – by examining their responses, considered 'wrong' in one practice and yet a competent relation of signification within another (in this case, the home).

School and experiment

The work which produced this examination grew out of an attempt to understand why a group of nursery school children made a particular mistake in a group lesson with the teacher which sought to explore size relations and seriation as part of the teacher's scheme for these children whom she felt to be 'ready' for this aspect of 'mathematical development'. Certain issues about the nature of the task and the comprehension of the relational terms involved led first of all to the development of a small experiment and subsequently to a detailed analysis of certain relational terms as they are used in home and nursery school mathematics practices. This was followed by a questioning of a number of basic assumptions about early learning and the transfer from home to school. It also led to a questioning of certain assumptions about the interpretation of experimental data, made possible by treating these data like the home and school recordings. That is, the transcripts were analysed by constructing the experiment as a discursive practice and the positioning of the participants, experimenter and child, within it. What is striking about the data derived from each method and practice is that they would each alone lead to different views of the linguistic capabilities of young children.

The first part of the chapter explores the initial school lesson and the experiment which followed from it, while the second part develops the themes taken up by exploring the practices for the comprehension and production of size and family terms at home.

Size and family relations in a nursery mathematics lesson

The following transcript forms a written record of a lesson undertaken by a nursery school teacher as part of her introduction to mathematics, in this case an aspect of size relations with a small group of children who she believed to be 'ready' for work at this conceptual level. Her introduction to size relations followed precisely that format described in current approaches to mathematics for young children (Williams and Shuard 1976; Matthews and Matthews 1978) in that the children were to be given opportunities for classification using the terms *big, small, bigger, smaller, biggest, smallest* and so on based on their active manipulation of objects to be classified: it is through this activity that children are assumed to discover size relations and therefore develop appropriate concepts. Williams and Shuard state the pedagogy in the following way:

> A child's first interest in size (of any kind) arises through contrasts: big or little, soon or long time, fast or slow (of movement), a little or a lot. Sorting at this stage means putting all the 'big' shapes into one box or pile and putting all the 'little' ones into another. . . . When a child comes to school he will need many experiences which will stimulate him to take the next step, i.e. to make judgements about a difference between two things which he will describe in words such as smaller, quicker, more, heavier. . . . The importance of the pre-measuring stage cannot be over-stressed.
>
> (42–3)

> We have seen that *seriation* depends on using the relations 'bigger' (or smaller) to connect each successive pair of things in a sequence. Such relations can also be added.
>
> (18)

Matthews and Matthews in their *Early Mathematical Experiences* (1978) scheme stress the 'indiscriminate' early use of size terms by young children:

> Children begin by making statements like 'this one is big!', 'this one is small', and only later use the comparative form 'this one is *bigger than* that one'. They may ask for a 'big' piece of cake, meaning one that is thick, long, or wide, and, comparing their dinners, will say that the dinner which covers more of the plate is the bigger one, without comparing the actual quantity. . . . In fact most young children use the words 'big' and 'little' indiscriminately, and while it is most important not to make them feel wrong for doing so, they can be encouraged to use appropriate words by hearing them from their teachers.
>
> (*Spaces and Shape Comparisons:* 16)

They also provide an injunction against interference:

> The sensitive teacher, while planning some activities with a definite bias towards maths, will be careful not to spoil imaginative and

creative play by intruding at the wrong time, or trying to coerce
children who are not ready into mathematical games.

(*General Guide*: 5)

Let us examine for a moment the assumptions about children and
teaching implied in the above guidelines for teaching. First of all it is
assumed that understanding of size relations arises from sorting and
classification and the comparison of actual objects. Physical experience
is seen as paramount, as the way of achieving understanding of size
relations. The terms *bigger* and *smaller* are understood in terms of
'relations', in that no discrimination is made between using the labels
and having the concept. The labels are seen to be an unproblematic
accompaniment to the concept, though it is stressed that young children may use size words in everyday contexts without understanding
their 'real' meaning, which comes only from practice at appropriate
discriminations. The inference is also that young pre-school children do
not have many of the appropriate experiences to make those discriminations and so are indiscriminate and over-general. It is important,
therefore, that the expectation which is built up for teachers is one of a
lack of the appropriate kind of experience and an expectation that
children will *not* already understand complex size relations. We can also
add to this the advice that teachers should be 'sensitive': that is, that
they should be wary of approaching children before they are 'ready' to
learn mathematics. Advice such as this has produced teachers who are
likely to be wary about interference into children's play in case they are
not 'ready' or they spoil something spontaneous which is going on, and
when they do so interfere they expect that they will have to provide
children with experiences which will lead them to make the appropriate
discriminations, which they will not expect the children already to
have mastered. The framework for the interpretation of errors is therefore given by the pedagogy: that is, that children will fail because they
are not 'ready' for that kind of learning, which will in turn lead the
teacher to feel implicitly at fault because (by implication) she was also
not sensitive enough. This provides one aspect of a 'regime of meaning', a 'regime of truth' in which the teacher herself is positioned. This
creates her insertion as subject into the practice and provides both the
basis of her readings and the aspect of the regulation to which she is
subjected. The regime is not one which is provided by the teacher, but
which itself produces her consciousness of what teaching means: thus it
produces not only her assessment of the children but is bound up with

her assessment of herself. The teacher can in no way be judged as standing outside the practices in which she as teacher is positioned and which delimit, define, and evaluate her work.

This teacher presents certain 'experiences' to the children which she believes will help them to learn to make discriminations of size and also to learn to seriate size-graded objects. The children are gathered around a table where the teacher is about to introduce them to the new topic. They are seated quietly and rigidly in their chairs.

One of the children touches the cards that the teacher is going to use:

T:	That's to do the new things with. Put that on there.	1
	(*The teacher goes and fetches an adult-size chair.*)	
P:	Big one. (*Points to the new chair.*)	
T:	Big one, and what about the chair you're sitting on?	
	(*Points to the child's chair.*)	
P:	Little one.	
T:	Little one, we'll call it a small one	5
	(*untrans.*) and that's the small chair.	
	Let's have a look at this.	
	(*Puts two blocks of different sizes in the middle of the table.*)	
	Which one's the big one and which one's the small one?	
P:	(*untrans.*) (*The children point to the blocks and appear to label them.*)	
T:	That's (*points*) the big one and that's the small one.	
	Watch Janet, otherwise you won't know, will you.	10
	(T *puts out small pictures, the first of a spade, the second of a balloon.*)	
T:	What's this? (*Points to spade.*)	
	Not whether it's big or small, what *is* it?	
P:	Spade.	
T:	A shovel – uhm, for the garden, one you use in the garden. What's it called?	15
PPP:	(*variously*) A shovel.	
	A spade.	
P:	A spade.	
P:	A spade.	
T:	What's that? (*Points to balloon.*)	20
P:	Toffee apple.	
T:	No, it's got a string on it – it's called a balloon.	

PPP:	Balloon and a spade.
	(T *puts out pictures of a nail.*)
T:	What's that?
P:	Pin.
T:	Well, we'll call it a nail – right?
PPP: T: }	Nail.
	(T *puts out a picture of a flower and the children immediately shout out.*)
PPP:	Flower.
	(T *puts out a picture of a brush.*)
PPP:	Brush/toothbrush.
T:	Toothbrush (*puts out a picture of a doll*) and a . . .?
PPP:	Doll.
T:	Doll, right. I've now got (*rearranges pictures in a row*) . . . some pictures of them. (*Introduces pictures of similar, but smaller sized objects, gives one of a spade to one of the children.*)
T:	Can you put it on top – or no – next to the same picture?
P:	Shovel. (*Child correctly places picture.*)
PPP:	Spade.
T:	Jason, have a go. The right one. (*Hands picture of small doll.*)
J:	Here? (*Puts next to doll.*)
T:	Yeh.
J:	That's the little doll.
T:	We've got a spade, let's have them all in a row . . . (*untrans.*).
	(T *puts objects in a row.*)
T:	Can you put that one for me, where does that one go? (*Hands child picture of small flower.*)
P:	A flower. (*Puts next to picture of a brush.*)
T:	Is that a flower? No.
J:	That's the little . . .
T:	Wait a minute. What word are we using? We're not using little, we're using . . .
P:	Big.
T:	Big and? . . . (*points to a small object*).
PPP:	Little.
T:	Small.

25

30

35

40

45

50

PPP:	Small.
T:	Small means the same as little.
P:	My little one.
T:	Right, they're the same.

55

So what've we got? We've got a . . . (*points to pair of dolls*).

T:	⎱ Big doll and a little . . .
PPP:	⎰ Little doll.
T:	Alright, we'll have little . . . .

And a little doll.   60

T:	⎱ A big spade and a small
PPP:	⎰ Little spade.
T:	We've got a . . .
PPP:	Big balloon.
T:	⎱ And a . . .
PPP:	⎰ Small balloon.

65

T:	A big flower and a . . .
T:	⎱
PPP:	⎰ Small flower.
T:	We've got a big nail and a . . .
PPP:	Little nail. ⎱

70

Small nail. ⎰

T:	We've got a big toothbrush and a . . .
PPP:	Small toothbrush.
T:	Small toothbrush, right.

Now then, we've got to be clever now, because I'm   75
going to mix 'em up, and I'm going to ask you each to
put one up and it's got to be the right one . . . wait
a minute.

(T *mixes cards up so that they are not in two rows.*)

T:	Jason, find the small flower?

80

J:	What's the small flower?

(*Other* P *starts to point and* T *stops him.*)

T:	*No* – don't you tell him.

Well, look at the flowers and I don't want the big one, I
want the small one.

Go on – you had it then.

(J *points to small flower.*)   85

T:	What is it?
J:	The small flower.
T:	The smaller flower.

T:	What's *that* one? (*Points to big flower.*)
J&PP:	The big flower.
T:	Stewart, find me the small balloon. 90
	(S *points.*)
T:	Good boy.
	Are you watching Janet, 'cos you won't know, will you
	what we've got.
	We've got the big balloon, we've got the . . .
P:	Little balloon. 95
T:	We've got the little or small balloon.
T:	Uhm, Ashok, find me the big spade. Spade. The *big* one.
	(*He hesitantly hands it to her.*)
T:	Good boy – is that the big one?
A:	Yeh.
T:	What's that one? (*Indicates small spade.*) 100
A:	Small one.
T:	Janet, find me the small toothbrush.
	(J *does so.*)
	And Sarah find me the *big* toothbrush.
	(S *hands it to* T. T *puts the cards away and gets out another set.*)
T:	Now, we all know the story of the three bears, don't we.
	That story – three bears. 105
	(T *begins to sort out new cards and put them out in a row.*
	There are three cards with bears of three different sizes.)
T:	Which one do you think's the daddy bear?
	(PPP *all point to the largest bear.*)
T:	Why? Ashok are you watching?
	The three bears.
	Why is this the daddy bear?
	Isn't *that* (*points to the smallest bear*) the daddy bear? 110
P:	The small one.
T:	Which one is that? (*Points to smallest bear.*)
PPP:	The *baby* bear.
T:	The baby bear.
	So which do you think that is? (*Points to middle bear.*) 115
PPP:	The mummy bear.
T:	The mummy bear.
T:	Why is that (*points to largest bear*) the daddy bear?
P:	Daddy bear.
T:	Why? 120
P:	'Cos it's a big chair?

T:	'Cos he's the biggest bear, isn't he?
	The biggest bear is – is he bigger than mummy bear?
PPP:	(*They shake their heads.*) Noo!
T:	Is daddy bear bigger than mummy bear? (*Points from largest* 125 *to middle bear.*)
PPP:	No-ooo!
T:	I think he is, isn't he?
	Which one's the biggest there?
PPP:	That one. (*They all answer together and very promptly, pointing to largest bear.*)
T:	And which one's he? The daddy bear . . . 130
PPP:	(*They all point to middle bear.*) The mummy bear.
T:	The mummy bear and . . .
PPP:	(*They point to baby bear.*) The baby bear.
T:	No, which is the smallest?
PPP:	(*Point to smallest bear.*) That one. 135
T:	That's the baby bear. Right! Now, we've got our three bears, daddy bear, mummy bear, baby bear.
T:	And they all had three beds, didn't they? (*Puts out pictures of beds.*)
	Which one do you think that belongs to? (*Points to big bed.*)
PPP:	That one. (*They all point to largest bed.*) 140
T:	Say, don't point.
PPP:	Daddy bear.
T:	Daddy bear.
	'Cos its the . . .
PPP:	Biggest (*tentatively*). 145
T:	Biggest.
	It's the biggest one and he's got to have a big bed because he's so big. Which one d'you think that belongs to?
	(*Shows picture of smallest bed.*)
PPP:	(*Some point to mummy bear and some say*) the baby bear. 150
T:	Tell me, don't point.
PPP:	The baby. } The mummy bear.
	(T *gets out the middle-sized bed and puts it side by side with the smallest one.*)
T:	Which one's mummy bear's, that one or that one?
PPP:	*That* one. (*They point to middle-sized bed.*) 155

T: That one (*points*), I think so too.
       And which does *that* one belong to? (T *points to smallest bed.*)

PPP: Baby bear.

T: Why? Because it's the . . .

PPP&T: Smallest. (*This is not clear: some may be saying 'small'.*)   160

T: Good boy, so daddy bear's is the biggest and mummy
       bear's, sorry, baby bear's, is the smallest.
       Now then, they each have a chair. (*Puts out three chairs.*)
       Whose do you think is *that* chair? Jason? (*Holds out smallest chair.*)

J: Baby bear.   165
       (T *puts chair next to bed and bear.*)

T: Why?

J: It's the smallest.

T: It's the smallest. Whose do you think is that one?
       (*Points to biggest chair.*)

PPP: Mummy bear. ⎫
       Daddy bear.   ⎬   170

T: Is that one bigger than that one?
       (*Points from largest to middle bear.*)

A: Daddy bear. (*Points to largest chair.*)

T: Daddy bear! (*Puts chair by bear.*) Because it's the . . . .

T: ⎫ Biggest.
PPP: ⎭ Biggest!   175

PPP: Mummy.

T: And mummy bear's the . . . (*Puts middle chair next to
       mummy bear.*)

PPP: Smallest.

T: Wasn't the smallest baby bear?
       And what else have they got?   180
       (*Puts out three bowls.*)

PPP: Porridge.

T: Bowls of porridge.
       And let's see, whose d'you think that one is?
       (*Points to largest bowl.*)

PPP: Daddy bear. (*They point to daddy bear.*)

T: Why?   185

PPP: Daddy bear.

T: Why is it the daddy bear's?
       Isn't that the daddy bear's. (*Points to middle one.*)

PPP:	Yeh.	
T:	That one.	190
PPP:	Mummy bear.	
P:	No it's not.	
PPP:	Daddy bear.	
	(T *holds up mummy's and baby's porridge.*)	
T:	Which is the smallest of those two?	
	Which one is the smallest one?	195
PPP:	That one. (*Point to smallest.*)	
T:	That one or that one?	
PPP:	That one. (*Smallest.*)	
T:	That one, who does it belong to?	
PPP:	Baby bear. (*They point.*)	200
T:	Baby bear.	
	Which one – now listen carefully and look carefully –	
	which one is the biggest?	
	(*Holds up largest and medium bowls.*)	
PPP:	Daddy bear. (*They point to the bear and not the bowl.*)	
T:	Which one is the biggest, that one or that one?	205
	(*She holds up the porridge.*)	
PPP:	That one. ⎫	
	Daddy bear. (*Point to correct one.*) ⎭	
T:	That one, so whose is it?	
PPP:	That one.	
T:	Whose is it?	210
PPP:	Daddy's.	
T:	Daddy's, so where is, whose is the one that's left?	
	(*Holds up medium porridge.*)	
PPP:	Mummy bear's.	
	(*They point to medium bear and T puts bowl by bear.*)	
J:	Can I go and make frogs now?	
T:	No. (*Calls to nursery assistant*) Maureen . . .	215
	You're not making frogs yet, are you?	
	You can go in a minute, Jason.	
	We've nearly finished. All right?	
	You can go in a minute.	
P:	Can I make frogs?	220
	(*One girl wanders off.*)	
T:	So let's look, we've got . . . daddy bear. (*Points.*)	
PPP:	Daddy bear.	
T:	Mummy bear. (*Points.*)	

PPP:	Mummy bear.		
T:	⎱ And baby bear.	(*Point.*)	225
PPP:	⎰ And baby bear.		
T:	We've got daddy's big bed (*points*) and baby's small bed (*points*) and mummy's (*points*).		
P:	Small bed.		
T:	What can we use, what can we call her size bed?		230
T:	It can't be small bed because baby's is the smallest bed.		
P:	Little.		
T:	No, that's the same as small.		
P:	That's the same as small.		235
T:	Where is it – it's in the . . . (*points*).		
	(*Long silence.*)		
P:	Middle.		
T:	Middle.		
T:	In the middle – she's got the middle-sized bed – right?		240
T:	Daddy's got the big bed, baby's got the . . .		
PPP:	Small.		
T:	Yeh and mummy's got the . . .		
	(*No reply.*)		
T:	The one in the . . .		
	middle.		245
PPP:	Middle.		
T:	The middle, the middle-sized bed.		
T:	Daddy's got the . . .		
PPP:	Big.		
T:	Big bowl of porridge.		250
	Baby's got the . . .		
PPP:	Little ⎱ bowl of porridge.		
	Small ⎰		
T:	Small bowl of porridge, and mummy's got the . . .		
PPP:	Middle. ⎱		255
	Middle bowl. ⎰		
T:	Middle-sized bowl of porridge.		
	Right – you remembered.		
	I'll leave these (*untrans.*). Right?		
	(*Children leave the table. Lesson ends.*)		

In looking at the videotape of the above sequence, I became struck by the way in which, at lines 123–6, the children apparently mistake the size relation of the daddy and mummy bear by answering in the negative to the question 'Is daddy bear bigger than mummy bear?' Their response apparently fits the statements about young children's competence made by Matthews and Matthews in the *Early Mathematical Experiences* material quoted on pages 35–6; that is, they understand *big* and *small*, but that the comparative *bigger* and *smaller* are developmentally more complex. We would be led to conclude, then, that the children respond in this way because they do not understand the terms or the size relations. However, I felt unhappy at simple acceptance of this explanation. First of all, the manner in which the children responded was extremely strange: they chorused 'No-ooo!' on both occasions that they were asked. Why did they reply in such a pantomine fashion? Why did they apparently mistake this relation when they could answer correctly and with no problem the question of line 128, 'Which one's the biggest there?' and make no mistake in responding to the comparative term *smallest* on line 134.

It is important to appreciate the positive effectivity of the teacher's reading of the children's mistake. While there is no evidence within the transcript to infer a reading, we can examine that reading which is given within the discursive practice in which she is positioned, and which I outlined earlier. That is, a mistake of this kind can be read in a variety of ways, all of which lead to the inference of a failure in a central capacity, cognitive or linguistic: the children cannot make size discriminations or have not mastered the relational terms. Either of these might lead to an assumption of 'lack of readiness'.

The consequences are therefore no mere matter for theoretical speculation. They have positive effectivity in terms of the positioning of children and teacher. That is, the children could be 'kept back', because they are 'not ready'. The teacher could feel responsible and guilty for interference; in the words of Matthews and Matthews, 'intruding at the wrong time, or trying to coerce children who are not yet ready into mathematical games' (1978:5).

How, though, might we prise apart signifier and signified, to examine in a new light the relations which produced the positivity of the discourse in which the teacher is inserted?

At other moments in the nursery transcripts the children correctly make size comparisons. Is a way to understand this phenomenon in terms of something about the 'communicative context' which prohibits their demonstration of what they 'really know'? Such a reading depends upon a model of an underlying competence which stands outside the social practices of production. If, however, signs are created, multiply, within practices themselves, another possible reading would be in terms of the intersection between different and contradictory signs. It is this reading which I shall explore.

The teacher set her text within a particular narrative discourse. She created a size comparison first within the framework of the three bears story. This device, which I shall explore further later in the book, provides the basis for a reading of the task as story. It therefore exists at the intersection of two discursive practices: story-reading and school mathematics. The teacher uses the story format as a 'meaningful context'. In Margaret Donaldson's (1978) terms such a device would provide a way of 'embedding' a cognitive task within a meaningful context. Yet, if the task itself exists at the intersection of two discursive practices, we might produce a reading which suggests not a relative of 'embedding', or the story as 'context', but of double discourse, double-signification, in which two tasks – story-telling and mathematics – are set up and overlaid upon each other. In this reading, there is not a necessary clarity, the 'making-meaningful' which makes a task easier for children because it provides a context that they know, but rather a series of 'readings' in which each set of relations of signification overlays the other. There the same signifiers become possible signs within two, and competing, discourses. Let us examine this reading a little further.

The teacher relies explicitly on the children's knowledge of the story when she opens the three-term comparative task at line 104. And indeed, the children have no difficulty in describing the three bears as *daddy*, *mummy*, and *baby*. However, the *family* relations, referred to in the three bears story, coincide with the size relations which the teacher wishes to present. Materially the size difference between the figures is equal, but the family relationship into which they enter as *mummy*, *daddy*, and *baby* are not.

Although the narrative discourse itself within the traditional three bears story plays on the size relation, it also conveys aspects of family relationships, notably between daddy, mummy, and baby. The family itself also operates as a focus or nexus of a number of discursive practices. In Chapter 2 I pointed to certain aspects in the regulatory practices in which mothers and daughters are positioned. These point up an aspect of power implicated in the positions, notably between adults and children. How, then, are power and positioning implicated in the reading of family relations produced within these practices, and how do size terms function as signifiers within the relevant discourses? Although the mathematical task requires that the three figures differ in exact ratio, it is not the case that in the constellation of family relations this signifies an equivalent power difference. Nor is it the case in all families that fathers are taller than mothers. How, then, is height read within that constellation of family practices and how must that reading be in contradiction with the mathematical relation? It seems that the task exists at the intersection of a myriad of relations of significance, where the narrative form and mathematical task and the multiple signification of the signifiers *big, bigger, biggest*, etc. form an overlapping and interlinking nexus. It could be argued, therefore, that far from the story providing an enabling and 'meaningful context', it produces a complex and potentially bewildering confusion. The narrative discourse itself is pointed up by the children's chorusing of 'No-ooo!', which I found myself wanting to describe with the metaphor 'pantomime style'. That is, it recalls the response of an audience.

It is with these issues of multiple readings in mind that I set out to explore further the intersection of size and family relations. Initially, I thought that the problem in the children's response was produced by the confusion over the mummy–daddy relation as signifiers of power or authority over children, and therefore the problem of the relation between equivalent authority and differential size. This turned out to be over-simplistic. However, the experiment itself, read as a distinct discursive practice, provides important information about the complex and multiple discursive practices into which children, teacher, and I as experimenter were inserted.

The three bears experiment

The subsequent experiment set out to test the hypothesis that young children from another nursery would make the same mistake as that made by the first nursery children when they were asked the identical question in relation to three bears, but that when they were presented with three shapes of corresponding height to the bears, which were not labelled as bears or anything else, the same mistake would not occur. It also seemed important to provide a seriation and matching task, as the teacher had done with the bowls, chairs, and beds, and to provide a similar task again where no labels were used and the objects were plain geometric figures.

Here was a problem in my own thinking at the time, which was that objects not 'called' something would exist outside relations of signification. This is patently absurd. There is plenty of evidence to suggest that children create such relations out of those relations presented. I have discussed this discursive strategy (Walkerdine 1982), particularly the case in which children when asked such apparently nonsensical questions as 'Is yellow bigger than green?' would search for objects to justify an answer (Hughes and Grieve 1980), and I shall develop this point in relation to the analysis of the experiment.

I devised an experiment which consisted of two conditions: three bears and geometric figures. The experiment was therefore divided into two parts, so that the order in which the bears and geometric figures were presented could be varied. The three bears task consisted of putting out the three bears in size order. The children were asked if they remembered the story of the three bears. To make sure that they had heard it, I had arranged for their teacher to read it at story-time on the previous day. The children were then asked to label the bears as *daddy*, *mummy*, and *baby*. Having done so they were asked: 'Is the daddy bear bigger than the mummy bear?' They were then asked the reverse question, 'Is the mummy bear bigger than the daddy bear?' After this they were presented with the beds, chairs, and bowls and asked to 'give them to the bear you think they go with'.

In the geometrical shapes condition, the shapes were three rectangles of heights and widths equivalent to those of the bears and three circles of equivalent dimensions to the bowls of porridge. The rectangles were set out in size order. The children were asked two questions: 'Is that one bigger than that one?', pointing from the biggest to the middle rectangle and vice versa. In the circles condition they were asked to 'put these shapes next to ones you think they go with'. As previously indicated, the tasks were administered in two orders, one beginning with the bears and the other with the rectangles task. The children taking part in the experiment were from the nursery class of another school. Fourteen children took part, and these children were chosen because they were the oldest in the nursery and so of a comparable age to those in the transcript on pp. 37–44. The mean age of the children was 4.5 years. The entire experiment was videotaped. The results are given in Table 3.1.

It will be immediately noticeable that the majority of the children do not make the mistake made by the children in the first lesson: that is,

Table 3.1 *Three bears and geometric shapes task*

Task	Correct	Incorrect	No response
Labels three bears	14	0	0
Is the daddy bear bigger than the mummy bear?	12	2	0
Is the mummy bear bigger than the daddy bear?	6	6	2
Seriation chairs	12	2	0
Seriation beds	13	1	0
Seriation bowls	12	2	0
Is that one (biggest) bigger than that one (middle)?	11	2	1 not given
Is that one (middle) bigger than that one (biggest)?	7	6	1 not given
Seriation circles	11	2	1 not given

they answer correctly the question, 'Is the daddy bear bigger than the mummy bear?' However, there is a considerably lower success rate on the second item, 'Is the mummy bear bigger than the daddy bear?', in which over half the children give the wrong answer or no response. This means that, in any simple sense, my original hypothesis is not supported. In addition, a similar response pattern can be observed in the rectangles condition, so that it is not the case that there is a substantial difference in the children's responses to these items, contrary to the prediction.

An analysis of the response patterns of the children gives more insight into the responses. There are clear response patterns, as follows:

Bears condition

Four correct on both items.
Six say yes to each question.
Two say no to each question.
Two say yes to the first and no responses to the second question.

Rectangles condition
Five correct on both items.
Six say yes to each question.
Two say no to each question.

If we further examine how far the same children respond in the same manner across bears and rectangles items, we find that this is overwhelmingly the case:

Bears and rectangles
Four correct on all items.
Five say yes on all items.
Two say no on all items.
One says yes to bears items, but yes, no to rectangles.
One is not given the rectangles items.
One says yes/no response on the bears and yes on both rectangles items.

It is also important that the majority of children have no difficulty with the seriation task, in either condition, and it is the same children who fail the seriation task in both the bears and circles conditions. What is most marked is the way in which many children give the same response to both questions, although this most often involves giving the wrong response to the question about the middle item being bigger. Since there is no distinction in terms of the family versus size dimensions which I had imagined, how do we account for the response pattern of the children in this case? One child at least responds to the second question as though it was a repetition of the first by saying in answer, 'Yes, I said'. There appears to be a distinct response bias in favour of treating the second question as though it were the same as the first. In order to investigate this interpretation further. I decided to examine more carefully the videotape of the experiment and that of the classroom sequence, treating the two more carefully as interactions between adult and children. What typifies these interactions? In what ways are they similar and different? What might have led the children to give wrong responses to these two different questions in the different circumstances? On a closer inspection what features emerge?

Although seriation and matching of seriated objects is supposed to be conceptually more complex than simple size discrimination, it is clear that this did not prove a great problem for these children They had little difficulty understanding the task even when told simply to 'Put these with the shapes you think they go with': not the most explicit of instructions! Indeed, there is evidence that those children who did make errors tended to read the task in different ways. For example, one girl gave the bears their porridge by putting the bowls face down on top of the bears as if to feed them, paying no attention to what bowl was given to which bear.

Experiment as a discursive practice

Having available the videotape of the experiment made it possible for me to view the experiment as a discursive practice and therefore to render it amenable to the same kind of analysis as is possible with the transcript of the classroom lesson. We have already seen that the response strategies of the children are important for understanding the production of the actual quantitative data of the results. In order to understand why some children simply repeat the first response in answer to the second question, it seems necessary to examine how the task and situation are set up and the participants (experimenter and children) positioned. In this respect, it is important to note the positive effectivity of the experimental discourse in positioning me as 'experimenter' and the children as 'subjects'. This provides a set of rules, of regulations of practice, the interpretation of the practice, the interaction itself, in which certain things are done, said, and then read. If the participants are so positioned the experiment can be located and read within the discourse, and then claims can be made on the basis of it. Like the classroom, the experiment produces a discursive practice in which evidence is read and a regime of truth produced; in that sense, then, the dichotomies, objective/subjective take on a different significance. Similarly, those criticisms of experiments which treat observational data as more 'natural' or 'ecologically valid' fall into a trap, which fails to engage with the positive effectivity of the discursive practice in which any performance is produced.

In this respect, then, my aim is not to declare the experiment biased or distorted in relation to a true reality of natural observation, or the children's real competence. Rather, I want to examine how the truth of these practices is produced and look at the similarity and difference between the reading produced in the experiment and in the classroom. Treating the experiment simply as a means for devising a quantifiable analysis, and the classroom as the site for a naturalistic observation, evades and elides these issues.

One aspect which I wish to examine is that in the experiment, as in the classroom, the children are given the bases for possible answers and courses of action by subtle (or not so subtle!) verbal and non-verbal signifiers produced in the exchange. Before doing that it might be wise to pause for a moment to consider the tradition of work which has used the format of doing experiments to test out more closely phenomena observed using mostly ethnographic methods. I am speaking most particularly of the work of Michael Cole and his colleagues at the Laboratory for Comparative Human Cognition, who for some time have been examining and questioning the relationship between the assessment of cognitive performance as displayed on western psychological tests and the skills displayed in the everyday practices of Third World cultures. Cole and Scribner (1974) pointed out quite clearly the difference between the assessment of performance when assumptions were made about the absence of capacities which did not show up in the test results and the apparently similar skills being displayed in 'everyday contexts'. They showed the difference in resulting assessment if the experiments were conducted after observation, using those materials and inserting the tasks in those practices which were familiar to the participants. More recent work by Cole and Traupmann (1979) and Hood, McDermott, and Cole (1978) does, however, afford more detailed insights into the relational dynamics involved in the collection of experimental data. Cole and Traupmann analyse the particular case of a child who had been diagnosed as learning disabled and who was one of the children who took part in the study of classroom and experimental learning undertaken by Hood, McDermott, and Cole. Given the variety of data collected they were able to analyse the performance of the child, Archie, in a variety of situations. Their particular focus was on the way in which Archie consciously or unconsciously manipulates the other participants in the interactions so that they both help him and perpetuate his disability. For example, in a testing session, undertaken by an experienced psychological tester, who knew nothing about Archie, the tester strays from the standard format in response to Archie's display of discomfort and distress. Because he presents various signs to be read, such as putting his head in his hands, creeping low down in the chair, and so forth, the tester actually restructures her interaction with him. This test is repeated in a non-experimental session, though one which shares some discursive similarities with the experiment. In this case, Archie is among a group of children at a club run after school at the university. The club session takes the form of an IQ bee: that is, an IQ test presented as a quiz, with the group divided into two teams and taking turns to answer the questions. In this instance the group, including the adult who is administering the quiz, comment on the fact that Archie may not be able to answer the questions and finds the task difficult. Archie himself again displays the signs of distress which make the children and the leader, like the tester, feel that they are responsible for producing that distress and the necessity to alleviate it. After a struggle, in which the participants try to get Archie to let someone else take his turn, and Archie refuses, the leader actually changes the question so that Archie is given a simpler one than was expected. All the participants know this, but are relieved and pleased that Archie gets it right. This has a significant effect on Archie, who then actually becomes one of the children answering the most questions instead of the least. In other words, it significantly changes his perform-ance and therefore the possible evaluation by himself and others of his competence.

So we can see that, with this child at least, there is no fixed performance level which exists outside the confines of the way in which performance is constructed in the actual situation. The production of Archie as 'learning-disabled' is no mere label imposed willy-nilly. What this analysis makes clear is the relationship of interaction both to the production and change of displays of ability.

In this sense, the readings of performance and the positive effects of such readings are produced in relation to particular relational dynamics with classroom and test. In this case, the signs of distress and anxiety are particularly powerful. In taking further this analysis, therefore, it would be important to examine the relational dynamics in terms of their emotive power and the production of anxiety which is read. Archie's anxiety is manifest in both practices and is dealt with in particular ways, but we also need to examine the production of that anxiety within Archie's own history.

Analysing the experiment

In analysing the experiment as discursive practice, I shall draw on three sources: first, the explicit form of the task in terms of its discourse features; second, the interaction aspects of my performance not accounted for in the experimental design; and third, comments and responses given by the children both in the course of the experiment and the general conversation which followed it.

To begin the test sequence, and in order to make them feel at ease, I told the children that they were going to play some games. However, this is not without effects. Children of this age are very familiar with games, and the discourse features and subject-positions within games. In this respect, the use of the signifier 'game', like that of the 'story' in the classroom sequence, places the experiment at the intersection of two discursive practices and suggests to the children a reading and course of action different from that through which I create and read the 'evidence'. On another occasion the positive effectivity of such a reading was made apparent to me. A colleague, on giving a conservation test to a young girl, told her that he was going to do a trick. Afterwards, the girl whispered to me that she had not been fooled as she had watched my colleague's hands the whole time (Walkerdine 1982:16). Although there was no evidence of this kind here, we can still examine the effectivity of the 'game' discourse and its positioning of the participants. What is set up in a game, and how are the positions of the participants defined? How far does a device designed to lessen the effect of a powerful experimenter, by 'putting the child at ease', also serve to render the power invisible, by disclaiming its presence, while making the child the object of an evaluative reading from a different discourse? It could therefore be argued that, rather than helping, it is dishonest and disingenuous. Yet, of course, the purpose of such practices within experimental work has been to produce a more sympathetic reading of an underlying competence obscured by social aspects of the situation, as in Labov's classic work (1969). While such work has been tremendously important, it raises an issue about the retention of a competence/performance dichotomy in which competence is still understood as a phenomenon located outside the social, and the social as producing a performance or evaluative effect upon that competence. However, my purpose here is to question that very distinction.

Apart from the signifier 'game', which is applied to the experiment, other features actually offer conflicting information to the children. The form of the questions put to them is explicitly part of pedagogic and testing discourse. That is, they are those kinds of questions described by many classroom researchers (e.g. Barnes 1969) as pseudo-questions, because it is quite clear that the questions are not a request for information unknown to the questioner. The question in this case is a test. Thus the pseudo-question format denies the game discourse as set up by the opening metaphor. The children are thus provided with contradictory information. The pseudo-question format is what characterizes both this experiment and the classroom lesson. It is also the format of one test and the IQ bee given to Archie in Cole and Traupmann's example (1979). Questions such as 'Which one is the daddy bear?' and 'Is the daddy bear bigger than the mummy bear?' are quite clearly questions to which the experimenter knows the answer. This question format is contrasted later in the situation in which I ask each child about their own family, the comparative heights of members of the family, who eats what for breakfast, and so on. By comparison, these questions are ones to which I do not know the answers. In some cases this does have the effect of changing the interaction, though in other cases the children do not find an opportunity for a different kind of talk, as I shall explore with respect to the analysis of individual responses.

In addition to this, there is the issue of the relation of one question to another. For example, the questions 'Is the daddy bear bigger than the mummy bear?' and 'Is this one (biggest) bigger than that one (middle)?' always precede questions of the form 'Is the mummy bear bigger than the daddy bear?' and 'Is that one (middle) bigger than that one (biggest)?' The second question is therefore in a most peculiar position and children are left wondering why I asked it. Indeed, what information does it give the children? They have just answered one question, only to be immediately asked the reverse. In some practices this would be read as a trick, and indeed it does get one child to change his answer. It could lead others to think that it is a repetition of the first question, which one child implies by his 'Yes, I said' in response to the second question. There has been much written about the effect of such questioning in conservation tests. Indeed, Rose and Blank (1974) pointed out that asking the same question twice, namely, 'are they the same', was a peculiar form of questioning and might lead some children to infer that they gave the wrong answer the first time. As we shall see with respect to the classroom lesson, the teacher does just that: she repeats the question when she has been given the wrong answer the first time. What are the children to infer is the purpose of the double questioning? We cannot answer that question on the basis of the available data, but we can conclude that it does have some kind of effect, given the response patterns of the children, who tend to give the same answer to the second as to the first question. We could infer that the children understood neither question, that they did not understand the size relations, but we have no firm basis for preferring these above other possible readings. What would have happened if I had only asked one question, if I had changed the order of the questions, if I had used *smaller* rather than *bigger*, and so forth?

It is perhaps important to note that when experiments are devised it is usual to attempt to minimize order-effects, though clearly order and the relation of one question to another cannot entirely be removed and may have important effects which deserve study in their own right. Perhaps what is more important is that there exists a level of information given unintentionally by me as experimenter to the children which is entirely outside the techniques for evaluating experimental data. This would be present despite the most stringent attempts to avoid it, since it is axiomatic to interaction and provides an important aspect of the signification to be read.

The most noticeable of these phenomena is the way in which I, as experimenter, mark correct and incorrect responses. Although on a transcript of the test the words appear similar, the manner in which they are conveyed is remarkably different. There are two methods for replying to wrong responses which I use interchangeably. The first is to repeat the child's answer, but in the form of a question:

vw: Is the daddy bear bigger than the mummy bear?
ch: No (*shakes head*).
vw: No?
ch: No ...

What happens on these occasions is that the questioning responses on my part act as a cue for the child either to affirm her/his response, or to change it. The other response pattern is for me to follow the wrong response with a repetition of the child's response, but in a completely flat and unenthusiastic tone, which is in sharp contrast to the tone which follows a correct response. In these cases, while I might not actually say different words, the manner and tone of voice are very different. The words are spoken more loudly and in a markedly enthusiastic tone. For example:

vw: Which one is the smallest one?
ch: That one.
vw: That one!

Despite the information in the words uttered, the mode of conveying the information gives feedback which the children learn to read, just as they read the verbal signs. I will argue that the teacher marks correct and incorrect answers in precisely the same manner. In addition to this

I appear frequently to move my body towards, point, or touch the appropriate card for the children to respond to, in a manner of which, during the test, I was completely unaware.

By giving some examples of the children's responses I shall attempt to show how much they are dependent on the kind of interactional information which Cole and Traupmann (1979) describe. A very detailed analysis which considered the relations between gesture, word, and facial expression for each child would undoubtedly give a more complex reading. I suggest that such an enterprise would be an important exercise if we are to take further the importance and effect of experimental work. The two extracts that I shall give here are merely illustrative:

vw: Which one's the daddy bear?   1
      (CH *points to biggest bear.*)
vw: Which one's the mummy bear?
      (CH *points to middle bear.*)
vw: Which one's the baby bear?   5
      (CH *points to smallest bear.*)
vw: Is the daddy bear bigger than the mummy bear?
      (CH *shakes his head.*)
vw: No. Is the mummy bear bigger than the daddy bear?
CH: Wha?   10
vw: Is the mummy bear bigger than the daddy bear?
CH: He's (*points to biggest bear*) bigger than that
      (*points to middle bear*).

In this sequence of questions and responses the child gives the wrong response at line 8 and yet I had to code his response at line 12 as correct. However, this makes nonsense of the first negative response since the answer 'He's bigger than that' suggests that the child understands the relationship perfectly well. We are still, therefore, left in complete mystery as to why he gave the first incorrect response. Later in the same child's session are examples of explicitly pedagogic discourse on my part and of his response to that:

vw: Do you remember what else happened in the story was that they
      all had bowls of porridge. Do you remember that they all had
      bowls of porridge? Well I've got three bowls of porridge here, do
      you think you can give the bears their bowls of porridge?
      (*Gives him the bowl cards.*)

CH: Which one's the biggest? (*Touches the biggest bowl.*)
VW: Well I don't know, which one is?
      (CH *puts middle-sized bowl by largest bear and large bowl by middle
      bear.*)
VW: Mm, mm (*unenthusiastically*). Go on then, can you give the other
      bears their porridge?
      (CH *looks at cards already out and swaps them round.*)
CH: Oh, sorry.
      (*Gives small bowl to baby bear.*)
VW: That's it.

I then go on to ask, 'Why do you think the daddy's got the biggest
bowl of porridge?', to which he replies "Cos he eats big ones'. I ask him
about the amount eaten by mummy, to which he replies 'Middle-sized
one'. I then ask, 'Do you think mummies eat as much as daddies?' to
which he replies 'Yeah!' in the tone of, 'of course'. Thus, in this last
response, we have the total disjunction of the portions allotted to the
bears in the story and what he knows about mothers' and fathers' eating
patterns. One might ask, therefore, what is the effectivity of the three
bears narrative upon his reading of 'mothers' within the practices of the
family.

That is, another effect of the multiplicity of significations is that of
the imposition of one reading upon another. Even though this child
can articulate that his mother eats as much as his father, he may read
her power through those other discursive practices in which women and
mothers are positioned. Examples such as these occur throughout the
data and are a constant indication that a different kind of analysis is
necessary from that to which experimental data is usually subjected.

In order to understand why the children appear to give the wrong
answers, when there are other indications that they understand the
relationship which the question is aimed at revealing, it is perhaps
important to examine what are the parameters of the pseudo-questions
asked in this and the teaching situation. The pseudo-questions in this
case ask for a yes/no response. The very form of the questions indicates
that the child is being tested to elicit knowledge that is already known.
It may be for some children that this is what is salient and invokes a
wild guessing strategy, or a simple answer in the affirmative as being
usually what is required. To understand this it is possible to recall those
situations in a conversation where one is not paying attention but
realizes that a question has been asked. In these situations we take

other cues to work out whether the desired response is in the affirmative or negative. These are usually present in the speaker's intonation and we make a wild guess. The children might also wonder why a question is being asked about such a perfectly obvious matter. These thoughts are speculative, but I suggest that it is in this direction that our analysis should go if we are to understand more fully the responses given by children in experiments.

Other information from the experiment

As part of the procedure I asked children questions about their own families at the end of the test questions. Their responses are both illuminating with respect to their reading of my questioning and to the discourses in which they read and produce relations of size within the family. I shall give some examples to illustrate my point.

Damian
I have asked him if he has bowls of porridge at home:

vw: You have bowls like that? (*He pointed to the little bowl.*)
     And do you have a little bowl?
d: Yes, but, er, not as little as that (*points to small bowl*).

The construction used by Damian, 'not as little as that', certainly does not conform to the category of indiscriminate use of size terms suggested by Matthews and Matthews (1978). Neither do any of the following excerpts.

Camy
vw: Is your mummy bigger than your daddy?
c: Yes (*said very definitely*).
vw: Is she?
c: That's like Camy (*points to small bear*).
vw: Which one's the mummy?
c: (*Points to mummy and daddy.*)
vw: Both of them? Which one's like daddy do you think?
c: That fat (*points to daddy bear*).
vw: That one! Is your daddy fat (*laughs*).
c: (*Nods.*)
vw: Is he?

c: Yes.
vw: Is your mummy fat?
c: She's skinny ...!

Herbie

One way in which the pedagogic discourse which is used in the experiment affects the child is seen in this example, in which I ask Herbie what he has for breakfast, trying various suggestions, to which he will make no reply. He only opens up after I tell him that I have toast for breakfast, after which he tells me that he has Weetabix and turns it into a competition, in which his dad has four Weetabix, his mum five and himself six. This presents a striking reminder of certain advertisements, notably the recent 'Shredded Wheat' campaign. This is an interesting inversion of size and power in which he has most.

Michelle

Simply replies that she does not know to all my questions about her home, and becomes quiet where before she has been animated.

Scott

Like some other children he plays with the categories which I have set out in an amazingly sophisticated way. I ask him:

vw: Who's bigger in your house, your dad or your mum?
s: Me, 'cos I keep standing on the chair!

This response indicates that he is clearly not limited to an indiscriminate use of size, but can shift categories in a very sophisticated way. He also plays around with the test. When I ask him the question about the size difference in the rectangles, he replies by shifting round the positions of the middle and small ones and saying 'All right then, the baby's bigger than that one!' (said with great aplomb). He also spontaneously labels the rectangles as daddy's, mummy's, and baby's *doors*.

The classroom as discursive practice

I have argued in relation to the experimental data that in order to understand the reasons for the kind of response given by the children, it is necessary to examine the way in which the experimental situation is set up for them to read and to respond to it in particular ways. Although I have only offered tentative guidelines for the possibility of such an analysis, the tenor of the children's other responses, and the way in which the test situation uses a particular pedagogic and discursive style, seem to be particularly important. The pedagogic discourse of the experimenter hinges both on the uses of the pseudo-questions and on the way in which one kind of question is juxtaposed to another, the way in which correct and incorrect answers are differently responded to, and the use of particular questions and response patterns.

In the analysis of the classroom sequence, how far does the teacher do the same thing and therefore set the children up to produce the same kind of response patterns as in the experiment? If we focus first of all on the way in which she poses and responds to questions, we can see that almost all the questions fall into the pseudo-question format, since the teacher patently knows the information which is being requested. We can observe (see p. 37) that the teacher produces a very similar kind of questioning at line 3 and at line 4 corrects the child's response from *little* to *small*. The correction is common in the classroom discourse but is different from the testing one, where correction is not explicit, so that the children have to rely on other cues to judge the adult's reaction to their response. The form of pseudo-questioning appears throughout the transcript on numerous occasions. At line 10 the teacher tells one of the children to pay attention; this control strategy is also common and appears in the testing sequence on one occasion when I ask a girl if she is watching. The teacher continues by getting the children to name items which are pictured on cards. It does not take long before the children do not need her explicit question to work out what response is required of them. By line 28 the children are shouting the 'answer' immediately the teacher holds up the card. At line 43 she asks for a picture of a flower and the child gives the wrong response; she indicates this by asking the question at line 44: 'Is that a flower?'. Although this strategy does not appear in the experiment, questioning of the wrong response is something which is done, most often by the use of rising intonation or by the relation of the child's response. The next strategy used by the teacher, common in the pedagogic testing mode, is that she gets the children to finish sentences off for her rather than asking direct questions. She introduces this at line 58 and continues it for some time. On every occasion the sentence is not finished by her and ends with a rising intonation to indicate that it is a question. The children have no difficulty in recognizing the purpose of the strategy and accordingly supplying the end of the sentence.

At line 47 the teacher does get into trouble with the sentence completion strategy because the children give the wrong response. When she indicates that *little* is not the word being used, one of the children chips in with *big*, when she wanted the answer *small*. The difference between this and a non-pedagogic discourse is further amplified at line 81 where the teacher stops one child from telling the one being questioned the answer to a question with which he is having difficulty.

There are other relations used by the teacher which have to do with the management of more than one child, and which are therefore different from those applicable in a testing situation. These are discussed at some length by MacLure and French (1981) who point out that teachers often control the exchange by making sure that the children do not call out, that she says who is to answer, and so forth. This teacher does those things. She also indicates what kind of response she requires. At line 151 she tells the children to give her an answer rather than point. All of these strategies are repeated frequently throughout the lesson. When a new strategy is introduced it does not take long for the children to work out what is required of them by way of response. At the end of the lesson the teacher introduces the *middle* term, between *biggest* and *smallest*. She confirms the point of the lesson when the children manage to repeat the term and she says at line 258, 'Right – you remembered!'.

In these ways the purpose of the task is communicated to the children. The teacher actually imparts very little overt information to the children. She introduces the idea that *little* is to be referred to as *small* and that *middle sized* can refer to the mummy bear. Apart from these, the testing aspects of the discursive practice set the children up to supply 'answers', which then provide the basis of a reading of evidence of attainment and capacity or ability. The classroom and experimental practices therefore both provide the discursive sites in which comprehension and production are read as evidence of an underlying capacity. In both cases such readings have positive effectivity. With respect to the experiment, this concerns truth statements (see Walkerdine 1984) about 'children's development' as a generalized phenomenon. In the case of the classroom, this is the effect in terms of the teacher's subsequent pedagogy, her reading of her effectiveness, the abilities of the children and her own positioning of them, and the consequences for their schooling.

One of the striking things about the performance in the experiment is that children of this age are classically supposed to find this kind of task difficult. Piaget (1952) placed this in the ensemble of performance data which go to make up concrete operations. In Williams and Shuard's (1976) mathematics guide, seriation and matching are also seen as being achieved during the period of concrete operations. It is assumed that competence at seriation and matching depends on the children's *ability* to make a series of bigger/smaller comparisons. Although the task in the classroom and the experiment only has three terms, it is enough to constitute a seriation and matching task.

One aspect which may be important is the children's reading of the middle term. Although a lack of it does not hinder the successful completion of the task, it does seem to be the case that the children have simply to make a number of bigger/smaller comparisons, as the classic explanation would suggest. The term *middle sized* does actually focus on the pivoting of the other two around a central anchor. It is that term which the teacher tries to get across in her lesson. The middle term also means that the children can still simply use the terms *big* and *small*, rather than *bigger* and *smaller*. Failure to produce a middle term leads to errors for some of the children in the experiment, as when Andrea says of the daddy bear's bed, 'He's got a big one same as mummy' ... while Barry says in response to my question about the mummy bear: 'A big one like that over there' (pointing to the daddy). It is important that the mummy and the daddy are both seen as big, whereas Scott has no difficulty in using the middle term to apply to three brothers: 'Austin's baby, Barry's big, and I'm the medium.' One of the issues which I raised at the very beginning of this chapter is the way in which daddy, mummy, and baby do not represent an equidistant set of relations within certain discursive practices. Although this does not seem to interfere with their discrimination, the children appear to view parents and children as different categories. In Chapter 4 I shall seek to demonstrate that the young children and their parents, in the Tizard corpus, rarely use the middle term and that *mummies* are never referred to as *small* or as *middle sized*. Rather, *mummy* is a term which is often used as a synonym for *big*. This presents an example of the circulation of meanings within certain practices in which the family is inscribed.

4 Size and family relations in home practices

Analysis of size relations in home practices

In order further to explore the relations between the discursive practices in which signifiers of size and family relation are produced at home and school, I decided to examine the production of such signifiers from within three corpuses of spontaneous speech data: my recordings of children's activity outside of formal interactions with the teacher in the two nursery classes in which the previous work was undertaken, and the Tizard corpus of conversations between mothers and daughters (see p. 13).

In deciding how to work on the transcript data, I decided as a preliminary to note down and classify all size terms in the corpuses. I have noted the frequency of occurrence of each term within the corpus and also who first used the term in exchange (mother or child). This does not necessarily mean that in that exchange the first speaker was the only one to use the term, simply that she was responsible for its introduction. With respect to many of the extracts the terms would be used by both participants, adult and child, in the exchange. Table 2.1 (p. 17) contains the frequencies for the Tizard corpus.

Matthews and Matthews, discussing the use of size terms by nursery age children, comment:

> Children begin by making statements like 'this one is big', 'this one is small', and only later use the comparative form 'this one is bigger than that one'. . . . In fact, most young children use the words 'big' and 'little' indiscriminately.
>
> (1978:16)

It is immediately apparent from a cursory glance at Table 2.1 that these statements do not appear to apply to the utterances recorded here. Comparative terms form a large percentage of those recorded, although clearly in terms of frequency, *big* and *little* are most often used. However, it is not that children use these simple terms most often – the mothers also use them most often too. Thus it would seem over-hasty to infer that young children use these terms simply because of poorly developed conceptual apparatus. We shall see later that even these terms are used relationally and contrastively rather than indiscriminately, as Matthews and Matthews suggest.

It should also be noted that *little* is used significantly more often than *small* by children and adults. This certainly has implications in relation to the lesson discussed in Chapter 3. Here it was noted that one of the tasks presented to the children was to discriminate between and label pictures of large and small versions of objects such as a flower and a balloon. The children all automatically used the term *little*, but the teacher was most insistent that they should use the word *small*. It is not clear why she wanted this word: possibly she considered it to be mathematically more correct. However, she had extreme difficulty in getting the children to use the word, try as she might. One of the things which is most obvious from Table 2.1 is a possible reading of the children's difficulty. Quite clearly *little* is the word which is used most frequently with young children. It is not clear from the table why this should be, but I shall go on to argue that *little* is a term which has important and multiple significations in the lives of young children, in which it is used not indiscriminately, but to denote a specific set of relationships. However, whatever its function, *little* is the more common term, which means that for those children there was a specific difficulty of which the teacher was not aware: although the children would be familiar with the term *small*, they might more commonly refer to similar relations to those discussed in the lesson using the term *little*.

I shall argue that *little* and *small* function as relations of signification within distinct practices. The practice which includes intra-family relations uses the term *little* in these transcripts.

Table 4.1 refers to the occurrence of mother- and child-initiated sequences in which size and family relations are linked in the Tizard corpus.

Table 4.1 *Exchanges linking size and family*

Mother-initiated exchanges	
He didn't realize the *baby* was so *small*.	
	(MJ49)
Put some *little children* in there (*toy roundabout*).	
	(CW9)
It's only *little children* who have parties for their birthday.	
	(CW24)

Table 4.1   *(Cont.)*

When you were a *tiny baby*.

(JH47)

You're really a nice *big sister*.

(MJ24)

Look at those *little girls*.

(MJ57)

Three *little people* (children).

(LA43)

You let the *big boys* ride it (*bike*) don't you.

(JW25)

Tracy, you're not helpless, you're three years old – *big girls* can go upstairs. Only *babies* have to have big people running after them.

(TD81)

Grandad didn't get his teeth taken out when he was a *little boy* . . . (*but when*) a big man.

(MS15)

You'll have to do this (*darning*) when you're *bigger*.

(CW38)

(c: *Got to carry me down*.) Oh are you a *little baby*? I only carry *babies* down.

(DH22)

Baby one for him (*lettuce for rabbit*).

(AC9)

That's only a little *baby one* (*fly*). c: I don't like baby ones or *big* ones.

(AC14)

Oh a *little baby* are you? (c *is crying*.)

(TD39)

Mummy's just trying to think of the songs she learnt when she was *little*.

(TD50)

You're not a *baby*, you're a *big girl*.

(KG15)

(c: I'm nearly bigger'n you.) You've got a long way to go – you're just a *little tot*.

(JM13)

You do (*paint*) the *little boy*.

(JS23)

Table 4.1   (*Cont.*)

Child-initiated exchanges

A *little boy* and a *little girl* go out.

(CW9)

Cats like strokes from mummies and *little girls* and *boys*.

(LA2)

I'm a big *baby*.

(JW20)

Baby Joe's *tiny* head and *tiny* eyes.

(LA44)

The *little* ones (*make a noise at school*).

(KSB4)

Lucy went out on the *biggest* (*donkey*) and I went on the *littlest*.

(HR30)

When I was a *little girl* I did. M: What are you now? C: A *big girl*. M: Not *very big*.

(EG47)

I just want to do (*draw*) a *little boy*.

(LA42)

The *bigger* ones (*children aged 11*) can stay at home.

(SOT16)

Where's that *baby tiny* one (*drawing of cat*) gone?

(RP52)

Now the *mamma* (*drawing of cat*). M: What, the *big* one?

(RP50)

When I go to *big* school.

(EG58)

Oh what are the *baby* ones, the *weeny* ones (*birds.*)? M: They'll grow *big*. C: Like *mummy* birds.

(AC12)

Table 4.1 suggests that the relation between status and size is marked in the manner which I had expected. For example, the terms *baby*, *tiny*, and *little* are used synonymously, as are *big* and *mummy*. It is important that *big* and *daddy* are not used coterminously. This gives a firm basis for suggesting there is a problem about the use of *mummy* as the *middle* term, since if mummy is read as big it could prove difficult for some children to make the leap to using the term *middle sized* for designating her position. In several exchanges *mummy* and *baby* or *big/baby, little/mummy* are used as contrastive pairs. This suggests that certain relationships mix size and family terms to produce quite specific contrasting pairs. In this case, *baby* and *mummy* form a contrastive pair in which size, status, and power are coterminous. The relation between these terms and others, such as the *big/mummy* and *little/tiny/baby* synonyms means that there are specific relations of syntagmatic and paradigmatic opposition operating within this nexus of practices. For example, in RP50 *big* and *mamma* are both used to designate a cat being drawn. In RP52 the contrasting *baby/tiny* is used to refer to a small cat. In Table 4.1 the terms in AC9, 12, and 14 all refer to animals and birds, again where the relationship can be inferred from the size differences. The metaphor is further extended in AC9 where a portion of food small enough for a baby is called a *baby* one. *Little* forms a synonym with *baby*, particularly in those extracts invoking the regulation of behaviour considered inappropriate to the age (3 and 4 in the case of this corpus) of the child in question. Here the child is referred to as *baby* or *little baby*. The terms, therefore, have a regulative and evaluative purpose within the practice, and their multiple significations may be difficult to prise apart. Yet it is that prising apart which would be necessary for their articulation within mathematical discourse. Evidence for this is provided by an example from Coghill (1978) (quoted in Walkerdine 1982) in which a group of infant school children, during a lesson on *odd* and *even* numbers, booed the *odds* and cheered the *evens*. It is the pejorative significations contained within the signifier *odd* in other practices which would seem to be important here.

If, in this practice, at least within the corpus in question, children use *mummy* as synonymous with *big*, it does not seem surprising that within the experiment some children referred to *mummy* as *big like daddy*. The problem for the children's insertion within school mathematics practices becomes one of prising apart and rearticulating the signifiers as entering into different relations of signification, in this case one in which (and I shall refer to this later) evaluative aspects of the signifier are suppressed. In school mathematics, the quantitative and calculable size-difference is the signification which forms a relation within the discursive practice. It is not that the terms are used randomly or indiscriminately at all, they are used very specifically, though not in the way that is necessarily helpful in getting children to approach measurement, since the size differentiation which is marked by the terms is only quantitative in a very general sense, and since it refers at the same time to the relationship it is also qualitative.

Other aspects which emerge from an examination of Table 4.1 include the way in which *big* and *little* are used as contrasts with respect to children. I have argued how, in relation to size, adult and child terms form a contrastive pair; the terms are also used to make contrasts which relate to children. These contrasts (e.g. between *big girls* and *little girls*) are important in several respects. First, the terms are, as with mummy and baby, multiply signifying, because although the differences being marked refer to size they do not refer to size *alone*; what is also implied is increasing age, more adult-like behaviour, and so forth. Second, the terms are not used as fixed and determined attributes of the material bodies to which they refer; the same girls may be designated *big girls* or *little babies*, depending on their behaviour. If the girls are behaving in a manner judged unsuitable they are referred to as *little* or *baby*, and told to be a 'big girl'. If, on the other hand, they are asserting that they are really 'grown up' they may be 'brought down to size' by being told that they are *only little*. Thus, *big* and *little/baby* function as contrasts which apply to growing up as well as growing in size and appropriate behaviour in one moving towards adulthood. Any girl's designation as *big* or *little* is not fixed, therefore, but depends on the practice and her position in it. The girl may be a *little girl* but a *big sister*. Once again, we can see that although the terms are used in a way which is not specific to size they are not used loosely, nor are they used indiscriminately, but indeed in very specific practices and circumstances to represent a specific set of relationships.

In this respect, the position of the participants (in these examples, particularly the girl) is marked by shifting relations of signification, so that the signifier *big* or *little* may be used in this instance to position her within the family relations as 'big sister' or to position her regulatively as 'behaving like a baby' or being a 'big girl'. Thus the signifiers enter as relations within the discursive practice in ways which are not only specific within the practice, but help to establish positions within that practice too.

The terms may also be used in metaphoric extension to refer to phenomena associated with the qualities designated by the terms. For example, *big school* is a term commonly used to refer to the infant school, where it is implied that this is the school to which the children will go when they are 'big', rather than the 'baby' nursery. The term is not used to describe the size of the school building, but rather the relative size and age of the participants. Thus, here, as in the other aspects explored, size is certainly being referred to but in a way which is interrelated with other relations of signification. The terms may therefore be the same signifiers as those used in school mathematics, but they clearly do not form the same signs.

Additionally, comparisons in these extracts are made between children or between children and adults, rather than between adults themselves. That is, mothers and fathers are not compared, though it is possible that this might occur in exchanges in which both parents are present. There are few in this corpus.

Thus the terms *big* and *little* are not used either as fixed attributes or indiscriminately. Neither does the children's use of them within the practices appear to differ from that of the adults. I suggest that this latter point is important because it is common to talk (as do Matthews and Matthews) of *children's* use of terms as though there was something specific to children (i.e. their conceptual or lexical development) which made these terms be used in this way. What is important is that this does not appear to be the case. If the terms within any practice form specific relations of signification within that practice, their acquisition by children cannot be said to stand outside those practices in which they are positioned. Why, then, do we tend to examine rate of acquisition as though it were a spontaneous phenomenon, marked only by age or development, in which the social world acted merely as a 'facilitating environment' in which such terms were simply 'allowed to emerge'. While differences in 'rate of acquisition' exist between children, there is every reason for beginning to examine this as an aspect of the relational dynamics and positionings created within the practice itself. (I shall consider this with respect to girls in another volume, *Girls and Mathematics*, forthcoming.) Lieven (1982) demonstrates the way in which Eve, in the Roger Brown corpus (Brown 1973), first began to use time adverbials in very specific exchanges, in this case when she wanted to have a drink from her baby sister's bottle. This request was allowed, but always involved a discussion of turn-taking. But then Eve seemed to want to be *positioned like her sister*, and this highly emotionally charged aspect of family relations provided a space in which new articulation was required. Wanting to take the place of, or to be treated like one's baby sister, to become again a baby who has a bottle, is an aspect in which a position, relational dynamic, emotionality, and desire are bound together. In the same volume, Urwin (1982) discusses this with respect to Lacanian psychoanalysis (but see also Walkerdine and Lucey, in press). I shall refer to this in Chapter 9.

In this sense, then, there is every reason for examining relative rates of acquisition of aspects of positioning and the regulation of practices themselves. In addition, since the practices and their positions are multiple, shifting, and at times contradictory, it seems that concentration upon a fixed, unique developmental pathway obscures such multiplicity. If children are produced as subjects through their insertion as relations within specific practices, we should expect multiplicity and not singularity.

The insertion of different terms as relations in different practices can be explored with reference to the differentiation between *small* and *little*. *Small* is used very specifically to designate size, rather than those practices in which multi-dimensionality is signalled. All of the exchanges in which *small* is used expressively refer to relative size and are not used most often in practical activity. On some occasions they signify the relative fit of objects, such as whether a child can fit into a space, clothing too small for the child, and so on. Examples of such occurrences are JW21, ED3, RP3, EG40, (in Table 4.5). They also appear initiated by children in the same way, for example, CW47 (Table 4.2). The other way in which they are used is when a small amount or piece of something needs to be marked, usually by the mother – as, for example, needing a smaller pile of cards in a game of cards (LA62) or the necessity to cut paper into small pieces so as not to waste any (LA26) (Table 4.5). Again, the term as with *little* is used specifically and contrastively; it is not used to refer to objects in ways appropriate to the designation of those objects within the practice (elastic bands versus piles of playing cards). Thus the term *small* does not appear from these extracts to share the multiple signification of *little*, so that it is used when specifically *size* is the only attribute to be marked and most often within practical activities where size is a feature of the practice. This does not mean to say that on these occasions size is the *object* of the practice: the tasks are rarely explicit *about* size relations as the goals of school tasks are, but size is an attribute which has some significance in the accomplishment of the goal of the activity.

While *little* is also used to refer to size discrimination, *small* is *only* used when *size* is the focus. Thus the use of small is highly specific. It is *small* which is used in specific practices which approximate most closely to school practices leading to measurement. That is, *small* is used in practical tasks when there is a purpose for making a comparison of size. *Little* is sometimes used in this way, but in other multiply signifying ways as well. The teacher is correct to focus on *small*, but simply does not realize the massive entanglement of differential relations with which the children are having to cope.

Taking this analysis back to the issue of the family and size relations to the three bears task set by the teacher, we can see that *small* is the term which the children are likely to be used to using in discussion about size alone: it is not unfamiliar to them. However, it is not as commonly used as *little*, because it does not have the same wide range of applicability. However, the problem of its use in relation to the size task at school is that *small* may be the term used to refer specifically to a comparison of size, but *little* is the term used to refer to a comparison of size which is *also* a comparison of relationship. Thus, in referring to the three bears it would be more common and appropriate to use the designation *little*, and it would also be appropriate to refer to the *mummy* as *big*. Thus what is needed is a way of making the fact that it is the size relations alone which are the focus of attention stand out for the children. As it is, they are blurred by the terminology. Children older, and therefore more accustomed to school tasks, would be likely to be able to use other cues in the discourse to tell them what was the object of the lesson. As it is, these children are only just beginning to learn.

We can begin to see that there are many more features at stake than those which suggest that *bigger* and *smaller* are simply labels for a relationship of size and that children will be able to master tasks involving a size series when they can use size terms comparatively. These children can clearly make size comparisons, but these comparisons are relations within particular and specific practices.

It can be noted from Table 2.1 (p. 17) that although there are many instances of comparative terms these do not include *middle* terms; this is because there are no occasions on which it is necessary, for practical purposes, to compare a series (see Table 4.5). That the term is indeed a function of what is necessary in a particular practice rather than something to do with 'children's usage' is supported by extracts from the Tizard corpus in which *middle* does feature. In extracts concerned with *shape* and *space* there are three instances of the term *middle*, two initiated by the mother and one by the child. In each case it is a middle position which is referred to. For example, in the following extract, (SO49), the middle is the midpoint in a series:

c: I'll put this in my special dustbin, shall I? (*Refers to compost bin.*)
m: That's all right.
c: And it's that way.
m: Well you can put it in the middle compartment if you like.
c: Where?
m: For burning. . . . The middle one with all the big branches is for burning.
c: (*to self*) Right . . . in the middle. . . . It's for burning.

What seems to be the case with respect to size is that the specific practices in which size occurs in this corpus do not present problems in which it is necessary to use the middle term whereas, to a limited extent, some other practices do. We can infer from this that the term *middle* is not unfamiliar to children of this age. However, given the arguments about multiple signification referred to earlier it is important not to infer that because the term is used it can therefore be easily transferred from shape/space to size. The very fact that it occurs in those practices and not those concerned with size makes it likely that the sign which is produced is part of a particular practice which may not include the same relation as those in size discriminations. If the child has to be inserted within a difference practice, that of school mathematics, itself regulated in different ways, with different positions and relations of signification, we should not necessarily expect 'easy transfer', or indeed that the use of examples from home or 'meaningful contexts' will necessarily help, as I shall demonstrate in Chapter 7.

It is interesting at this point to include the one example of the retelling of the story of the three bears which appears in the Tizard corpus. In this instance the mother asks the child to tell her a story and the child retells the story of the three bears. Although the mother has to keep correcting her, it is interesting what stand out for the child as the salient features of the story. Although the relationships between the bears is mentioned (that there is a daddy, mummy, and baby is clearly stated and that they have beds, chairs, and porridge is referred to), size relations simply do not figure in the story that the child tells. She does, however, use comparatives such as 'too sweet' and 'too hot'. What is clear is that the size relations are not remembered by the child as salient to the story, nor does the mother consider them central enough to be remarked upon.

Three bears at home

M: No that's a song, tell me a story.   1
   Tell me that one about the three bears, I like that.
C: Three bears went out one day. (C *stops.*)
M: Yea?
C: In the forest.   5
M: Mm?
C: And little girl come along.
M: What was her name?
C: Poleck.
M: Goldilocks! (M *laughs.*)   10
M: Poleck.   ⎫
C: Goldilocks ⎭
   and she eat baby's breakfast but was too sweet.
M: Mm?
C: And she eat Mummy's breakfast but was too hot. Eat Daddy's   15
   breakfast, just right.
M: Yea? Go on.
C: She eat it all up, she broke the chair she was in . . .
M: Broke whose chair?
C: Daddy's chair.   20
M: Baby's chair, you're getting mixed up.
C: Baby's chair.
M: Yea, go on then.
C: And she got in baby's cot (M *laughs.*)
   and she said 'Who's sleeping   25
   in my one' and who's sleeping with my one, (M *laughs.*)
   who's sleeping with my one?
   (C *says these in three different pitched voices.*)
   (C *touches M's bust.*)
M: (Don't Trace, that's rude), go on, carry on!
C: I did.
M: Yes? Well what about the three bears, have they come back yet?   30
C: And they eat all the porridge up.
M: Who ate all the porridge up?
C: – and me!
M: Who?
C: *Sarah!*   35
M: Goldilocks.

c: Sarah did!
m: You're not, you're pretending, come on tell me properly.
c: I can't. (c *whines.*)
   Can't 'member it. (c *laughs.*)   40
m: Well tell me the one about little Red Riding Hood.
c: I've told you *that* enough times.

                                                                    (TD44)

Child-initiated home and school conversations

In order to examine further how the terms relating to size are used when initiated by children, I noted the exchanges in which this was the case for the Tizard corpus and the play sequences in the two nursery schools mentioned on p. 64. These are presented as Tables 4.2 and 4.3.

Table 4.2   *Child-initiated conversations: home*

I got a bigger bit. I'll put a bigger bit – now that's too big!
(AL50)
I got a big bit (*of mushroom in a salad*).
(JB21)
It's a very bigger (*Ref. unclear*).
(MJ27)
Get me big plate out.
(EG3)
It's a nice little doll.
(EG1)
She's learned to hold my cup, haven't you little Meg.
(MJ24)
I want a big bowl.
(JH1)
A great big hole (*in her tights*).
(CW37)
It'll make you bigger! (*To m drinking tea.*)
(MS20)
Children can have a little dustbin, a toy dustbin.
(CW36)

Table 4.2   *(Cont.)*

I've got a lot of holes in my tights – they're all little ones.

(CW34)

He needs a big car. (*Ref. unclear.*)

(CW29)

I want to come in. Little pig – no, no, no. (*Recites story.*)

(CA26)

That was a big blow (*nose*).

(AC2)

It'll be too big. (*Toy to fit in a toy school.*)

(CW21)

Isn't that a bit big for your supper?

(ED32)

Mummy, this is a big apple. Who told you to do big apples?

(ED17)

That little baby . . .

(CW22)

Have you just done a little bit? (*Ref. unclear.*)

(MS14)

I just a little stroking him (*cat*).

(MS37)

He can't get in, it's too small – I know they can get in big houses.

(CW47)

She's not big enough. (*Ref. unclear.*)

(SS5)

That's a nice little dress.

(RP29)

(*While cutting out in paper*) Got tiny, tiny, tiny, tiny . . . teeny teeniest line . . .

(RP48)

Mum they are tiny bottles.

(SO2)

She's (*sib*) a bit little to do hangman.

(SN4)

Table 4.2 *(Cont.)*

I'm going to do (*draw*) another big monster with small legs and small arms.

(RP55)

I got a little house in here (*a tent*).

(JB34)

. . . my pillow's falling out and it's too big, too big.

(AL34)

(*I want*) some Ribena in the little bottle (*baby's bottle*).

(ED31)

Some (*cats* c *has drawn*) are big, some are little, some big, some little . . .

(RP40)

You can have each stools if you like mummy – the little stool or the big stool.

(ED11)

Look you see, one must have the big spoon and one must have the little spoon.

(ED25)

I'm a big baby.

(JW20)

(c *is drawing.*) Baby Joe's tiny head and tiny eyes.

(LA44)

Some of the little ones (*make a noise at school*).

(K8B4)

Lucy went on the biggest (*donkey*) and I went on the littlest.

(HR30)

She doesn't want to grow bigger . . .' cause she wants to stay at the same school.

(SOT52)

I just want to do (*draw*) a little boy.

(LA42)

The bigger ones (*children aged 11*) can stay at home.

(SOT16)

I don't think the children can sit in that, I don't think there's too much bigger and bigger (*furniture in doll's house*).

(CW17)

Table 4.3   *Child-initiated conversations: school*

I'm bigger 'an my mum and I'm not even bigger 'an Melissa.

(St CJT2)

It's a big dolly.

(St CHT1)

It's a bit small (*about a hat* c *wants to wear*).

(St CHT2)

Mine's having a fatter body than your 'un (*Plasticine model*).

(St CHT2)

I'm up to there (*drinking milk*).

(St CHT2)

Toby, make our sandcastles big up to the sky!

(St CHT1)

This is a big daddy giant! 's batman giant, daddy one! (*Refers to own drawing.*)

(St CST2)

A little wheel and a big wheel. So'e know 'ow little wheels and bigs go, don't you Toby? (*Drawing of a car.*)

(St CST2)

c1: Would you be my baby?

c2: (*Shakes head.*)

c1: I want a *little* girl to be my baby.

c2: I'm too big for the pram now, look, look, see I'm too big. (*Gets in pram.*)

(St C Sa T2)

c1: This big crane look, trying to make a long, b . . . one.

c2: No, I'm not making a big car.

(NNTA)

c1: Make you grow strong milk, won't it.

c2: Big, big, big.

c1: No the milk will make her strong and big and big and big won't it.

(NN 14/3 T2)

I saw spiders in my Nanny's bathroom and they came with big 'ammers.

(NN 14/3 T2)

Table 4.3   *(Cont.)*

A long time ago there was a big, big grey spider, that big, on my wall.

(NN 14/3 T2)

Tarzan don't kill the little boy though that lives with 'im.

(NN 14/3 T2)

Lots of little red spiders.

(NN 14/3 T2)

No leave a bit (*space*) for the lorry to get in . . . bigger, bigger, and bigger.

(NN 14/3 T1)

I can get a big pile (*of bricks*) up.

(NN 14/3 T1)

c_1: I'm on the little one (*horse*).

c_2: You're on the little 'orse and I'm on the big 'orse . . .

c_1: I'm on the small one.

(NN 15/3 T2)

c_1: I'm on the little 'orse.

c_2: You're a little man!

(NN 15/3 T2)

c_1: Long, long car.

c_2: Yeah, long car.

(NN 14/3 T3)

From these extracts it can be seen that the children use the terms in precisely the ways referred to earlier. They might not use the same range of terms as in those requiring comprehension and not production, but the conversations are of the same order and the same distinctions between *little* and *small* are present. It is interesting that St CST2 in Table 4.3 gives an instance of a link between *big* and *daddy*. Here the child is drawing a giant and since giants are usually male, he links *daddy*, *big*, and *giant*. This illustrates clearly that the practice in which the exchange occurs is crucial to an understanding of what terms are judged synonymous and which form contrastive oppositions.

In each case, school and home, these exchanges are a sub-set of discussion in which size is mentioned. In the home exchanges, mothers to some extent take the position of a playmate, which the staff of the nurseries rarely do in the same way: after all, there are plenty of children to play with. The exchanges are necessarily more limited in scope than those involving adults, but the same distinctions and relationships occur if on a more limited basis. The children's use alone does not appear indiscriminate nor does it appear to be differentiated from examples of instrumental exchanges with mothers (see Table 4.5). However, the testing pedagogy is not a significant feature of those exchanges, at least, though later children learn to take the position of the teacher within the discursive practices in complex and important ways (Walden and Walkerdine 1982).

There is one particular exchange from the nursery examples about size which mentions no relational terms but which reveals the children making the transition from qualitative judgements based on relational terms to quantative. They make that transition easily and the exchange is sophisticated. The two boys are measuring themselves against a chart on the wall which is in the form of a man, but marked off in gradations (in what form of measure I am not certain: the boys were outside the classroom and this does not appear on video):

c1: Let me see where you're up to.
    You're just up to that line right there.
c2: And there.
c1: No – you're up to this mark, eyebrow there.
c2: Where 'm up to?
    I'm up to 'is eyebrow!
c1: No.
boy's voice: You're up to 'is eyebrow.
c1: You're up to there.
c2: You're up to there, you're up to 'ere. One, two, three, four, five,
    six, seven, eight, nine, ten, eleven, twelve, thirteen, fourteen,
    fifteen, seventeen.
c1: Sixteen.
c2: Yeh – you're sixteen.
    How, 'ow many I am – oh.
voice: No you ain't – you're seventeen.

It is important that the children move to the use of numbers, which they do with some accuracy, even though the use of counting is often taken as an indication of 'rote-learning' rather than 'proper-conceptualization' (Walkerdine 1982; Corran and Walkerdine 1981).

However, in the other examples, children are clearly aided and stretched by adults. This may well be important because it is quite common in early education to assume children learn best when uninterrupted by adults. This is because the analysis of development which is used assumes that development is a process which depends on children's manipulation of concrete objects, which the adult can only assist. What is suggested by the analysis in terms of practices is that parents and other adults are not mere bystanders, but rather themselves are centrally positioned within the practices, as I have attempted to demonstrate with the teacher in the three bears example.

Mother-initiated exchanges

In order to investigate the ways in which size is discussed in mother-initiated exchanges and to compare these with the classroom and experimental examples, it is necessary to establish how far the practices in which size is used at home are similar to or different from the examples we have of a school lesson. In order to do this it seemed important to devise some procedure of classification of the excerpts. As a beginning I decided to use that which I had used on previous occasions to describe certain sorts of tasks in relation to mathematics in the home (Corran and Walkerdine 1981; Walkerdine 1982). This classification used the designations *instrumental* and *pedagogic* to describe certain kinds of tasks at home and was a distinction originally devised in relation to practices involving *number* in the home. In the Tizard corpus it appeared that those exchanges in which numbers featured could be classified using these two typifications. Instrumental referred to tasks in which the main focus and goal of the task was a practical accomplishment and in which numbers were an incidental feature of the task, for example in cake-making, in which the number *two* might feature in relation to the number of eggs needed and so on. In the pedagogic tasks numbers featured in a quite different way: that is, numbers were the explicit focus of the task. On such occasions the focus was predominantly the teaching and practice of counting. So, for example, a child might be asked to count her coat buttons for no other purpose than to practise the count. Thus I was able to argue that children and mothers do engage in school-like tasks at home in some circumstances. It therefore seemed that such a classification system might be equally appropriate to the examination of size relations, since it could well be the case that the same distinction could operate. My attempt at this classification can be found in Tables 4.4 and 4.5.

Table 4.4 *Pedagogic: mothers*

c: I want to see them (*babies*) small.
m: You want to see them small? Well, they may. .... They may be born when they're small ... if they're too small they have to stay in hospital. To be looked after.

(LA50)

Grandad got his teeth taken out when a big man and not a little boy.

(MS15)

You'll have to do this (*darning*) when you're bigger.

(CW38)

c: Mummy I shall grow up before Anna won't I?
m: Not much darling, she's about the same age as you.
c: Oh, 'cos I'm bigger than her.
m: Yes, but Anna will probably always be a bit shorter than you, 'cos Anna's mummy and daddy are much shorter than mummy and daddy, so Anna will probably never be as tall as you even when she's grown up.

(ED14)

c: Have they (*tigers*) got small mouths?
m: No, they've got great big mouths.
c: Your size? ...
m: What, do you think I've got a great big mouth? ... Oh, are their mouths the same size as me?
c: Mm.
m: No, not that big.

(MJ10)

We must seem big to ladybirds.

(SOT23)

Flies have smaller eyes than us but big compared with its body. (m *and* c *are watching a* TV *programme about insects.*)

(HR26)

m: Well, no I think they (*ants*) told the beetle to go away and there's so many ants that they, even though they are smaller than the beetle, they could push him away ...
c: Cause they're smaller than him.
m: Mm, they are smaller than him, yes ... but there's lots and lots and lots of them ...

(HR24)

Table 4.4 *(Cont.)*

Only little children have parties for their birthdays.

(CW43)

c: You ate all those biscuits, which means you're greedy.
m: But don't forget, I've got a bigger tummy than you've got ... I need more
food to fill it.

(MJ11)

... look, that bit of Mars is a big as the bird and yet he can pull it along,
look!

(CA42)

c: I'm going to invite little persons to my party.
m: But you'll be bigger by then.

(SO21)

It *(cutting toe-nails)* doesn't hurt little toes.

(EG19)

Somebody's put a thin body on that big head – that can't be right.

(JB40)

G is for grandpa, like the Big G you put for Grandma.

(JB35)

That's big, that's a stone really, you have pips in oranges ... it's bigger so you
call it a stone.

(GS15)

(Goldfish) eat little tiny flies' eggs.

(AL12)

(c *is drawing* m.) Nearly right, but you don't have one small one and one big
one *(arms)*.

(MS45)

m: Did you put them in there? *(Objects in a bag.)*
c: When I was a little girl I did.
m: What are you now?

(EG47)

Table 4.5   *Instrumental: mothers*

(*Child wants a ring on*) Your finger's too small.

(JW21)

(*Making Wendy house*) How many short and how many big pieces are there?

(KOK6)

(c *refers to big cat she has drawn as 'mamma'.*)
That's a big one.

(RP50)

(c *tries to sit in baby's buggy.*) That's a silly place to lie!
c: Why?
m: 'Cos you're too small.
c: Too big you mean.
m: I mean *it's* too small.

(AL51)

(m *and* c *are looking at goldfish in a bowl.*)
m: They look a bit bigger through their glass, don't they . . . look over the top
   and see it, it looks different.
c: No, that's a little one now, when I look from the top and it's bigger when I
   look through the glass.

(AL14)

You can have your big bike out now can't you . . . you let the big boys ride it,
don't you. . . . James and Darren are looking for that bike. Jenny's not too big,
but James and Darren are. They're far too long for your bike . . .

(JW25)

Can you get a big spoon and fork for you and a small spoon for Ben?

(1A7)

(c *wants biggest tomato.*) Let me see how big they are.

(HR4)

Skates are a bit big for you – meant to fit (*sib's*) feet.

(SN31)

Get two plates your size – not bowls, plates.

(MJ1)

Put some little children in there (*toy roundabout*).

(CW9)

I think he's (*teddy*) too small to have a nappy.

(ED3)

Tights are a bit big for her (*baby sib*).

(MJ21)

Table 4.5 (Cont.)

(c *wants to use round block for printing eyes on a figure of a man.*) They're a little bit big – just do a little dot 'cos otherwise his eyes'll be bigger than his head and my eyes aren't bigger than my head are they?

(MJ44)

Make a little mummy for her this time (*Plasticine cat*).

(EG36)

You'll have to cut the paper up small, won't you?

(LA26)

He's got a nice big tail this rabbit, hasn't he.

(LA35)

Try and copy these little words.

(MS39)

I don't think there's any place for you to dig yet, but soon your flowers will be big enough and you can dig around.

(SN41)

I don't think that it'll stretch around the egg box – it's only a small elastic band.

(EG40)

You're not to bring that bike in 'ere – it's too big to be in 'ere.

(MS8)

Which jigsaw do you want to do – one of the big ones?

(LA56)

There's a big pad of paper and a little pad . . . big pad is for painting . . . because painting is better on big paper on the whole, isn't it?

(SS7)

It's too small for you (*coat*).

(RP3)

Cutting apricots is not so hard for mummy 'cos my hands are bigger.

(SO51)

Haven't we got a bigger packet (*of apricots*) than that?

(SO43)

Aren't they getting big? (*Plants in the garden.*)

(CA13)

I did keep a tiny bit of pastry for you last night.

(ED27)

You mustn't touch them (*plants*) because they're only little aren't they.

(CA17)

Table 4.5   (Cont.)

There's some tiny little screws here.

(AL3)

I've only got a tiny bit (of flour) left.

(MS24)

Remember that big sausage we had the other day.

(LA12)

(m and c are playing Snap.) OK – but let's get two piles the same. You make those two piles the same. Put them together like that on the ground, now you make those two piles about the same. Can you do that? Put some *more* of that onto there.

c: No that will make the same and my will be smaller.

m: No, it won't make them smaller, make them the same size. That's what you want.

(LA62)

One thing which will become apparent immediately from an examination of the tables is that I found the exercise difficult. The usages did not always seem mutually exclusive and I was not convinced by my own categorization. In addition, there appeared to be some exchanges that did not fit either of the classifications. In these exchanges the mother appeared to be *commenting* on an activity or on something which had been done or seen. In these cases the mother did not appear to be instrumental, in that the exchange was not actually part of a practical activity, but then neither was the purpose explicitly didactic. I have therefore classified these exchanges separately in Table 4.6.

Table 4.6   *Mother commenting*

(m *looks at contents of* c's *bag.*) Lots of little things.

(EG20)

Colin put his finger in the cage and the big bird bit him.

(MS55)

It's her birthday today. That's why we had a little party last week.

(ED30)

A tiny little cauliflower coming (*in the garden*).

(RP7)

I went to see if they had one of these big pencil sharpeners.

(HR2)

Table 4.6 *(Cont.)*

Is that the little pink mouth? (c *has drawn a baby.*)

(LA5)

Who put these little pigs (*toys*) in a row?

(LA55)

I want some little plates.

(MS16)

He bought a big dolly's house.

(EG28)

It was one of the little girls' hamsters.

(MS52)

He didn't realize that she (*the baby*) was so small.

(MJ49)

Is honey bunny smaller than the other one? (*Rabbit.*)

(EG46)

He's tiny, he's not growing very much this one, is he?

(AL9)

(*That's*) when you are a tiny baby. (*Photo of* c.)

(JH47)

She's thinking you're a really nice big sister.

(MJ24)

(*Cats*) don't really like little children, you know.

(LA2)

Look at those little girls out there, they're carrying drinks – can you see the big drinks?

(MJ57)

(c *says she is going to draw three of her young friends*) Three little people.

(LA43)

c: Have you ever seen an elephant walk upstairs?
m: You'd need big stairs for an elephant, wouldn't you.

(LA8)

c: Mum, when will you go to work?
m: When you go to school.
c: I already go to school ...
m: When you go to the big school with Hannah.

(EG58)

One of the things which stands out is that while the mothers do engage in pedagogic discourse it is different from those exchanges with respect to number. In the number pedagogy (Corran and Walkerdine 1982) the mothers engage in the same kind of testing discourse as the teacher in the classroom lesson, while in these examples the mothers appear to be teaching, but it is teaching of a different order. First of all, size is not the main object of the lesson and the lessons are informative rather than testing. In each case the mother appears to be imparting information which while it relates to size, does not have discrimination of size relations as the main focus. Testing does occur, but the focus of that testing is predominantly number and reading. What does this suggest, then? It may well be that the mothers in this corpus do not treat size as the object of pedagogy in the same way that the teachers do. The topics most commonly forming the object of pedagogy are number work: counting, addition, and so forth.

Several points are worth noting here. The first is the assumption that development occurs within a 'facilitating environment'; this often means that mothers are expected to prepare their children for school mathematics by providing them with the 'right kind' of experiences: in order for words to provide a practice which matches that of the school. It has been a common policy to castigate parents, particularly working-class mothers, for their conceptualization of pedagogy in traditional terms, thereby holding them responsible for their children's failure. In such cases, where teachers and parents are operating within a different set of discursive practices, this seems both particularly unfortunate and very punitive. It forms a part of that pathologization of difference which I shall examine in Chapter 10. There have also been those studies which have claimed that mothers are *better* than teachers, thereby castigating teachers (Wells 1982; Tizard and Hughes 1984). Again this seems most unfortunate, since clearly pedagogic practices are different from home ones. The basic question, in both cases, which remains unasked, is why mothers should be expected to teach their children when a system of state schooling exists for the purpose, and why, when children fail, teachers should themselves be blamed for a system which, through its insertion into a system of social inequality, has failure built into it. However, the discourse of child development does not recognize failure. It operates as though practices of schooling did not produce subject-positions, but served to facilitate a basic and underlying system of conceptual development. Sociality is thus denied in a very basic sense.

Even given such considerations, however, and given the qualifications that I have set out about why we should *expect* mothers to teach, and the questions which could be asked about that expectation, nevertheless the *form* of pedagogic discourse in which mothers and teachers are inserted is remarkably similar. Both practices utilize testing discourse, although the object of the pedagogy varies. This suggests that children on entry into school practices will have some familiarity with the form if not the content of such practices. However, even here I am aware of the danger of making over-generalized statements as though they were general truths. The mode of analysis I have attempted rests on grouping the data, which is open to the objection that I have not looked at differences within the sample itself. It leads to the possibility of generalizations of the form 'mothers do...', 'teachers do...'. This is unjustified and suggests the necessity for analyses of a different order; which enables the examination of similarity and difference (see Walkerdine and Lucey, in press). MacLure and French (1981) also point out that mothers and teachers alike use pseudo-questions with great frequency. However, their mode of analysis, like that of other work within the field of discourse and conversational analysis, tends to rely solely on form at the expense of content. This has the effect of making statements which infer an over-simplistic similarity. In addition, they tend towards an ahistorical account of discourse. I shall explore this further in Chapter 10.

I would suggest that this difference of content matters, for it could begin to explain why the children are more tuned in to the form of the pedagogic discourse of the teacher and experimenter than the content to which it refers. This then could provide the basis for and explanation of the responses observed in both the classroom and the experiment. Thus while the children are accustomed to the form of the experiment, they are not accustomed to this form being applied to this particular content. To explain this we do not have to look to some detriment in the mothers: it can be explained by recourse to the fact that the teachers are operating according to a different pedagogic discourse from the mothers. Thus testing discourse with *size* as the focus is likely to be new for the children.

If we examine the contents of Table 4.5, which shows the instrumental activities in which size is used, we can compare these to the school use of size. One of the things which stands out about the discourse which informs early mathematics teaching is that it is centred around activity, that is, building up mathematical concepts on the basis of what the children do. Therefore one of the things which Matthews and Matthews (1978) urge teachers in nursery classes to do is to comment on the size aspect of children's play activity or some instrumental activity directed by the teacher. For example:

> When playing with bricks, children often call adults to admire their work, thus opening the way for questions. You have built a tall tower. Can you see some other things that are as tall? That's a long road you have built. How much longer can you make it? How can you make it wide enough to push the pram along? Do you think that John's tower is taller than yours?
>
> Questions like this will help a child to answer with more than 'yes' or 'no' and the conversations which follow may produce even more mathematical ideas.

(Shape and Size Comparisons: 17)

These examples compare in some respects with the instrumental tasks in home practices, although they are more like those using the contrastive pair *big/small* than those in which *little* is used. As I argued earlier, *small* is the term used specifically with respect to precise size comparisons. What is different in the school example given above are the positions taken by the participants in the exchange. In the home task, at least those in which mother and daughter are working together, the mother is no mere bystander. The two are engaged in a joint task, either the child helping the mother or the mother playing with the child. In the nursery example, the teacher is supposed to comment on some activity which the child has done without the teacher. Thus the kinds of conversations which ensue appear to be considerably more stilted than the home ones. Again, to account for this I suggest that it is necessary to look to the pedagogic discourse which informs the teaching: that is, that adults should not over-interfere with children's spontaneous play, which is the motor of development. Indeed, this is stressed in Matthews and Matthews' introductory notes to guide teachers. They say:

> The sensitive teacher . . . will be careful not to spoil the imaginative and creative play by intruding at the wrong time.

(1978:5)

The mothers here do not comment on size aspects of the task in which the child is engaged; rather, size comes up as an important dimension to solving some practical problem. Again, the aspect of the relational dynamic is important. The relationship between 'mother and daughter' is not coterminous with that of 'teacher and child'. Further, the stress for the teacher both here and in the infant school is on the 'activity' of classifying and sorting objects *big* and *small*. For example, Williams and Shuard (1976) suggest that teachers should get children to engage in activities which focus on the comparison of size, for example comparing two rods. These activities can be recorded:

All such discoveries through comparing need to be recorded, for example by placing all longer ones of the couples into a particular box, or by putting an appropriate word or letter on the objects, or by putting drawings or pictures into blanks in given sentences such as the following: 'The (blue) rod is longer than the (red) rod.'

(Williams and Shuard 1976:43)

This extract reveals two more differences between the home instrumental and the school practices. First, the school practices have as the practical outcome (like the pedagogic number tasks) some school mathematical statement, such as the recording of the differences in lengths of words or reciting a number sequence. The instrumental tasks at home do not have this as a practical outcome. I will discuss in Chapter 6 how important this is in understanding what typifies school mathematics as a practice. Second, by stressing the 'activity' of sorting and classifying, as Williams and Shuard do, they are focusing on different aspects of the task at home. At home the classifications are made as part of a topic or purposeful activity. In the activity as defined by Williams and Shuard, the action of classification and sorting itself is stressed as the end-point. In statements such as 'the blue rod is longer than the red rod', the statement does not form part of a discursive practice with a clear metaphoric content or topic in the way that the home tasks do: the tasks here have no topic and no purpose other than the act of classification itself. This can only be comprehensible to children by being understood as part of those practices which go to make up what school is about. Thus it is quite possible that precisely the same sentences may be presented at home and at school (for example, a statement which remarks on a comparison of size), but that does not mean that the two utterances exist in the same relation in the practices at all. Indeed, since in some examples the mothers are not setting out to teach or make explicit for pedagogical purposes anything about size, then we would not expect them deliberately to point out the size aspects. In addition, the teachers do not have an intimate relationship with the children that they teach. But their teaching is aimed at, sooner or later, getting the children to operate in school mathematics. That could never be the function of the mothers. It would be unfair to blame the teachers or the mothers for shortcomings. I have tried to show how the discourse in which the teachers read their task is instrumental in deciding both what counts as mathematics and thus how they are positioned. If we are to change teaching we must change those discursive practices in which they are sited.

The idea of the development of concepts through experiences represented unproblematically by size terms can be shown to be over-simple, to say the least. There is not unproblematic transfer of experience from home to school. What exist are discursive practices which operate according to relations of signification, utilizing different systems of syntagmatic and paradigmatic opposition. School mathematics practices with respect to size discrimination take the discrimination as a focus in a way which is not the case with respect to size in other practices, though it is so in respect of other mathematical practices, such as counting. To enter early school mathematics, therefore, children must become subjects within those discursive practices and recognize the lesson as an example of pedagogic testing discourse with size as the focus. Using size terms at home does appear to be of some help, since it prepares the children in the use of the signifiers, though since those signifiers are united with different signified to form signs as part of different discourses their helpfulness is not of an all-or-nothing kind. Transfer is therefore not a simple and straightforward process. It is not a case of getting children into a supportive context which allows them to express what they already know since this knowledge may well be different.

I have attempted to demonstrate in this chapter the effectivity of different discursive practices, the way in which they produce relations of significations, and different relations of signifier and signified. In that respect they cannot be read as distorting some set of relations which exists outside or before them, but themselves in producing regimes of meaning, signs which function as truth-tests. These have real effects in positioning the participants in systems of regulation within the practices. In taking the experiment, the home, and the classroom as practices we can examine the constitution of their truth. This does not lead to the kind of analysis which dismisses experiments as biased and observation as a source of true naturalistic data. In each case I have tried to display ways in which the truth within each practice is constituted in and through relations of signification themselves. That is, discursive practices in producing regimes of meaning create particular intersections of the material and discursive, signified and signifier. The same signifiers may exist across practices, but this does not mean the same signs are created. In addition I have tried to suggest that the multiple signification of many signs within particular practices demonstrates the way in which the participants are positioned and regulated, and how emotionality and desire are carried within these relations themselves.

5 Practices in which numeracy is produced

In this chapter I want to explore further some of the ways in which mathematical signifiers form part of non-mathematical practices, and to distinguish those from practices for producing formal academic, or school, mathematics. I shall suggest that the practices in each case differ in crucial respects and that although the same signifiers may be used we are not justified in inferring, as is common in early education, that 'mathematics is everywhere'. Although it is commonplace to assume that numeracy consists of concepts or skills in which mathematical understanding is utilized or applied in 'everyday settings', I want to question this view.

> Mathematics for very young children is an incidental and integral part of their general activity and they need a variety of experiences from which they may generalize later. At this stage their play may be free and experience apparently random, but it is in this range of experience that they encounter ideas (such as, 'inside', 'next to', 'taller than', 'heavier than') in a variety of contexts, and from which they gradually acquire concepts.
>
> (Matthews and Matthews, *General Guide*, 1978:2)

Within practices of mathematics education this conforms to a position consonant with that taken by Margaret Donaldson (1978) in relation to 'embedding', that is, that numeracy represents the use of mathematical concepts in known and familiar settings which facilitate their performance. However, although practices outside formal mathematics utilize mathematical signifiers, I suggest that we are not justified in assuming they are 'the same thing'. I shall look at this assumption in the chapters which follow by an examination of certain home and school mathematics practices. I will suggest that non-mathematics practices can be used as the foil for, and therefore be transformed into, mathematics practices, but that this requires a shift in the relations of signification involved in the transition from one discursive practice into another.

Let me begin with some examples. Maier (1980) describes what he calls 'folk mathematics', by giving an example of the difference in modes of calculating what is a practical problem and a pseudo-practical problem presented as a written test item. He takes the example of an actual question in a national mathematics test:

A parking lot charges 35 cents for the first hour and 25 cents for each additional hour. For a car parked from 10.45 in the morning until 3.05 in the afternoon, how much money should be charged.

This kind of question is included in the curriculum precisely because it is supposed to be an example of real-life mathematics. But, as Maier clearly points out, solving a school mathematics problem and working out one's parking charges are not equivalent:

Obviously in a parking lot the problem of figuring one's bill is never so clearly or so explicitly stated. One is not handed a piece of paper on which all the necessary data are neatly arranged. Instead, information must be gathered from a variety of sources – a sign, a wrist watch, a parking lot attendant. Paper and pencil are seldom available for doing computations. One is unlikely to go through the laborious arithmetical algorithms or procedures taught in school and used in tests. One is more likely to do some quick mental figuring.

(1980:21)

Maier outlines particularly the difference in mode of calculation in the task. In Chapter 6 I will take this examination further by looking both at this and the goal of school mathematics versus other tasks. Although it is common to understand them as the same thing, there are many differences in terms of the discursive practices, and therefore task-demands of the school and non-school tasks even if, superficially, they may appear similar. On the national numeracy test utilized by Gallop and designed by the ACACE (Sewell 1981), all of the items contain practical tasks such as working out a bill in a restaurant, paying a phone bill, filling a car with petrol, and buying items in a supermarket. One question presents two bottles of tomato sauce, of different sizes and prices, and asks which is the 'best buy'. This is assumed to be a practical application of a particular kind of mathematical calculation. But let us consider how, in practice, I might make a choice in a supermarket. Do I have time to make a calculation? Are there non-mathematical reasons for preferring one bottle to another? For example, I may not think the taste or quality of the cheaper sauce is as good, or my family may dislike it. It may come from a country whose goods I do not wish to purchase. Or, of course, on the other hand, I may only be able to afford the cheaper brand. This means that whether or not I calculate it is not simply about my 'ability' to do so. Readers, I am sure, could add other associations. Every item in the test could be subjected to the same evaluation.

In Chapters 3 and 4 I explored the way in which signifiers used in mathematics, unlike the other practices, were multiply signifying: 'big girl', for example, stated not only a relation of size, but of regulation, value, behaviour, etc. In these practices, in which what is described as 'numeracy' is produced, the same criteria apply. They are not formal mathematics because the relations within the practices are not the same, nor are the practices regulated and accomplished in the same manner at all. Indeed, if we were to carry further Maier's 'folk mathematics' analogy, we may conclude that traditional practices in which numeracy was produced themselves produced practices for making appropriate kinds of calculations. These are not coterminous with formal mathematics. Formal academic mathematics, as an axiomatic system, is built precisely on a bounded discourse, in which the practice operates by means of suppression of all aspects of multiple signification. The forms are stripped of meaning, and the mathematical signifiers become empty. This is central to its power as a system or discourse which may be superimposed onto and read into all others. When nature is seen as a 'book written in the language of mathematics', certain things follow which have profound implications for the possibility of the natural and human sciences. I shall explore these in Chapter 9.

For the purpose of this chapter, my point is that non-mathematical practices, or those containing what we describe as 'numeracy' are not mathematics any more than cognitive tasks are 'the same' when contained within 'familiar contexts'. The point of contention, then, is to examine all practices as systems of signification which produce subject-positions within them. This reading produces a very different form of analysis.

I want to take this further by examining one particular practice, cooking, which is commonly taken in nursery and infant schools to be mathematics or pre-mathematics, if viewed as an opportunity for the concrete manipulation of certain objects. It is therefore instructive to consider that when a traditional developmental reading is imposed upon such a practice, it utilizes a quasi-mathematical discourse to do so. Logico-mathematical structures become a reading by which the psychologist or teacher 'sees' mathematics or cognition *in* the activity in question. On the basis of this reading, the practice 'becomes' cognition or mathematics.

However, I want to examine various examples of practices at home in which numbers appear as signifiers, to examine the way in which the practices are regulated and how such practices, in providing a *foil* for formal mathematics, can become the site for the move into a formal discursive practice in which external reference, or the multiple significations of the signs, is suppressed. We might therefore ask, what is the positive effectivity of treating all practices as undifferentiated aspects of a blanket 'experience'? Again, I pose the question this way, rather than as one of 'distortion of the real' in order to point up the constructed and therefore productive quality of the discourses through which we understand the social world.

By examining utilization of numbers and arithmetic operations in the home practices it should be possible to see how far the signifiers, signs, and discourse are similar and different. Let us begin by examining more closely what is meant when it is asserted that the same signifiers may be used in the different discursive practices but that they do not produce the same signs.

There are many words which form part of school mathematical discourse which are commonly used in other discourses. One example of such words are the terms *odds* and *even*. In school mathematical discourse they form a contrastive oppositional pair describing aspects of the cardinal and ordinal features of the number system. The following example, taken from a lesson reported by an infant school teacher (Coghill 1978), will serve to show that these terms have a multiplicity of significations. Coghill was teaching a lesson on odd and even numbers in which she asked the children to call out numbers and then to say whether they were odd or even. She found that children cheered the even numbers and booed the odds. When she asked why they did this the children replied, 'We like evens better'. The only possible explanation for such behaviour on the part of the children is that odd and even as signifiers are also part of other discourses, joining the other signifieds to form different signs. We can immediately think of the pejorative connotations attached to 'odd' – 'the odd one out', 'odd' behaviour, and so on. The point is that although children will meet in school mathematics terms with which they are already familiar, those terms may be used in very different ways in their articulation in, and signification within, other practices.

In Chapter 2 I argued that those relational terms which are understood to be very important for mathematics learning are inserted very specifically into home practices, so that very specific signifiers are used within particular relations in practice. For example, although *more* and *less* are assumed to be an important contrastive pair, it is often assumed that young children do not understand the meaning of *less* and, indeed, interpret questions involving *less* to mean *more* (Donaldson and Wales 1970). This failure is taken to imply, and in some accounts to be caused by, a failure to understand quantity relations. In the analysis of the terms *more* and *less* in home practices, I argued that children have plenty of practice in activities involving quantity relations. However, the terms used to signify similar relations in the relevant practices do not appear to be the contrastive pair *more* and *less*. Other terms, such as *a lot* and *a little* are far more common. While there were in the corpus inspected many instances of *more* and none of *less*, it is important to point out that the term *more* was not used in practices involving the contrast of quantity relations. More was used almost exclusively in the regulation of consumption by parents and the children's requests for extra helpings. In these practices the opposite of *more* is not *less*, but something more like *no more*, since the opposite of *more pudding* in such an example is clearly not *less pudding*.

In order to examine these relations I shall look at the occurrence of numbers and arithmetic operations in the home transcripts. These exchanges seem to operate in several ways. Numbers or other 'mathematical signifiers' can form a relation within those discursive practices which have a variety of aims, from gardening to learning manners. In each case, then, it would be important to examine what precisely was their relation and the multiple signification contained within the practice itself. Apart from this, the signifiers can form a relation within explicit attempts at a pedagogy concerning mathematics when, as I shall argue, the relations and practices are remarkably like those of school. In other exchanges the relation itself is still often pedagogic, but with other aspects of the focus: sharing, game-playing, appropriate behaviour, correct dress, and so forth. Although, classically, these would be exactly the kinds of exchanges in which Matthews and Matthews (1978) would 'see' mathematics, are we justified in so describing the practices? Or even assuming that they are, in some simple sense, *pre*-mathematical?

Table 5.1 *Numbers from one to six and fractions (other than 1 – 1 correspondence and counting)*

___

One

___

(c *asks for another ice-lolly.*)
M: No I've given you *one* lolly today.

(TD22)

c: (*I'm*) getting some spoons out . . .
M: Only one!

(EG6)

M: Run and get the milk quickly . . . one at a time.
c: One at each side.

(KG31)

(c *is making cakes.*)
M: Now do one more.

(JS6)

___

Two

___

c: What's that?
M: Two little cats.

(MS19)

M: How many small, short ones have we got?
c: Two.
M: Any how many big ones?
c: One.

(JO'K)

c: When is Steve going to be home?
M: Two minutes.
c: Two minutes, one, two?
M: Mm.
c: He won't, he'll be a long time.

(LA62)

M: You going to lay the table? – two knives and two forks.

(KSB1)

c: I'm not going to eat any more.
M: . . . just two more mouthfuls.

(RS5)

Table 5.1   (*Cont.*)

c: You've only got two cards left.

(LA84)

m: They're two pink cards but they're different (*in Snap*).

(LA76)

c: Snap! There was two the same.

(LA73)

c: You didn't know there was two the same.

(LA66)

Three

---

c: I'm just go to do (*draw*) Ben, Lucy, and Sam.
m: Three little people.

(LA43)

m: They must be three ends of sausages I suppose (*looking at ends of sausage on dinner plate*).

(SO'T5)

m: You've got a lot of holes in your tights ... three now ...
c: I got three.

(CW30)

Four

---

c: Can I have all of them? (*Sausages*).
m: Let's leave Dad four – you can have four if you want.

(DH4)

Five

---

c: How old is this baby? (*A doll.*)
c: Five.
m: Five? Good heavens! She's very small for five. Five years old?

(AL56)

Six

---

m: (*explaining a board game*) You have to get a six to start.

(JB10)

Table 5.1   *(Cont.)*

Fractions

M: I'm not sure if another piece (*of bread*) is out darling, did you eat half of it? Yes you did.

(JB27)

M: We can take those few out (*biscuits*) – there's half a one.

(RS39)

M: There's an apple out – so you can have a quarter of that. Olivia has hers.

(ED35)

M: Could I have one and a half to London please?

(EG22)

C: I'm going to have a whole apple.
M: I'll cut them in half for you, Molly.

(MJ2)

M: There's one (*walnut*) left – break it in half, and you two can have it between you.
M: (*to c1*) One.
M: (*to c2*) Two.

(HR13)

M: There are six rooms (in a dolls' house) and you can both choose three each . . . you can choose half.

(KSB31)

M: There's only one (apple) there . . . you'll have to share it.
C: Cut it in half mummy.

(EG17)

C: Half for you – half a pear for you.

(GS13)

C: I want some more.
M: No . . .
C: Only one biscuit?
M: No.
C: Half a biscuit?
M: No.
C: A little of a biscuit?

(EG59)

They are involved in locating numbers of objects, therefore using the cardinal aspect of number. Clearly this gives children practice in the concrete use of the appropriate signifiers. It is important that small numbers are used by both adults and children. This may or may not reflect parents' expectations or children's capacities, but there is no basis for making an inference about this on the basis of this data. However, if we examine the practices in which these references to number occur, an examination of Table 5.1 suggests that the practices of which these instances form a part are ones in which large numbers would not ordinarily be involved, for example, numbers of knives and forks to lay the table, numbers of mouthfuls of food before stopping eating, numbers of sausages to be eaten, cakes to be made, and so on. It is also crucial to note that in those sequences involving counting, some of which are instrumental (such as making and counting cakes), much larger numbers are used. Therefore it becomes clear that it is important not to draw hasty conclusions as to competence from instances contained in a limited range of practices. However, it is these practices which most often reflect the views of early mathematics educators about the understanding of number arising from the handling of actual objects, and of one-to-one correspondence involving small numbers. If we examine the traditional categories which are taken to provide the experiences which produce mathematical concepts, we find instances of one-to-one correspondence, sorting, and classification. One-to-one correspondence tasks are quite common though they occur more frequently when they involve counting. Sorting and classification occur in other tasks, such as that in which the mother and daughter are constructing a Wendy house, using a kit which has a frame made of metal pieces slatting together. The mother asks her daughter about particular numbers of pieces:

m: How many small, short ones have we got?
c: Two.
m: And how many big ones?
c: One.

What is interesting about this exchange is that it clearly requires the child to sort and classify using number, and the child apparently has no difficulty with the task. The mother phrases her question as though there were no problem in posing questions of this sort to the child. She clearly therefore assumes that the child can understand small numbers. In addition to this, it is important to notice the discursive construction used by the mother, which is instrumental in order to complete a practical task. The discursive form of the question 'How many?' is identical to that used in pedagogic exchanges in which the question is testing, because the adult already knows the information requested of the child. It is not, therefore, the discursive form of the question which, in this instance, allows the participants to discriminate between kinds of tasks, but more clearly the nature of the tasks in which the discursive forms are contained. It is, however, important that the sorting and classification tasks do not form part of exchanges in which the purpose of the task is pedagogic, nor do one-to-one correspondence tasks which do not involve counting. Thus, those aspects which do form the subject matter of the parental pedagogy are not entirely equivalent to those of the teacher. However, it must be remembered that instrumental tasks in school, that is, ones which involve children in practical accomplishments, are judged pedagogically by the teachers of children. Although tasks such as these do explicitly form that part of the mathematics curriculum for young children that aims to give them appropriate experience of objects, are we justified in assuming that the children will recognize the tasks as mathematics, and does it matter? In Chapter 6 I shall examine certain aspects of some primary school children's understanding of the mathematics curriculum, which suggests that it is certainly not understood as an undifferentiated aspect of everyday experience, but a highly differentiated and specifically reg- ulated practice. However, as I argue later, many tasks within the curriculum are presented as *though* they were aspects of a different discursive practice: story-telling, a game, shopping, etc. This sets up two competing systems of signification for reading the tasks and it is in these misreadings that mistakes often occur. Thus, although in the Piagetian scheme children's understanding of their tasks as mathematics or not does not matter, and although in Donaldson's the 'human sense' is taken to help, I remained unconvinced, on the basis of the alterna- tive reading that I am setting out here.

Other aspects of number which are used in non-school practices are fractions. Fractions appear in a variety of ways which can be quite complex (see Table 5.1). They usually involve the sharing of objects between siblings, most often a fruit to be cut into halves or quarters. However, there are aspects in which the division is more complex and allusion is made to the fact that when one object is divided the end result is more objects. This occurs in HR13 in which a walnut is divided in half, one half given to each sibling, at the same time the mother counting out the halves, 'one, two' as she does so. Another example (KSB31) involves not the sharing of *one* object, but *six* rooms in a dolls' house between two children, giving them three, or 'half each' as the mother says. In these cases, the children are being introduced to the practical aspects necessary for the beginnings of division. However, they are also introduced to sharing as an aspect of moral regulation. Again here it is important to point out that clearly the topic of the task is equivalent to that which is used in schools, though the form of the task may well be different. The signifiers here seem to be used in a similar way to the examples the children will meet at school. However, one instance in the fractions exchanges shows that this similarity is not total. In (EG22) the mother and daughter are playing at going on a journey to London. As part of this fantasy the mother says 'one and a half to London please'. This example comes from the discursive practices of public transport travel. In this instance the 'one' and the 'half' are used as indicators of full adult and half child fare, even though the child fare may not always be exactly half the adult. This usage is metaphoric: a child being equivalent to half an adult and so on. This usage of half, as with some other examples of numbers, is different from that contained in school practices and expected from the discourse of early mathematics education, which recognizes those instances which arise from the operation of objects. For example, there is one instance of a child using a number to refer to age, in this case, five. The children do not make the mistake that the number refers to a number of children, but use it in a way consonant with the practice, that is to refer to age. They may not know precisely what eleven years means but they recognize the usage of the number as different from the labelling of numbers of objects. There are other examples in the Tizard corpus (see Walkerdine and Lucey, in press) in which the two children are made to recite their addresses in true pedagogic fashion. In these cases the addresses contain numbers. In another exchange a child finds a piece of paper with the numerals 382 on which she reads out as 'three eight two'. Her mother instantly recognizes this as the grandmother's telephone number. Again, the child learns that there are other usages of number. In (JB10) in Table 5.1 the mother and daughter are playing a board game which involves throwing a dice and getting 'a six' to start. Although the six has six dots the term a 'six' is understood differently from that in other usages. Another example in the Tizard corpus (Walkerdine and Lucey, in press) occurs when a child asks whose space hopper her father is sitting on. He looks underneath, and on this surface is painted the numeral 3. He asserts that if it is a three it must be Claire's. Here the number is used to differentiate the objects belonging to different siblings and does not refer to the cardinal or ordinal aspects of number. Here, also, the numerals are used to designate possession and private property.

Children do indeed come across numbers and understand them when used in a variety of practices other than labelling numbers of objects, or from one-to-one correspondence. Their experience of, and understanding of, number is therefore not limited to those usages contained in school mathematics. Numbers are used in a variety of other everyday practices in a variety of other ways. In those other modes the numerals may be the same signifiers but they are not the same signs. It is important that in these cases children do not appear confused. When faced with 'a six' they do not expect six dice.

Counting

Table 5.2 contains the instances of exchanges around counting in the Tizard corpus (see. p. 106).

In these examples it is apparent that counting is not always adult initiated. On several occasions children initiate a counting sequence and often count spontaneously. They do not always count objects but sometimes simply recite a counting sequence. The importance of such child-initiated counting is amply testified by Gelman and Gallistel (1978). On one occasion in Table 5.2 the mother counts objects and simply appears to be counting to the child who is present (EG11). There are several exchanges in which mothers take a practical task and appear to use it, by seizing the moment for a maths lesson. This is exactly what teachers of young children are supposed to do, to seize the right moment, when the child is engaged on a practical task, and use it to extend the child's understanding. Quite clearly the mothers recognize an area of practice which is pedagogically important and do use that moment. It is important that they recognize this with respect to counting and arithmetic operations in ways that they do not with other aspects of early school mathematics.

There are several examples in the home transcripts of discussions about time. These consist of qualitative uses of time in which the amounts of time which make up 'short' or 'long' duration are not quantified and are indeed subjective and variable. While they introduce children to the dimension of time, such experiences do not relate to the mathematical quantification of time. There are other exchanges which do so. These are instances in which children ask what the time is or

Table 5.2   *Counting*

(c *is drawing a picture.*)
M: I've only got three fingers – I'm not having that – I've got five fingers, one, two, three, four, five.
(M *counts fingers on her hand.*)
    How many more you got there?
c: One, two, three, four (*counts drawing*).
M: No, you've got three, silly you've gotta put another two.
c: Four, five.

(SN24)

(c *is drawing a donkey.*)
c: Now, one foot, two foot, three foot, four, five foot, six foot. One, two, three, four, five, six, six.
M: Six what?
c: Feet.
M: Six feet, my goodness!
c: (*laughs*) look, one, two, three, four, five, six.
M: More like a caterpillar than a donkey!

(HR34)

(M *is referring to an apple cut into four.*)
M: How many have you got?
c: One, two, three, four.
M: Mm.
c: That isn't a lot is it?
M: Not really.

(MJ13)

(c *wants more knives for laying the table.*)
M: Oh! you can't have one, two, three ... you can't have five because I don't think I've got five. You've got one already haven't you? You can get four now.

(EG89)

(M *and* c *doing number jigsaw.*)
M: Is there anything with five .. anything with five things on there?
c: No.
M: They've all got more, haven't they?
c: Mm. That (*finds one with six*).
M: Well, count, I think there may be more.

(ER59)

Table 5.2   *(Cont.)*

M: How many have you got (*printing blocks*).
C: One, two, three, four, five.
M: Five. That's enough to be going on with.

(JO'K)

(M *is looking through a drawer.*)
M: Some of Hannah's badges in there: one, two, three, four.
   There's a big one, five, six, seven.

(EG11)

M: How many red ones are there? Count the red ones.
C: One, . . . two, three, four, five.

(JH19)

M: Hold your breath and count to ten, if you've got hiccups.
C: Ten, eight.
M: Hold your breath, one, two three four five six seven . . .
C: One two three.
M: Don't say it. Say it under your breath while you're holding it.
C: One two three four eight six nine two three four seven two four.
M: What about one?

(JW28)

C: Fourteen, fifteen – my plate's empty!

(ED13)

C: One pretend, I'm pretending this one, does two and two make four?
M: Mm, mm.
C: Three and three makes . . . one two three four five six.
M: Mm.
C: Count this (*holds up eight fingers*) . . . one two three . . . four five six seven
   eight.
M: Well done.
C: One and one makes . . . you remember, you say it.
M: One more than eight?
C: Two!
C: What does two and two make?
M: You tell me, you've just done it.
C: One two three four.

(S'OT'6)

M: Just eat those three little bits.
C: Look there, one two three.
M: Mm.

Table 5.2   (Cont.)

c: One two three four five.
m: Well eat those – how many's left then?
c: There's five, look one two three four five six.
m: Oh six now – they're getting bigger are they?
c: One two three, one two three, got three.

(SO'T)

(m *is counting tags into bag – counts to 65 –* c *tries to join in.*)
c: One two three four five.

(SO57)

(*Counting money.*)
m: . . . count it for me.
c: Yeah.
m: That's it.
m: That's ten.
c: Mm.
m: Twelve.
c: Yea.
m: Fourteen.
c: Yea.
m: Sixteen.
c: Yea.
m: Eighteen 'p'. Eighteen pence.

(JM19)

m: Do you know any numbers then?
c: One.
m: Mm.
c: Two three four, one two three four, one two three four.
m: Yes, what's after four?
c: Five, six seven, eight nine ten.
m: Oh clever aren't you? What's after ten?
c: One two three four five six seven eight nine ten eleven five!
m: Ten eleven *twelve*.
c: Ten eleven twelve fourteen sixteen nine eighteen sixteen four nineteen
     seventeen twenty-one, twenty-two, twenty-three, twenty-eight.
m: Oh that's not bad.

(TD52)

mothers seek to test their daughters' knowledge of clock times. All of these clock examples concentrate on testing. Where they go beyond this they relate the time on the clock with an external event, as in:

c: Is it afternoon?

m: Yea, it is three o'clock. Michelle – Aunty'll be picking Michelle up from school now.

In another sequence the mother tests the child on 'meaningful' times, such as 'one o'clock, dinnertime', 'seven o'clock, bedtime'. In such instances it is important that the meaningfulness is conveyed by the relation of the clock time to an external event within the child's home life and not, for example, an adjacent clock time. The meaningfulness is not presented as 'one o'clock is next to two o'clock', but that one o'clock is dinnertime. This usage is similar to that advocated in Matthews and Matthews (1978): 'All schools have a daily routine in which the children find a great deal of security. This routine can be a help in displaying the link between events and the passage of time' (*The Passage of Time*: 3). They then go on to a list of ways in which precisely those relations pointed out in the home exchanges can be demonstrated in relation to school practices. While this relation is clearly of vital importance, I would argue that it is significantly different from that in which the internal relations of the quantitative relations of time are focused on. In order to operate on the mathematical dimension, the focus has to be away from the practical and external relations to the internal relations of the numerical sequence of the measurement of time. This transition is blurred in both their approach and the experiential one.

Qualitative not quantitative

There appear in the home transcripts a considerable number of terms which feature in school mathematics in relation to measurement. However, these tend to be used in some cases in different ways from that assumed in school mathematics. For example, terms which refer to size and distance are often used qualitatively rather than quantitatively. In the following extracts such usages are exemplified:

m: . . . look, that bit of Mars is as big as the bird. And yet he can pull it along, look!

(CA42)

M: It's too small for you, that.

C: What is!

M: That coat.

C: No, it isn't.

(RP3)

(M *and* C *have just put a ladybird outside.*)

M: That's alright, he won't come back in now.

C: Why won't he?

M: It's a long way to the door.

(SO'T24)

In these examples, as in many others, while size and distance are discussed they are not understood in any absolute sense, but qualitatively, that is, as a function of the relation between the objects being compared. Size and distance are *relative*: the distance from the door to the table in SO'T24 is only long for a ladybird, not for humans. Where examples are used which focus on absolute quantity numbers are used, as in the measurement of clock time. This move from quantitative judgements seems an enormously important transition. The children involved in qualitative judgements are clearly not engaged in the same practice as that requiring quantification in school mathematics. In each of the examples quoted above the children are not taking part in a practice where it would be necessary to quantify their experiences. We can hypothesize that it is the insertion of the children into practices requiring the quantification of size and distance relations which would produce the appropriate usage. Such practices could be do-it-yourself jobs around the house, cooking, dressmaking, and so on. It may well be the case that for many children school is the first example of the use of such quantifications. In the Matthews and Matthews approach, like others in early mathematics, it is assumed that qualitative judgements are the precursor to quantitative ones. They do not discriminate between such usages. The problem is that while there is indeed ample evidence to suggest that such qualitative judgements are a crucial forerunner to quantification, it does not mean that they are the same thing. Indeed, the *differences* between the two systems and the transition and translation required to move from one system to another might (like the examples involving number which we have examined) be very important in helping children into measurement.

For the Matthews, and Williams and Shuard (1976), however, children are taken to *discover* measurement. Their introduction to it is therefore autodidactic and spontaneous, and does not require them to come to quantification through their insertion into specific practices. Indeed, quantification comes only as a representation of relationships which the children have already mastered through the simple manipulation of concrete objects.

One of the important features of the home exchanges is that often terms are not used simply to indicate one dimension at a time, but several different dimensions at the same time, depending on the practical situation under discussion. For example, the two following exchanges taken from the conversation of a mother and daughter in the garden show how commonly the practice in which the exchange occurs (in this case the garden) defines the set of relations which will be described and the connections which are made:

c: Which one is yours?
m: The *big* one.
And yours are the seeds that we put round the *side*.

(CA15)

m: They grow *big*.
c: They grow *fast*.
m: Grow *fast* when the summer comes, yes.

(CA24)

We can say that in these two exchanges there are examples of terms used in size, geometry, speed, and time. In a mathematical exchange these particular relations would not occur together like this, although a statement containing a similar selection of lexical items could take place in scientific discourse in which the speed of a plant's growth and the height it attains may be related to the amount of sunlight, etc. Thus, this episode on gardening is an example of the production of relations in a practice which could provide the foil for a scientific lesson. But if the focus were mathematics, one would have to calibrate particular aspects, such as the time taken to grow to particular heights and so on. However, in this instance it is the practice of gardening which provides the setting for those terms to co-occur in this way. The example suggests clearly how gardening might be used as a foil to teach mathematical relations, but I suggest that if gardening were to be used as such a foil the relations would be presented in significantly different ways, such that possibly only one dimension was the focus and gardening would not be the instrumental end product, but rather the *mathematical* product would be a mathematical statement. I explore this in Chapter 7 with respect to the use of shopping as a school task to teach subtraction. In the case of gardening we can take the example further. I have argued that it would be possible to use gardening as the basis for a science lesson, in which case, for example, the increasing height of the plant might be mapped onto or correlated with the time taken to grow. We would not in this case be doing mathematics. We would, however, express that simple physical relationship by transposing it into mathematical discourse, for example, as something like:

$$H = f (T)$$

But the physical relation which we have noted, while it can be *expressed* in mathematical terms, cannot be *reduced* to them. The physical relation cannot be deduced from the mathematical formula: the process is not reversible, but of course the mathematical formula might be produced in an attempt to transform and to work out the generalization of the physical relations. The mathematics in this case comes in the mode of quantification, the mode of signification, but not in the physical relations. This extends the point which I was making in relation to the home pedagogy examples. When the mothers and teachers use cooking to teach mathematics they both single out a mathematical aspect and use a particular form of discourse to represent the relation which they are pointing up. Similarly, shopping and gardening remain shopping and gardening until they are used as a foil for teaching mathematics, when particular relations will be focused on with particular kinds of discourse. An associated point is that one word when used in an exchange in any particular practice outside mathematics may simultaneously point up several dimensions, whereas in mathematics the term would be used to describe one relation at a time.

The use of particular terms to represent specific relations of practice does not appear to be arbitrary. The terms are used in quite specific ways, though psycho-linguistic analyses of the lexicon would suggest that words form particular contrastive oppositions and associations, given their position in a particular adult lexicon. What is missing from such an analysis is that the use of the terms within particular practices as demonstrated above may not coincide with the expected pattern at all. The contrastive oppositions and so on which are taken to be relevant to mathematics education are those which are presumed to operate within particular cognitive contexts, such as conservation experiments. The assumption is then made that children can use such terms in the manner predicted in cognitive experiments. If the children fail such tasks then we can assert that they have not acquired either the requisite cognitive or linguistic apparatus. It can be demonstrated, however, that the terms within everyday practices in which the children are brought up may not be used in the way predicted from cognitive tasks. What has been missing from this work is a detailed analysis of precisely how such terms are used in everyday practices. These linguistic relations do not always correspond to the usage that we would expect, or the one which is taken to be central for the acquisition of mathematical concepts.

In the unsupervised play sequences in the nursery school transcripts which I examined (see p. 64) the type and range of activities is remarkably similar to some of those engaged in by daughters and mothers in the home transcripts. Because spontaneous play is taken to be a central pedagogic device the kinds of play are similar, as are the range of topics which occur spontaneously: number, shape, size, time, distance, age, board and card games, puzzles, spatial activities, cooking, and constructive play. Such activities are repeated in both locations. However, certain differences are worth noting. In the first place, although the type of activity is similar, the way in which these activities are carried out does differ. At home, in the Tizard corpus as well as in my own recordings, there is one child (or at most two children) interacting with one adult. This means that often play activities are carried out jointly by parent and child, with either the child 'helping' to work or whatever, or the mother acting as playmate in jigsaw puzzles, card-games, fantasy play, etc. There are many such activities which are carried out jointly by adult and child. In the nursery, however, the pattern is different. Although such activities occur they are carried out by children playing together. When adults intervene they tend either to intervene very minimally, or to use the task as a foil for pedagogy (e.g. for testing questions). They very rarely act as equal participants in a game or activity: such positions are left to other children. It is not clear to me precisely what effect such differences in adult positions have, but it certainly does produce significant differences in interaction.

The mothers join in and extend the children's knowledge because of their participation. Perhaps it is because the nursery teachers receive so many injunctions against ruining the spontaneity of children's play that they do not intervene in this way with any frequency. Clearly, of course, the ratio of adults to children makes a crucial difference, since it is doubtful if mothers would intervene in this way if their child had other children to play with. Because, however, the mothers do join children's activities as participants and indeed, conversely, the children join adult activities as participants, the relationship between the two must be different. The children in nursery school do not join in adult activities because there are none to join in. Similarly, perhaps, it is precisely the distance from children and the diktats of spontaneity which prevent the teachers from organizing jointly participatory activities. It is therefore difficult for the teachers to extend rather than test the children's knowledge because of the difference in their relationship with them.

It is important to remember that the school is an institution for the production of school mathematics. It is clear that certain pedagogic practices do appear to help children in their mastery of school mathematics. What is not clear is how far the participation of adults and children in other practices outside the school actually does help them in mathematics.

Two of the categories of activity which are noted as 'pre-mathematical' and are frequently undertaken are construction and spatial activities and the playing of card and board games. Two examples are particularly worthy of mention. One is of a girl who plays knockout whist with her mother, having mastered the names and sequences of cards, ace-high, picture-cards, trumping, and so on. What is not clear is how far such a complex activity will aid the child in the mastery of school mathematics. Perhaps an analysis of some of the similarities and differences between this card game and school mathematics will help.

The child is playing a game which is called 'knockout whist'. It is not called mathematics and is, therefore, unlikely to call up the same sequence of activities. My argument would be that such activity would help with the progress of school mathematics in those, and only those, aspects of the game which are both *contained* in school mathematics, and presented in the same manner. Scribner and Cole (1981) have argued in respect of cross-cultural studies of cognition and the effect of literacy on thinking, that literacy only helps those aspects of cognitive activity which mirror the use of literacy in the specific practices in which it is used. They use this study to criticize Olson (1977) who had argued that literacy *per se* was at the basis of the move towards formal thinking for children because it permitted concentration on the 'meaning in the text'. Scribner and Cole's point is in favour of the *specificity* of the acquisition of particular kinds of knowledge, suggesting the crucial importance of the relation between a mode of representation, such as writing, and the set of practices in which it is inserted.

Similarly, I would argue that playing knockout whist will only aid the acquisition of those aspects of school mathematics which enter into similar relations of signification.

Let us examine what these might be. The card game that they played relies on:

1. Accurate knowledge of the number sequence in ascending order from 2 to 9.
2. A recognition that 1 (i.e. Ace) can be a high number.
3. The ordering of the picture cards as higher in value than 2–9, but ordered according to a royal hierarchy: Jack, Queen, King.
4. A recognition of the classification of the cards by their designation as diamonds, hearts, spades, and clubs.
5. An understanding of 'winning a trick', either by a higher card of the same class (suit) or by a trump (of another, specifically designated suit).

Yet, stating the requirements in this way immediately presents them as abstract capacities or skills, which can then be transferred. My major contention has been that examining the regulation of the specific practice allows us to examine how the subject is inserted as a participant in that practice. The game of knockout whist is rule-governed and regulated in a particular manner, which presents correct play, cheating, winning, etc. These significations are vital and are different from, for example, 'getting the right answer'. Thus, although aspects of the practice are similar to school practices, its successful participation requires the subject to be positioned in different ways with different relations of signification. The position of the Ace, for example, requires that the numeral 1 can operate in different positions, that 'royalty' signify as having quantitative and high values, while the practices of suits, tricks, and trumping, all of which require systematic and complex relations of action combined with iconic signifiers, numerals, are related to spoken signifiers. In other words, it is a complex sign system in its own right. An examination of the transcript from which this example was taken illustrates the way in which the girl's insertion into the discursive practice of knockout whist is regulated and her status as successful player accomplished.

. This suggests to me that only those aspects where the relations of signification overlap will present points for what has been described as *transfer*. Other points of intersection, namely, the inclusion of the same signifiers, forming different signs within the two practices, will produce possibilities for error in this misunderstanding. In Chapter 6 I shall examine in more detail some examples from home and school practices in which 'mathematical' signifiers are prised out of their relation within the practice and rearticulated in school mathematical discourse.

6 School mathematics as a discursive practice: beginnings

Experience leading to 3 + 4 = 7

Pre-arithmetical: –––––––– Arithmetical: –––––––– Formal:

Some children were playing ball. Others joined in. There are a lot of children now.	Three children were playing ball. Four children joined in. There are seven children now.
This plant has some flowers. So has that one. They have many flowers.	This plant has three flowers. That one has four. They have seven flowers.
John saw some butterflies. Mary saw more. They saw several butterflies.	John saw three butterflies. Mary saw four more. They saw seven butterflies.
Mary had some sweets. Mother gave her others. She brought all of them to school.	Mary had three sweets. Mother gave her four. She brought seven to school.

$3 + 4 = 7$

(Lee 1962)

In the example above, taken from a textbook for teachers, the provision of certain kinds of activity is seen to lead unproblematically to the production of formal arithmetic, as in the equation, $3 + 4 = 7$. The 'understanding' underlying the transfer from one system to another is seen as all-important, while the actual discursive structure of the statements in each case is not worthy of comment. The statements and the practices of which they form a part are only similar at the level of a hidden and underlying structure (syntax, logico-mathematics, etc.). Each of the activities contained in the first column of the illustration is contained in different practice. The second column is only different from the first if the number of objects in each case is pointed out or made salient to the children in some way, for example by a practical purpose for examining the number of objects, children, and so on. As for the final column, comprising an addition statement, which unifies all previous experiences, there are many differences between that statement and what it follows from. The statement is written, like all formal mathematical statements. It is composed of signifiers which are different from those contained in the previous statements. Those written signifiers have no content in the way the other statements have and the formal statement is transformed in important ways as soon as it is translated into speech. If we speak that statement, we might say it was, for example:

> three plus four equals seven
> three and four is seven
> three add four makes seven

These statements, converted into spoken or written words, contain elements which are not present in the formal statement. For example, as I have explored elsewhere (Corran and Walkerdine 1982) *makes* and *equals* do not have equivalent effects upon the statement. The former makes one read it as a process of production of the answer, the latter points up the equivalence of distribution of both sides of the equation.

The specific effect of these metaphors is to locate the learners within particular practices. For example, within early education, actual physical construction of objects (making) is understood as the basis of many mathematical operations. Consider, for example, the remark of Dienes (1960) in the introduction to his book on mathematics teaching, *Building Up Mathematics*, which continues the discourse of 'making':

> The teacher should not use mathematical terms unnecessarily in extending or generalizing the game, but make suggestions in the

child's own language. For example, he should say, 'Why not put a window in there? Don't you think it's rather dark inside?' rather than 'instead of taking that square, you should take some rectangles and cubes and make a square in the middle'.

(Dienes 1960:xi)

The discourse which Dienes himself adopts is in itself very interesting. Compare, for example, the explicit moral regulation in his statements to teachers of the form 'the teacher should not . . .'. Children, on the other hand, are not to be approached in this way, but rather with softer tones, 'Don't you think . . .'. This aspect of discourse aimed at teachers is typical, in which statements of correct practices are stated as a combination of known fact 'this *is* how children learn', 'at this age children can/cannot . . .', etc., and moral regulation: 'teachers should/ should not' (on the basis of the facts . . .). They produce a very powerful form indeed.

If, as for most early mathematics educators, such statements are taken to be factual, then the *production* of their truth is elided. Piaget suggested, for example, that the formal statements in mathematical discourse of the form $3 + 4 = 7$, or $A + B = C$, if A then B, etc., are produced through a gradual realization that the physical properties of objects are unimportant to their function in logico-mathematical operations. This is consonant with those positions which understand logico-mathematical statements as 'de-contextualized' or 'content-free'. However, if we understand such a position as a reading, we might examine the positive effectivity of its truth. A position which I have adopted is that the object world cannot be known outside the relations of signification in which objects are inscribed. In this sense, then, the shift into mathematical discourse becomes a shift or transposition from one practice and system of signification to another. I want to examine both what the qualities of this system might be and some possible ways that this shift is achieved. I want to go on to compare the notion of 'de-contextualization' as a freeing, to an opposite position of insertion into a new practice, premised not on a freeing but on a 'forgetting' or 'suppressing' of aspects of the multiplicity of significations contained within other practices.

Using various examples of home and school pedagogy, I want to exemplify how it seems to me that significations from a non-mathematical practice become transformed and rearticulated within mathematical discourse. This is not so much a case of the disembedding of a skill, but the prising apart of relations of signification and rearticulating them to produce new signs. It is the achievement of that prising apart and rearticulation which I want to examine.

I want to begin by examining several exchanges between mothers and daughters from the Tizard corpus (see p. 13), in which routine exchanges become transformed. In the first example, Transcript A (see p. 129), the mother and daughter discuss how many friends the latter will have to play in the garden and how many glasses of juice and biscuits they will have. This could be seen as a one-to-one correspondence task, but what I am interested in here is how the relation between numbers of drinks, biscuits, and children is made to signify. The relation is first made by the daughter naming the children she wants to invite (from line 11) and her mother helps her to put up one finger to correspond with each name. Here we have the first relation of signifier to signified. In this case we might describe the names as already signifiers of the actual people, but in the shift they have become, or dropped to, the level of signifieds to unite with the iconic signifier (finger). The next move in the construction of this chain of signification is for the signifiers (fingers) to drop to the level of signifieds to become united with new signifiers, in this case, spoken numerals. Although the child has difficulty in reciting the counting string (line 33) she none the less is led to the set of relations which makes the task meaningful. This kind of exercise is repeated over and over again, in many examples, and it appears to be the way in which the move out of the relations of a practice and into the internal relations of the number system is achieved.

In the second example, Transcript B (p. 130), the mother takes the daughter further than a simple counting string. Interestingly, this is also another example involving food, this time a discussion about cakes to be baked for the family. After a general discussion about the kind of cakes and how to bake them, they begin a discussion of how many cakes to bake. This opportunity is seized by the mother to move into a simple addition (line 75). By line 80, the mother has moved the child into similar relations of names and fingers, although on this occasion the numeral and person's name are articulated jointly and then related to the fingers. But by line 86 the mother has begun to leave the external referents (names and cakes) out of the string, leaving the relation of signification (the tie into the practice being left behind) as the fingers. She begins to articulate strings of the form: four and that one makes ...; five and one more is ..., allowing the child to complete the utterance. At line 96 she returns to the external referents, by mentioning the people again. However, what I am suggesting is that it is by means of the construction of signifying chains such as these that the mother facilitates the transition into mathematical discourse. She does this by producing a particular chain of relations of signification, in which the external reference is suppressed and yet held there by its place in a gradually shifting signifying chain, held in this case by the fingers as signified. These 'hold' the practice left behind and permit the articulation of the new signifiers within a discourse in which all external reference is displaced.

This continues for some time until the mother attempts to get the child to make the correct counting sequence. An interesting exchange occurs at lines 116–118 when the child attempts to challenge her mother's counting string by reference to the position and authority of her teacher. Her mother counters by telling her the practical purpose of counting within cooking practices. After more practising, the child initiates the discourse herself, making the utterance and holding her own fingers. The mother gives her further tuition at line 154 and the sequence continues.

It seems to me that several aspects of these two episodes are worth noting. First, although traditionally it is the object relations which are focused on, with the discourse understood as representing a relation discovered through manipulation, the specific sequencing and articulation of material, signified, and signifier, and the move from one practice and discourse to another seem crucial. Second, although traditionally the mother's position would be understood as interfering, and the use of fingers and counting objectionable, they seem to be central and vital. The fingers are iconic signifiers which serve a strategic importance and it is the presence of the mother which facilitates the discursive shift. Why, then, are such practices often understood as harmful and immediately wrong? My reading is that teachers do remarkably similar things to these mothers, even though the discourse they use to explain their pedagogy is at variance. In each case here, there is no meaningless rote learning, but the creation of a complex chain of signification and a meaningful shift from one set of relations of signification to another. I will return later to the issue of the pejorative connotations of traditional practices.

However, let me briefly allude to a third example, before moving on to discuss the issue of pedagogy. Here the focus is also on food, though this time in the form of a song about currant buns (see Transcript C, p. 135). The sequence begins with the mother trying to get the child to sing for her. The song 'Three currant buns in the baker's shop' is built around the decrease in the number of buns each time one is bought, and makes a traditional one-to-one correspondence leading to subtraction. Here again, the presence of the buns is signified by the fingers and the mother begins with three and folds a finger down every time a bun is bought, or 'taken away'. In this exchange, as in the last example, the mother moves out of the discourse of the song and into that of subtraction. At line 59 she says: 'Well if you've got three currant buns in the baker's shop, look, and I take one away how many are left?' As she says 'look', she holds up three fingers and folds down one. She then continues the move out of the song and into school mathematical discourse by excluding external referents, as in line 64, where she says: 'How many's left if I take one away from three?' Again, this is accompanied by the fingers. They continue the sequence down to nought.

In the nursery school example which I am going to examine in detail, it is not iconic signifiers that the teacher uses, but written mathematical symbols. However, the mode of transition from a non-school practice to school mathematics is almost identical.

The classroom production of the union of sets

The nursery teacher in this example is working with a small group of four-year-olds, who she thinks are 'ready' for action on objects leading to simple addition as the union of sets. What the teacher does is to introduce the children to the mathematical statement which she wants them to learn using a series of exercises. What I want to focus on particularly is the simultaneous relation between object, action, and spoken or written signifier. The teacher begins by putting two piles each of two blocks on the table in front of the children. She does not say anything to open the lesson, apart from moving straight into an examination of those aspects of the blocks which she wants the children to take note of. She begins:

T: ... and I know Debbie did so we're just going to go over what you did at home and what you started before. How many's there?
C: Two.
T: How many's there? There? How many's there?
    Two and put them altogether. How many have we got already?

Notice that in these opening comments she moves straight into pedagogic testing discourse. She asks the children questions to which she clearly knows the answer, and by doing so achieves the focusing on the aspect of the blocks which she wants the children to consider. As she says the words, 'put them altogether', she gathers up the two piles and makes one pile. This is important, because what she achieves is the relation of discourse and practice: that is, she acts upon objects and begins simultaneously to provide the terms in which to read those actions. It could be argued that by this she begins to achieve the union of signified (blocks) and signifier (words), her own actions providing the uniting force. Here she produces the first sign. This is important because the current interpretation of such actions in the discourse of new mathematics would be only to note that she acted on objects. The argument here is that the simultaneity of the relation between action, object, and word is what matters. Action on the signified does not in any sense precede the production of the signifier to understand that action. In other words, actions or objects do not make sense without a discourse in which to read them.

The next move which the teacher makes is discursively interesting. She practises the same actions and objects twice, using different numbers of blocks, thereby retaining the same discursive unity in terms of the relations in the string while changing the numerical values and thus the content. She then goes on to another two piles of blocks with, this time, three in one and four in another. She gives the piles to two different children. She then says:

T: Good boy, let's count them altogether. One-two-three-four-five-six-seven. So Nicola had four, Debbie had three, so three and four make . . . (*she puts the blocks together*).
C: Seven.

This time, she again performs the same actions on objects, but she changes the discursive statement which she makes. After counting the blocks, she says 'three and four make . . .' and leaves the statement for the children to finish. This way she produces in speech a statement of the form which approximates more closely to the written $3 + 4 = 7$. Notice that she uses the metaphor *make*, appropriately here because she is actually making a new pile of blocks: by this she points up the product of her actions. Indeed, she simultaneously points it up in discourse, since it is that which she makes the object of her pseudo-question: she waits for the answer, *seven*. Moreover, what she does is again to unite signified (blocks) with a different signifier, the new statement linked by her actions. When she says 'three and four make . . .', she is suppressing the metaphorical association of the blocks as the object of the statement by leaving them out of the discourse but by retaining them for the children as the signifieds. The next move by the teacher takes the children from spoken to written signifiers: mathematical symbols. The teacher has drawn three large circles on a sheet of paper which she places on the table. The circles are connected by lines drawn between them as follows:

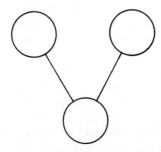

What the teacher does is to practise the actions on the same objects saying statements of the same form as before, but this time she moves the blocks from the top two circles, along the lines to the bottom circle.

т: Seven, when they're together and we wrote it down. Debbie did this – do you remember those funny pictures? And we had four up here and a three down there and these mean you've got four and they all go along there and we've got three and they all go along there so we put them altogether and count them and how many have we got? Seven. We've still got seven let's do another one. Right, see if Nicola can do this one for me just like I did then. Put them altogether, see how many you've got in each one and put them altogether.

n: Seven.

This is practised several times and the children are encouraged to articulate the statement '– and – make ...', at the same time moving the blocks down the lines and into the bottom circle. The relation between word and action is carefully timed since the teacher articulates the word 'make' at the precise moment she gets the two piles together and into the bottom circle. The children copy her. The next stage in the transition is to take further the written discourse, removing the blocks and replacing them by drawings of blocks, accompanied by the articulation of both statements of the same metonymic form and the same actions, though this time without the objects. Thus, the signifier/signified relationship is transformed. We can then say that the signifiers (spoken words) drop to the level of signifieds to be united with new signifiers, that is, the drawn representation. This drawn representation, being in a process of successive approximation to the production of the written statement, $3 + 4 = 7$, is done in the following manner. The teacher says:

T: Good girl. Now we've got some on cards like this . . . and to make it a little bit easier we're going to trace over so it won't take us a long time. Right, Nicola, can you get me the pencils from over there? Three we want, three nice pencils. Right now, Debbie, are you watching? Thank you. Now that's what you're going to have and you've got to trace over first of all everything that's on there. Right? Then you go round the squares and count them as you go. One two three and one and then you've got to draw when you've got there. So we've got to draw three and we've got to draw – are you watching me 'cos you won't know what to do – so I'll put those three in there instead of moving them 'cos we can't pick them up, so I've drawn that one in, and three and one make?

N: Four?

Thus the children learn to replace actual objects – blocks – by drawings of blocks, produced by tracing round the actual blocks. Again, the teacher emphasizes the action even though there are no longer any objects. She moves her hands down the lines exactly as she did when there were blocks, making the same movements at the same moment at which she articulated the spoken statement. She says:

I'll put those three in there instead of moving them 'cos we can't pick them up, so I've drawn that one in, and three and one make . . .?

She says again later:

If we had them in there like this we could pick them up couldn't we and move them, but we haven't so you've got to draw how many you've got in the circle.

One of the children soon picks up the relationship the teacher is trying to get across and refers to the metaphoric aspect spontaneously when she says:

I carried them up and then I drawed them.

It is important to note here work by Martin Hughes (1981) which explores children's representations of number and arithmetic operations. Hughes argued that children could understand and respond correctly to statements of the spoken form 'three and four make' but only when they had been produced by other examples with concrete or imagined referents. The children did not respond well to statements where there had been no previous referents. This gives support to the view that it is the relation of object to action to word which is important and the process by which the children are brought to produce statements of a particular form which, while they have no referents, themselves refer to objects or imagined situations to which they are metaphorically linked. The second point to make is that when the children have drawings instead of actual blocks they now have squares in both the top and the bottom circle. This means that they actually have too many iconic signifiers of objects for the sum that they are doing. If they were using a concrete strategy, which relied solely on their action on the objects to provide the answers, they ought to keep ending up with the wrong answer.

The next stage in the teacher's operation is to move from iconic signifiers in terms of drawings to the symbolic form of written numerals. This is achieved by getting the children to write the numeral next to the drawing of the blocks which it represents. This further translation connects the drawings as signifieds with the numerals as signifiers, held together by both the articulation in speech of the same form and the movement of making hands going down the lines:

T: And we draw those two and those three altogether they made? What you said before. One, two . . .

D: Three, four, five.

T: Right can you draw a five? Do a five there. Now in our books just one stage further. . . . Now then in our books. That's how a five goes. Do me a five there. Now then Nicola do you remember you did this at home?

N: Yes.

T: Now this is exactly the same except I've written in the numbers and what you do. Let's do another one first. How many have I written there?

S: Two.

T: So then you think, oh I need two – (*she gets two blocks*) – and I need another two because it says two and then you do exactly the same you move them altogether and count them up . . .

N: It says four.

T: . . . but you don't draw them you write the number. Right, let's do another one. How many does that say?

In the end the teacher has got the children into written symbols. She tells them not to draw the blocks but just to write the numerals. Although the written form, 3 + 4 = 7 is never achieved, a written representation is, namely:

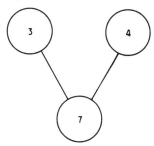

which can be articulated in speech as 'three and four make seven'. Thus we have a process which does not appear to consist simply of the production of a concept through action on objects, but the important co-ordination and articulation or relations between practice and discourse, between signifier and signified. The children have been brought to a practice, the object of which is the production of statements of a particular written form. I have exemplified the process which gave the possibility of the production of that form of statement by the children and its articulation within a discursive practice.

I want now to pause briefly to examine one instance when the teacher works with a child in the group who appears to be having difficulty. After the teacher and the children perform the joint exercise, she gets them all to do similar tasks in individual work books in which she has already drawn the three linked circles. It is interesting that, with one child having difficulty, she does not make the task more 'concrete' in that she does not do anything which could be described as more at the level of action on objects. What she does is to keep precisely the same action on the same objects, but to transform the metaphoric axis. She calls the circles houses and the blocks people, going one step back in an elaborate fantasy, thus introducing more 'meaning' for the child, not more action:

т: Got to go down, these lines. Right that's my house and that's your house. Right and that's you and your sister. Right and that's me and my brother and my sister . . .

n: Seven, one, two, three, four . . .

т: Right and we're all going to visit somebody and that's their house, so I've got there with my brother and my cat and you've got there with your sister. So (. . .) and two of you and we've all gone in the same house and they're altogether and how many's in that house altogether now?

d: Five.

What seems crucial is not any link to concrete action, but the metaphor which allows the task to be located within the framework of a familiar discursive practice. This practice also has the effect of allowing the child as subject to enter the discourse more readily than the action on the blocks as blocks would do.

In the Hughes (1981) example, noted earlier, an imagined referent worked as well as an actual one. This move into fantasy seems important, for it provides a narrative, rather like the three bears example examined in Chapter 3. The story form is a familiar aspect of practices in which children are inserted and in which they are positioned (Walkerdine 1984). Entering fantasy provides an important point of practising existing relations. In all the examples of nursery play which I have examined there are no instances in which object play and fantasy play can be read as distinct categories. Action on objects is also read through a discursive framework created by the children. I shall explore the importance of this in Chapter 9.

The focus of this chapter has been an examination of the way in which non-mathematics practices become school mathematics practices, by a series of transformations, which retain links between the two practices. This is achieved, not by the same action on objects, but rather by the formation of complex signifying chains, which facilitate the move into new relations of signification which operate with written symbols in which the referential content of the discourse is suppressed. In the next chapter I shall explore this transition further by examining differences between non-mathematics and mathematics practices and some problems for transformation.

Transcript A (SH16)

c:	Mummy?	1
m:	Mm – mm?	(m *and* c *are eating midday meal.*)
c:	Must put seven juice out. Because, because, three juices out.	(c *wants 7 glasses of juice for the picnic she's going to have in the garden with her friends but then changes her mind to 3.*) 5
m:	Three?	
c:	Yeah.	
m:	How many children are there?	(m *and* c *discuss how many children will be having juice and biscuits in the garden.*)
c:	Three.	10
m:	There's Michelle.	
c:	Mark.	
m:	Mark.	
c:	Kirstie.	
m:	Kirstie. Now have you got the right number of fingers? Michelle . . . put these down.	15 (c *has all the fingers on her hands up.*)
m:	Michelle.	(m *pushes all the fingers except one down – the one is for Michelle and then* c *puts 1 finger up for each person they remember.*) 20
c:	Yeah.	
m:	Mark.	
c:	Yeah.	
m:	Kirstie.	(c *doesn't finish* – m *interrupts.*)
c:	Kir –	25
m:	Her little sister Katie came along and don't forget Stephanie.	
c:	Yeah.	
m:	How many is that?	
c:	Four.	
m:	No.	30
c:	Seven.	

M: No. Count.

C: One, two, three . . . seven.   (C *counts the fingers one after*
                                   another but puts seven after
                                   three.)

M: Four.

C: Four.   35

C: Five.   (C *counts last finger.*)

M: Mm – mm.

C: Five.
   You have to give me . . . five juice out, give biscuits out.

M: Mm.   40

C: Five beakers.

M: Are you going to pour   (M *means is* C *going to pour*
   everybody?   *everyone's juice from the jug.*)

C: Pardon?

M: Did you like pouring?   (C *N.R. – no response*)   45
   Did you like pouring the
   juice out for everybody?   (C *nods.*)
   Can you pour that many?

C: Yeah.

Transcript B (TD72)

M: Ooh sorry, thought it was nine.   1
   Don't know whether I'm coming or going lately.
   Do I?
   Oh well, sit down and drink   (M *sits down at table and drinks*
   me tea. Then, must get that   *her tea;* C *is also sitting with her*   5
   washing done and . . . and   *tea.*)
   I've gotta go and make that
   pie.

C: I will, I'll make some.   (C *means she'll use some of the*
                                   pastry.)

M: Yeah?   10
   Alright, if we have enough time.

C: I will make some.

M: Make some little rock cakes you made before, there will be a
   bit of pastry over, they were nice they were. Do you remember
   the ones you made when Nanny D . . .   15

C: Mm.   (*Nanny referred to earlier was* M's

		mother who lives close by. Nanny
		D *lives further away.*)
M:	With little currants in?	(M *and* C *sitting at table drinking*
		tea.)
C:	Mm.	
M:	Could make some of them for Daddy tonight.	
C:	And . . .	20
M:	Mm he likes them.	
	You make 'em and I'll put them in the oven and cook 'em.	
C:	I can't make them.	
M:	Remember you gotta roll the pastry out.	
C:	Mm.	25
M:	Spread some currants.	
C:	Mm.	
M:	Then fold over your pastry, and roll it up in a ball.	
C:	Mm.	
M:	And Mummy'll grease the tray.	30
C:	Mm.	
M:	And you put them in the tray, like you did before, little rock cakes. They were nice.	
C:	Oh I know, the little rock cakes!	
M:	Like you were making when Grandad come down that night.	35
C:	Oh yes.	
M:	And . . . you made them little rock cakes.	
C:	I can still make them.	
M:	Mm, mm.	
C:	But I can't make the other ones.	40
M:	What other ones?	
	What the ones with the . . . (*No time for* C *to respond.*)	
	shapes?	
C:	Mm.	
M:	Oh they're the ones you mean yea, no well d't know where the	45
	shapes are? See you can make little round ones tonight, can't	
	you? (C – N.R.)	
	Eh?	
C:	Mm.	
M:	Daddy likes them.	50
C:	Well I don't.	
M:	Oh you ate enough of them last time. Kerry had one didn't	
	she?	

c: I'm gonna eat all of them.
m: Oh you're being selfish are ya?   55
c: And Daddy can have one.
m: That all?   (c – N.R.)
Poor old Dad's been working all day, getting some money to
buy your slippers and you only gonna give him one.
c: Two.   60
m: Two?
S'that all he's gonna get?
c: Three.
m: Three?
How many Kerry can have?   65
c: Two.
m: Kerry can have two, how many I'm gonna have?
c: Same as me.
I'm gonna have one, two and you're gonna have two.
m: Two and Daddy can have three, that right?   70
c: I'll have them.
m: Well how many's them?
c: Three.
m: Three?
Well if you're gonna have   (m holds up first two fingers and   75
two and Daddy's gonna   then another two fingers.)
have two, how many's that?
c: Three.
m: No.
c: Four.   80
m: That's right.
And if Mummy's gonna   (m holds up another 2 fingers.)
have another two, that's
what four and two . . .
c: Four and . . .   85
m: If that's four, and that one   (m holds up 4 fingers and then
makes . . . ?   adds another one.)
c: Five.
m: And that one makes . . . ?   (m adds another finger.)
c: Four.   90
m: No these are five.   (m points to the 5 fingers on 1
                                     hand.)
c: Five.
m: Five and one more is . . . ?   (m holding up 6 fingers.)

c: Six.

m: S'right. 95

   Now if you're gonna have   (m *holds up* 6 *fingers and then*
   two and Mummy's gonna   *adds 1 more.*)
   have two and Daddy's
   gonna have two that's six,
   and if Kerry's gonna have 100
   two that's, that's six, and
   one more makes?

c: Five.

m: No.

c: Six. 105

m: Yea and what's after six?

c: Eight.

m: No.

c: Nine.

m: No. 110

c: Ten?

m: No.

c: Eight.

m: No after six, what comes after six?

c: Nine. 115

m: No, seven.

c: No, now seven!

m: Nine doesn't come after six, definitely seven.

c: My teacher says one, two then six.

m: Well you got to count 'cause you wanna know how many little 120
   rock cakes you gotta make.

c: Go on then.

m: Alright, well if you gonna   (m *holds up* 6 *fingers.*
   have two Mummy's gonna   m *holds up* 1 *more finger.*)
   have two and Daddy's
   gonna have two that makes 125
   six. And if Kerry's gonna
   have two, what's after six,
   one more makes . . .

c: Four. 130

m: No.

c: Five?   (m – N.R.)
   Six?
   Seven.

M: Seven and one more is ...?   (M *holds up 1 more finger.*)   135
C: Four.
M: No, what comes after seven?
C: Six.
M: Yea well what comes after seven?
C: Ah ...   140
M: Eight.
C: Eight.
M: So you gotta make eight rock cakes ...
C: Make that one that one ...   (C *holds up 1 hand and starts*
                                  counting on her fingers.)
M: And if you make, if you make ten that's two more, then you   145
   can have them for school tomorrow. Or take 'em with you to
   eat on the way to school.
C: I gonna make ten.
M: Gonna make ten.
   You're gonna, so you're gonna leave two tomorrow for school?   150
C: I'm gonna make ten.   (C *holds up 1 hand.*)
M: Gonna make ten? That's only five.
C: Well I'll make five.   (C *holds up her other hand.*)
M: That's five and that's five.   (M *points at both hands.*)
   And then two makes ten.   155
C: I'll make eleven.   (C *holds up only 1 hand.*)
M: You're only making these,   (C *nods.*)
   you're only making five?
   Oh that won't be enough,
   that means there's only one   160
   for me, one for you, one for
   Daddy and one for Kerry
   and one for school.
C: I making them for school.   (C *holds up her other hand.*)
M: Oh you're making them *and*   (M *points at both hands.*)   165
   them.
C: Mm, I'm making them for   (C *holds up 1 hand and then the*
   t'day and I'm making them   *other.*)
   for t'morrow.
M: You're making five for today, and five for tomorrow? So you're   170
   gonna take five with you tomorrow, and you're gonna have,
   we're all gonna have ...
C: One each.

M: . . . one each day.
  Who's gonna have the odd one?   175
C: You.
M: Oh I'm gonna have two and you gonna have one, and Daddy's
  gonna have one and Kerry's gonna have one?
C: Mm.
M: Oh right.   180
  Glad we sorted that out.
  You gonna make ten?
C: Mm.
M: Come on then.

Transcript C (EG41)

M:	Oh that's a funny noise.	1
	Right, now leave it like	(C *pings the rubber band which is*
	that.	*round the egg box.*)
		(M *and* C *sitting in dining area*
		playing with an elastic band
		around an egg box.)
C:	Make a funny noise.	
M:	—————	5
M:	Will it go right round the back?	
	Wait a minute.	(M *stretches the band a bit more*
		and it pings higher.)
C:	That's better noise.	
M:	That's better yea.	
C:	It'll be a, it'll be a um – music box.	10
M:	A music box, mm!	
M:	Play a tune on it then.	(C *pings the rubber band.*)
M:	What's the tune?	
C:	You have to sing at the same time.	
M:	I don't know what the tune is.	15
C:	(*Baa baa black sheep have*	(C *sings.*)
	you any wool? Yes sir yes sir.)	
C:	How do . . .	
	What's the next bit?	
M:	'Yes sir, yes sir, three bags	(M *tells* C *the words.*) 20
	full.'	
C:	Full.	

(*Yes sir, yes sir, three bags.*)   (c *sings.*)

c: What is it now?

m: One ...   25

c: (*One for the master, one for*   (c *sings.*)
   the dame, one for the little boy
   who lives down the lane.)

m: Mm, you'll have to do another tune. How about 'Three
   currant buns in the baker's shop'?   30

c: (*Three currant buns in the*   (c *sings.*)
   baker's. Three currant buns in
   the baker's.)
   Oh what does it go like?

m: Shop!   35
   'Three currant buns in the   (m *tells* c *the words.*)
   baker's shop.'

c: You tell me first.

m: 'Round and fat with sugar on top.'
   'Along comes a ...'   40

c: (*Boy, with a penny one day*   (c *sings.*)
   bought a currant bun and took
   it away.)

m: Right.
   Then there are?   (c – *N.R.*)   45
   Two currant buns.   (c *and* m *sitting in dining area.* c
                                 pinging the rubber band and trying
                                 to sing songs.)

c: One!

c: How many was there?

m: Well, you can have as many as you like.
   Three I should think.   50

c: (*Three currant buns in the*   (c *sings.*)
   baker's shop. Round the fat [sic]
   with sugar on top. Along
   came boy with a penny one
   day. Bought a currant bun   55
   and he took it away.)

m: That was very nice.

c: Now what is it now?

m: Well if you've got three   (m *holds up 3 fingers and then*
   currant buns in the baker's   *folds one down.*)   60

	shop, look, and I take one away how many are left?		
c:	(*A three currant buns in* . . .)	(c *sings.*)	
m:	How many's left if I take one away from three?	(m *holds up 3 fingers, and folds* *down one.*)	65
c:	Two!		
m:	That's right.		
c:	(*Three* . . .)	(c *starts to sing.*)	
m:	No! two current buns in the shop . . .		
c:	(*Two currant buns in the* *baker's shop. Round the fat* *with sugar on top.*)	(c *sings.*)	70
m:	'Along . . .'		
c:	(*Came a boy with a penny* *one* . . .)	(c *sings.*)	75
c:	Put your hand up with two fingers. (*Along came a penny* . . . *A bought with a penny one day* *Bought a currant bun and* *took it away.*)	(m *holds up 2 fingers.*) (m *laughs.* c *sings.*) (c *folds 1 of M's fingers away.* m *laughs.*)	80
m:	How many's left now then?		
c:	(*One currant bun in the* *baker*)	(c *sings.*)	
c:	Put your finger out.	(m *holds 1 finger up.*)	85
c:	(*One currant bun in the* *baker's. Round the fat with* *sugar on the top. Long came a* *boy and bought a currant bun* . . .)	(c *sings.*)	90
m:	No! 'Along came a boy with a . . .'		
c:	(*Penny one day.* *Bought a currant bun and took* *it away.*) None left!	(m *and* c *sitting in dining area,* c *pinging her rubber band.*)	95
m:	None left now.		
c:	Now come back.		
m:	What? Put them back again?	(m *thinks* c *wants the fingers back* *up.* m *presses.*)	
c:	No!		100

M: Oh the little boy's coming back.

C: Want to go back again.

M: Right.

M: Is that all the tunes you   (C *nods.*)
   know?   105

7 2p doesn't buy much these days: learning about money at home and at school

> Money is used only for buying and he pays in coins for what he asked for, two pence, four pence, etc. The idea of money as meaning the exchange value of goods will be beyond him for a long time to come.
>
> (Williams and Shuard 1976:51)

> She got a job as a barmaid. It was good money at £20 a week. Jeannie bought Linda a bike to ride and Melissa a doll and their friend Lisa a dog.
>
> (Steedman 1980:19)

These two passages exemplify the difference which I want to explore in this chapter. The first passage comes from the most important reference work to date for teachers on infant school mathematics and describes the assumed capabilities of primary school children with respect to money. The second extract is from a story written in 1976 by three eight-year-old girls. The first assumes that children's understanding of money comes first through their manipulation of coins representing very small amounts of money, and that the notion of exchange value is a highly abstract concept and therefore outside the conceptual power of such young children who are tied to learning through concrete manipulation. The second displays an understanding of the relation between labour, money, and the purchase of goods – the three elements in the exchange relation as understood by most working people – which in Williams and Shuard's terms is a highly abstract complex of concepts, though one which is part of the extremely concrete materiality of the lives of working families.

In Chapter 6 I explored how relations of transformation might be effected. Here I want to take a different example, to demonstrate further some of the problems in assuming that 'transfer' is effected simply by the insertion of mathematical relations into a 'meaningful context' without examining the differences as well as the similarities in the two discursive practices. Paying attention to the features of transformation and making them a conscious aspect of the pedagogy might, therefore, rather than impeding learning, be an important aspect of the support of transformation and the repositioning of children as subjects within school mathematics practices. I shall exemplify this with extracts from the Tizard corpus (see p. 13) and from video recordings made in a top infant classroom.

Learning about money at home

In order to examine how money exists as a relation in some non-school practices I have extracted from the Tizard corpus all the conversations in which money features at all. They form a stark contrast to the view endorsed in infant school mathematics. Importantly, there is a homogeneity about these extracts which is very striking. Of fifteen exchanges between mothers and their pre-school children concerning money, in all but one the focus of attention is the domestic economy. In almost every case there is concern about the high costs of necessary goods and the material effect of this for the children; that commodities are therefore precious and should not be wasted. In five of those exchanges the relation is made between the value of labour, the receipt of wages, and the purchase of goods, the very relation so clearly understood by the eight-year-old girls in the extract from their story which opened the chapter. Let us examine more closely the salient features of these exchanges.

The high cost of goods is discussed, such that small amounts of money are quite clearly shown as not worth much in terms of purchasing power. Children are encouraged not to be wasteful of commodities because of high costs and the labour involved in earning money to pay for the goods being consumed. On other occasions the exchanges bear witness to a struggle for power between children and adults, in which the children want the parents to buy goods for them to consume, while the parents retort with the high cost of such items and their lack of money to buy them. So we can say that although, in one sense, arguments about exchange value and the money economy are highly abstract and complex, the elements of the arguments are presented to the children in such a way that they have actual *material consequences* in their day-to-day lives. I would argue that the children are made to understand at least the implications of such practices only too well. Williams and Shuard treat exchange value as an abstract concept which forms a part of a complex economic discourse, failing to recognize or to understand the implications of the fact that the children live this exchange as part of modern family life. Let us examine some of the exchanges themselves:

M: Joanne, if you have everything you wanted for your birthday I'd need to be a millionaire.

(M *tells off* C *for mistreating her slippers.*)
C: Will you, will you buy me some more today?
M: No I will not!
C: No, no, Christmas, no, Christmas, Mum. Mum, Christmas, when you get paid.

(*The same mother–child pair in a later conversation:* C *had just asked if it is afternoon yet.*)
M: It's gone dinner time, (*father*) doesn't come home for lunch does he? Not now, works too far away.
C: Why doesn't he come home for lunch?
M: 'Cause it takes too long for him to get home and get back to work again.
C: And he's not allowed to?
M: No.
C: Or he gets, or he won't get lots of money?
M: No, he won't get lots of money and then you won't get new slippers.

(C *is giving* M *pretend money and gives her three pennies.*)
M: Oh, can't buy much with three and a quarter pennies!

M: You know that bottle of medicine, Daddy? Sarah tipped it down the sink this morning.
(D *tells younger sibling the medicine was expensive.*)
M: How much was it then?
D: Thirty-nine.
C: The nose drops?
M: Yes, the whole bottle!

(M *is telling* C *that she can't have too much rose-hip syrup.*)
C: Why?
M: Because the rose-hip cost a lot of money.
C: Is Megan going to drink it all?
M: Megan only drinks a little weeny bit, so it lasts quite a long time, but if you drink it, you drink about a whole bottle a day.

This is the most sustained exchange about money, but it reflects the same elements as the above exchanges:

> (M *and* C *are talking about the window cleaner who is in the street cleaning the windows of various neighbours.* M *has mentioned that one of the neighbours, Irma, often pays the window cleaner for cleaning the windows of those neighbours who are out and then collects the money from them later.*)

C: Why they all out?   1
M: 'Cause they're working or something.
C: Aren't they silly.
M: Well, have to work to earn money, don't you . . .
C: Ummmmmm Mummy.   5
M: Mm.
C: Um, she can't pay everybody, er, the win, er all the bills to the window cleaner, can she?
M: What?
C: Irma can't pay all the bills, all the bills.   10
M: No, she can't pay all, everybody's bill.
C: To the window cleaner.
M: Well, she sometimes pays mine if I'm out. She sometimes pays Jane's up the road if she's out. I always pay her back though.
C: 'Cause its fair.   15
M: Mm, it is . . .
C: Mummy, can I tell you something?
M: Mm.
C: Um, but where does she leave the money?
M: Where does she leave the money?   20
C: Yes.
M: She doesn't leave it anywhere, she gives it, she hands it to the window cleaner, after he's finished.
C: And then she gives it to us.
M: No, no, she doesn't have to pay us.   25
C: Then the window cleaner gives it to us.
M: No, we give the window cleaner money, he does work for us and we have to give him money.
C: Why?
M: Well, because he's been working for us cleaning our windows.   30
   He doesn't do it for nothing.
C: Why do you have money if you have people clean your windows?

M: Well, the window cleaner needs money doesn't he?
C: Why?   35
M: To buy clothes for his children and food for them to eat.
C: Well, sometimes window cleaners don't have children.
M: Quite often they do.
C: And sometimes of his own to eat.
M: Mm.   40
C: And for buying curtains.
M: And for paying his gas bills and electricity bill.
C: And everything.
M: And for paying petrol for his car.
   And sorts of things you have to pay for, you see. You have to   45
   earn money somehow, and he earns it by cleaning other
   people's windows, and big shop windows and things.
   (*The conversation continues with a discussion about the number of
   times previously that the window cleaner has cleaned their windows
   and, since it is lunchtime, whether the window cleaner has his lunch
   in a pub or brings sandwiches.*)

In the last example the same set of relations as in the other examples
is developed and extended. It can be observed that although the child
in question is not actually handling concrete money in any sense, she is
learning to deal with a very important aspect of her family and society's
life, not some set of concepts abstracted from the practices in which
they occur. Since these exchanges all occurred in the children's homes,
there are no examples of practices involving shopping. However, even
if we had recorded children on shopping expeditions, whether or not
they actually handled money in the shops, it is hardly likely that they
would have been dealing with the small amounts of money about which
Williams and Shuard speak. It also seems the case, from the above
exchanges, that the last child does not entirely grasp what it is that her
mother is trying to explain. However, it is equally apparent that she
does pick up the idea despite its 'abstract' quality. At line 40 and
beyond she has recognized that the window cleaner needs to earn
money to pay for 'everything'.

While it would be foolish to argue that four-year-old children are
capable of immediately grasping the most complex of problems in
economic discourse (and I will take up the question of the different
ways the same relations can be presented later in this chapter), I would
maintain that these examples at least indicate that the distinction

between a mathematics comprehensible to small children, because it is based on concrete manipulation and small numbers, and abstract concepts is a false opposition. The concrete manipulation of small numbers in relation to money is simply barely appropriate to the domestic and other practices in which the children lead their daily lives. However, they are constantly surrounded by other, more sophisticated relations which have *concrete and material effects* on their lives and those of the people around them. Money, therefore, lives as a relation within very specific practices of the domestic economy. (For a further analysis of this example, see Walkerdine and Lucey, in press.)

In infant schools children are introduced to more formalized approaches to mathematical topics, although these are most often presented as enjoyable and playful activities. The particular exchanges I am going to examine are taken from the top infant class of one school, which means that the children are aged between six and seven. In this classroom the teacher has divided the children into groups and presents topics according to her understanding of their readiness. Her stated aims and her classroom practice amply testify to her adherence to the view of mathematics education outlined earlier. In the following extract from an interview with her she discusses the importance of keeping the children to small numbers so that they can develop a thorough understanding:

> You see (the headmistress) is very keen on – er – if a child can't, um, sort of analyse mentally beyond six and hasn't much concept of what numbers beyond six are – you know, how they break up and so on – that everything as far as you can should be limited to that – so that they're not trying to grasp hundreds of grammes which – they can't understand what a hundred is if they are only able to grasp, say, six.

On the particular occasion of the recordings the teacher is introducing the group to the topic of subtraction from ten. Over the course of several sessions they practise the same set of mathematical relations as exemplified in a ten pin bowling game, a game with counters and dice, and a shopping game. In each case the children are handling concrete examples of the small numbers and then recording them on paper as, for example, in the bowling game in which they record their score as a subtraction sum. The games are enjoyable and the children introduce a considerable element of fantasy. Although not part of the recorded episodes I also witnessed an example of spontaneous shop play among the same children which I recorded in field notes. What is important is that the same degree of sophistication and understanding of roles apparent in the nursery is apparent here. For example, those girls playing shop assistants put on marked versions of their own London accents whereas the girls who played customers put on middle-class accents, demonstrating an implicit understanding of another feature in the set of practices and relations in which an understanding of money is a relation for them.

The teacher's shopping game appears to conform to all the parallels set by Williams and Shuard. The children are given a pack of cards on which are pictured items to be bought accompanied by a price in pence, below ten pence (e.g. 2p). The children are to take turns to pick a card. They each have ten 1p pieces in plastic money and they are to work out the subtraction operation with the coins and then record the change from 10p in the form of a subtraction sum on their paper (see Transcript D, p. 149). First of all it very quickly appears obvious to the children that this task is not like real shopping, and I will analyse its disjunction in a number of ways. Let us note that it is the fact that the teacher has deliberately chosen to use small amounts of money that makes the task quite unlike real shopping for the children. What they talk about are those relations which we witnessed in the exchanges between mothers and children in the home (see pp. 141–3). There is an immediate recognition that such small sums buy virtually nothing and certainly not the goods which they have been asked to purchase. That at the same time renders the game both silly and fun precisely because they are disobeying the rules of shopping by conforming to the rules of this game. At line 46 it is the teacher herself who first cites the disjunction between this and a real purchase when she buys an aeroplane for 5p and says, 'it couldn't be a very big aeroplane, could it?' And again, at line 67, when Tracy comments 'cheap', the teacher replies: 'Right, very cheap. It's a very cheap shop I've got, right.'

At lines 83 and 84 the same relation of cheapness is stated and then Tracy comments that 'polar bears are usually five hundred thousand pounds' (line 85). The same relation of cheapness is reiterated throughout the game and at line 243 Alison states it even more clearly:

It's Hilary's go now. It's good innit. What you buying? She's buying a basket 2p, isn't it cheap. My mum's shopping bag was £6.

At line 249 Alison comments that since she did not like her bag the shop gave her her money back, to which Lisa replies that she is lucky. In this exchange the risky nature of the possible reversibility to the exchange is clearly noted. This is further confirmed at line 255 when Lisa has copied the idea but is taking her bag back because 'it's too much money. Couldn't afford it.' Again, the realistic assessment of prices is clearly related to other conditions which impinge upon the domestic economy. Later Alison buys an aeroplane (line 346):

> Oh I wanted one of them. I'm going to go on holiday soon . . . 'cos I've saved . . . oh dear my aeroplane broke, didn't it. I've got to buy another one. I am rich.

Thus Alison gets into a fantasy about being the kind of person who could buy an aeroplane, only to be brought back to grim reality by Gordon who, in the next line, points out to her: '2p's not rich. It's not enough to buy bubble gum and a bazooka.'

In this transcript the children display an understanding of money compatible with that which appeared in the home extracts: they show a reasonable and realistic assessment of prices, they can talk about large amounts of money, and they show some understanding of the relations of exchange value and the domestic practices into which money and shopping are inserted in the lives of their families. The teacher, on the other hand, is using shopping as a foil to give the children a real concrete experience of handling small numbers inserted into a real situation. It is the insertion into the giving of change in shopping which is supposed to make the exercise meaningful for the children, and also render it of practical value. Yet it is precisely this which makes it unlike shopping: the children relate to it in the only way which they can, that is, they treat it as a fantasy, since it bears little relation to shopping practices. When people calculate their change in shopping not only do they work with larger amounts of money, they also rarely if ever use pencil and paper: they do not write subtraction sums. They are most likely to engage in quick mental arithmetic or approximation and estimation of amounts. The problems here do not resemble practical problems either in their content or in their methods of solution. In this sense they are 'fake' practical problems and most of the children seem to recognize this. The practical context is a foil for the teaching of certain mathematical relations, so that everything about the task is different from shopping. In school mathematics the goal of the task is to compute the answer rather than to make a purchase. The purpose here is not to purchase shopping but to calculate a subtraction. In this sense, the practical format can be misleading and sometimes downright unhelpful.

While in this exercise most of the children successfully negotiate the disjunction, one child, Gordon, makes the mistake of actually treating the task as though it were practical: that is, he spends all his money. At line 209 Gordon says that he has no money left, and later has to be told by the teacher (line 295):

'each time you get another ten pence to go shopping with'.

Later, at line 310:

I know what you did, you spent two pence there didn't you and that left you with eight pence and so the next time when your toy cost eight pence you thought you had nothing left, but it says start with ten pence every time doesn't it so you can work out again ten pence take . . . spend eight pence and work out how much you'll have left.

Ironically the error which Gordon has made would be correct practice in shopping, that is, that the money is exchanged for goods and therefore decreases: the very central feature of the exchange. In shopping no money is returned for a fresh turn!

In the last line of the teacher's explanation above we also have another clue about the difference between this task and shopping. She nearly uses the words 'take away' and then corrects herself to 'spend'. This transformation of signifiers is exactly what the children have to do too. Right at the beginning of the exercise, when the teacher is explaining what to do, she takes a card with an aeroplane for 5p (line 45): 'It couldn't be a very big aeroplane could it. So, anyone know what my sum's going to be that I'm going to write down?' Lisa quickly replies: 'Ten take away five leaves five.'

This appears to be remembered from previous lessons, but although it is the correct answer and in the appropriate format for 'sums', the teacher wants the sum stated as 'change' (line 55). When the children are doing the calculation for themselves, however, they often simply state the sum in the form of 'take away' and 'leaves'. This method gives them the required answer, the goal of the pedagogic mode. That children recognize that getting the answer is the goal of their mathematics is evident throughout the work of the infant school children.

Everything about this task, then, testifies to the disjunction for the children between this task in mathematics and the knowledge of money which they have obtained outside school. The two practices barely overlap. The pedagogy assumes that children learn about money only from the handling of small coins which leads to the real understanding of arithmetic processes, whereas the understanding of money on the part of the children is one in which large sums of money are involved, these sums have important value attached to them and are inserted in crucial domestic economic practices. Furthermore, their practical understanding barely encompasses those very handling and paper and pencil techniques which are the mainstay of their school work.

It is also interesting to note the way in which, in fantasy, what the children in this exchange and the one I noted earlier (p. 145) do is to use the disjunction between actual shopping and these low prices to shift their position within the practice. In fantasy they can 'become' what is not possible in real life, namely rich and monied people who can buy expensive items, have exotic holidays, return goods they are tired of and, equally, behave badly towards shop assistants. In a play example in the nursery a young girl, on taking the position of the mother in a domestic play sequence, becomes the one who can buy expensive food items – in this case chicken, bacon, and steak – for her daughter (see Walkerdine 1981).

Children's insertion into practices, therefore, is not totally dependent on 'real life', and their positioning relates also to the imagined through their insertion as subjects within story-telling, the media, and other cultural practices (Walkerdine 1984; Walkerdine 1986b). I want to suggest that it is often the case that we live our daily lives as fantasy and this provides a source of signification which is not at odds with other aspects of insertion into practices.

However, the practices presented here in which money forms a relation suggest, by the examples from the domestic economy and the fantasy play, that *positioning* within the practices is central for the production of a particular reading of the relations within them and how those relations attain value and are regulated. It may well be the case, for example, that in families in which money was not a factor to be monitored, the children's recognition of certain relations would differ. This position is supported by a study of Varnava-Skouras (1981) in which poor children read the wage-relation far more clearly than wealthier ones in all countries. These eight-year-old children's readings of the significance of money and work appeared to be closely related to the readings of work within their families and in the hegemonic discourses of their culture. These latter were variable. For example, Greek and Turkish children freely gave 'exploitation' as the reason for the unfair distribution of wealth among manual and non-manual workers, whereas children from advanced industrial societies (Britain, Sweden) cited factors such as hard work bringing higher rewards and the greater difficulty of intellectual work. Such differences are also apparent in our data and form the basis of a different analysis (Walkerdine and Lucey, in press).

Positioning within cultural and social practices, therefore, can be read as variable – culturally and historically specific and not fixed and timeless. Insertion into school practices, then, might be facilitated by means of the production of transformatory relations of signification, but children have become positioned within historically and culturally specific schooling practices in order to operate effectively. In Chapter 8 I shall examine certain aspects of the operation of infant school practices and the positioning of children within them. It is thus suggested that successful positioning depends upon successful insertion within a distinct set of relations of signification embodied in school mathematics practices.

Transcript D: School shopping game

L = Lisa; TR = Tracey; T = Teacher; G = Gordon; A = Alison;
K = Karen; H = Hilary; C = unidentified child

T:	Oh I can see what you clever things have done . . .	1
L:	I put my name on . . .	
T:	. . . made 10p up in lots of different ways, haven't you. But I'm afraid I did particularly want you to have ten one-penny pieces. Alison, Tracey, sorry. But I do think	5
	you might find it easier to do the work I am going to give you if you've got ten one-penny pieces today. If, when you know what the work is, later on you want to change you can do but try it first of all with all the pennies.	
TR:	One-two-three-four-five-six-seven-eight-nine-ten . . . I need four more one-two-three-four.	10
T:	OK?	
TR:	Yeah, I'm OK.	
T:	I'll clear the box away so that you can see me. Right, we're going to play a shopping game today.	15
G:	I know we're going to run around the chairs and get back before the last one and then you get some points.	
T:	No. I'm afraid not. I've got a pack of cards here.	
G:	Easy to shuffle. I know how to do that.	

T:	Can you shuffle?	20
G:	Yes.	
T:	Good, 'cos I can't – you do it then.	
L:	That ain't how you shuffle 'em.	
T:	Can you shuffle?	
A:	I can.	25
T:	Pass them to Lisa and let her have a go. They'll be well shuffled by the time they're finished.	
L:	I always do it like that.	
G:	That 'ain't how you shuffle 'em.	
L:	I always put them in the middle as well. I don't just turn 'em over.	30
T:	Right, well we don't need to shuffle again. That was just to get them really well mixed up.	
L:	I've got 'em mixed up.	
T:	I'm going to . . . thanks. Now I hope you're going to be able to reach 'cos the pack of cards stays in the middle of the table. I'll take my turn first so you can see what I've got and I'm going to borrow Gordon's ten pence. Right. You've got a ha'penny in here.	35
L:	Ha'penny. What's ha' penny? Oh my God.	40
T:	Right. Halfpennypiece . . . and I'm going to take the top card. The top card and you mustn't look before you take it. Alright. So you take it like that . . . I've got two so I'll take the one I looked at – ooh I had three . . .	
L:	Five pence.	45
T:	. . . it couldn't be a very big aeroplane could it. So, anyone know what my sum's going to be that I'm going to write down?	
L:	Ten take away five leaves five.	
T:	Right. And I'm going to use my pennies. I've got ten pence . . . I'm going to spend one-two-three-four-five pence buying my aeroplane . . . that's altogether . . .	50
L:	Leaves . . . ?	
T:	. . . leaves me. Gordon? How much does it leave me. How much change. I had five pence change. Now, very important thing. When you've worked out your shopping you put your card back.	55
L:	underneath . . .	
T:	. . . underneath.	

L:	Can we go round . . .	60
T:	You could probably pass the pack round couldn't you. Right, Gordon I'll give you your ten pence back.	
G:	2p. . . . A basket.	
T:	Right, you leave that while you spend two pence. Right, how much will you have left?	65
G:	Mm . . . I'll have . . . eight.	
TR:	Cheap.	
T:	Right, very cheap. It's a very cheap shop I've got, right.	
L:	Don't.	
A:	You've got to put it underneath.	70
L:	Is that the one?	
G:	I dunno.	
A:	Yes it is.	
T:	When he's finished, he might need it just to look at for a moment. Perhaps he just wants to look at it. Write it down.	75
L:	Oh nine p. . .?	
T:	Every time the cards come back to you . . .	
L:	I've got to buy a teddy bear for nine pence . . .	
T:	You should have your sum written down ready.	80
A:	You'll only have one pence left.	
L:	I've got a teddy bear . . . nine pence.	
T:	That's cheap for a bear isn't it. . . . How much did you spend Gordon?	
TR:	Polar bears are usually five hundred thousand pounds.	85
L:	They ain't.	
TR:	Real ones are.	
L:	Yeah, yeah they are. Too much money. God . . . my my it's my cousin's birthday on bonfire night oh God . . . we had a bonfire party . . . oh . . .	90
TR:	It's my cousin's birthday . . .	
L:	. . . take away nine pence leaves . . .	
T:	. . . pass the cards round darling, try and pass the cards round fairly quickly so people aren't waiting.	
L:	Ten take away nine pence leaves . . .	95
A:	. . . four pence.	
A:	. . . four pence.	
TR:	. . . you can sail under water. How much is it?	
A:	Four pence.	

L:	. . . for what, for what?	100
A:	Boat . . . sailing boat.	
L:	Yacht, a yacht, a little yacht, a toy yacht.	
A:	Not a little, a big one.	
L:	No.	
TR:	Four pence, come on.	105
L:	I've write my sum down. . . . Mine was easy . . . come on Tracey. . . . What you got?	
TR:	I've got a nice little kitten.	
A:	Three pence! Just for a kitten.	
L:	Three pence. . . . Tracey put in underneath.	110
TR:	Ten take away three.	
A:	Ten take away four.	
L:	C'mon Karen. . . . Ten pence take away nine pence leaves one pence.	
A:	Four pence leaves one-two-three-four-five-six pence.	115
L:	I got a teddy bear, mm I always get a teddy bear.	
A:	You don't always you might get something else . . . like a boat . . . four pence.	
TR:	Seven.	
A:	You might get it six hundred pence . . . you'll have to get all the money and give it.	120
L:	Where is Karen? I'll be here all day.	
TR:	He'll be taking the back of Karen's head . . . 'cos the cameras . . .	
L:	I was sitting there and you was sitting there wasn't you, she took . . . the back of your head.	125
TR:	He's going to take the back of Karen's head.	
L:	And Hilary's.	
TR:	No.	
L:	Yeah he is.	130
TR:	Karen they're gonna take the back of your head that camera is 'cos you're facing this way they're gonna take the back of your head.	
A:	It's your go.	
L:	Now it's your go.	135
A:	. . . . What you got? Oh. Put it underneath and take another one.	
TR:	Miss – if you get nothing on the card what do you do?	
T:	What do you think? What do you buy?	

TR:	You don't write nothing.	140
T:	So you have to write nothing.	
TR:	Karen picked another one up.	
T:	Oh no Karen that's your card so when you go to the shop you buy nothing.	
T:	So how much money will you have for change?	145
K:	Nothing.	
L:	Ten pence.	
T:	You'll have nothing left if you spend nothing will you?	
G:	No, you'll have ten pence.	
K:	I'm lucky I've got ten pence left.	150
L:	You have to put ten take away none, you have to put nought . . . leaves ten.	
A:	C'mon Hilary. Hurry up.	
L:	What you got. . . . Ah, a kitten.	
TR:	I got that.	155
A:	I got my four pence all.	
L:	Put it back underneath.	
TR:	Gordon sit back down.	
A:	It's your go.	
A:	It's your go.	160
G:	Good, and I got a lovely . . .	
K:	I've spent nothing so far. I got a lovely . . .	
G:	A young doggie . . . eight pence.	
A:	Oh he's won a doggie, eight pence.	
L:	Oh I've got a doggie at home.	165
A:	Me too. Guess what I've got . . . I bought a boat.	
L:	I bought a teddy bear.	
A:	We could draw pictures of them.	
TR:	I've bought a little kitten.	
K:	I've bought nothing.	170
TR:	My kitten died his name was Timmy.	
A:	My boat died, my boat falls to pieces.	
L:	My teddy bear died. C'mon pass them on.	
A:	My . . . my . . . my boat fell to pieces.	
L:	So did my teddy bear all the fluffing came . . . oh.	175
A:	It's my go.	
L:	I got to put the same as you Karen.	
A:	I'm buying a watering can . . . one pence.	
TR:	That's cheap.	

L:	Ten take away none leaves ten. I didn't buy nothing today.	180
G:	I buyed everything . . . I got no money left.	
A:	I did a watering can for ten pence.	
TR:	I've got a lovely little teddy.	
L:	I got that and it's . . .	185
G:	Here all silly girls.	
A:	I . . . I . . . I bought a watering can ten . . . one pence.	
G:	Teddy bear.	
A:	I bought a watering can.	
K:	I bought nothing so I've still got ten pence.	190
TR:	I bought nothing.	
K:	I've got a nice little teddy bear.	
TR:	Ten take away . . .	
L:	Ah, Tracey has that . . . teddy bear. . . . You forgot to put that teddy bear underneath.	195
C:	Oh.	
G:	I'm telling.	
L:	Karen you better pick another one.	
TR:	You got two now.	
K:	I got a sailing boat like you look look I got a sailing boat look look.	200
A:	Oh I got that.	
L:	Yer four pence. Gordon. You've got a doggie eight pence. No, put it back underneath.	
G:	A dolly hahaha a dolly.	205
A:	What you buying . . . a baby?	
L:	A dolly.	
A:	A dolly.	
G:	I haven't got any more money left.	
A:	You have, look you've got all that ten pence.	210
G:	Alright.	
L:	C'mon put it back underneath.	
G:	Alright, alright.	
L:	Show the cards, don't show the cards.	
K:	I forgot to put that underneath.	215
L:	Hilary did you have a dog?	
G:	Seven.	
L:	You forgot to put it underneath.	
TR:	Hilary you never had her go did you?	

L:	Oh I got a watering can.	220
A:	Like me I bought a watering can.	
L:	How many? One pence, ooh mine's not cheap is it?	
A:	Mine was cheap as well. . . . Oh I'm buying a teddy bear, nine pence.	
L:	I bought a teddy bear . . .	225
TR:	I bought a teddy bear as well.	
L:	Aaa all the fluffing, all the fluffing came out so I had to have another one. Ten pence. Take away . . . pence . . .	
TR:	Oh I got a sailing boat.	
L:	. . . leaves . . .	230
G:	I got a poor old dolly polly.	
L:	. . . nine pence.	
A:	Ten pence take away nine pence . . .	
L:	I've finished mine . . . Karen got an aeroplane.	
K:	I got five . . .	235
A:	How much have you got?	
K:	Mine's cheap mine's five pence.	
L:	Mine was one pence. I what did I buy? I bought a dog. No I bought a um er.	
TR:	No, Karen I'm gonna put it underneath.	240
A:	It's Hilary's go now. It's good innit. What you buying? She's buying a basket 2p, isn't it cheap. My mum's shopping bag was £6.	
L:	So was mine.	
A:	But I threw my shopping bag away . . . I didn't like it . . .	245
L:	So did I.	
A:	So the shop gave me my money back.	
L:	You're lucky then. I like the basket I got 'cos it had all flowers on it.	250
A:	How much was your basket?	
L:	£12 . . . I took it back.	
A:	Dear isn't it?	
L:	Yes but I took it back, it's too much money. Couldn't afford it.	255
A:	I've only got ten pence that's how much money I got.	
L:	Two pence basket.	
G:	I got a basket.	
L:	Give me the cards.	

G:	Why? I just want to have a look at it.	260
L:	He's looked at it . . . put it back.	
TR:	You're putting it back the wrong way.	
A:	Right, right what are you buying?	
G:	How much, how much was it?	
L:	Tracey, that's what I bought.	265
A:	She didn't buy it. My go.	
K:	What did she get? What did she buy?	
A:	Nothing.	
L:	Ten pence take away one leaves ten pence.	270
TR:	Oh dear I think I'll buy a watering can . . . ten pence take away one pence leaves . . .	
K:	I've got another aeroplane.	
TR:	One-two-three-four . . .	
L:	Ooooh you've for an aeroplane. You can go hiding them.	
A:	Yes if I could afford it I'd get an aeroplane.	275
L:	Yes, how much is the aeroplane?	
K:	Five pence.	
A AND L:	Ooooh.	
A:	Can afford it, if I can find one. . . . what you buying?	
L:	Oh, Hilary . . . teddy bear, oh ten pence.	280
A:	Seven pence mine was nine pence my teddy bear.	
L:	Teddy bear? Must be wrong.	
A:	Mine was nine pence.	
L:	P'raps there's two teddy bears.	
A:	P'raps there's hundred of them.	285
L:	Teddy bears.	
G:	A dolly.	
T:	I hope you're all getting on there, you're making. . .	
TR:	He's got a dolly.	
T:	Well, buy it for me Gordon. I should love a doll.	290
G:	I've just got one pence.	
L:	No you haven't you've got all them.	
G:	That's over there. I spent that.	
T:	Oh, I see what you're doing, no, it's alright you . . . each time you get another ten pence to go shopping with ... so you just put it on the bottom. That's six pence.	295
G:	I got a dolly.	

A: I got a dolly.

L: Oh there's two dollies, there's two dollies . . . six pence   300
     that is ten pence take away six pence leaves two-three-
     four-five-six, one-two-three-four, four pence.

A: I'm going out shopping . . . aeroplanes and go out.

L: I've only spent six pence. I spend six pence, I spent six
     pence on dolly.   305

T: Right let's have a look what you've spent. . . . Are you
     sure? If you had ten pence and you spent eight pence
     how much would you have left – Gordon?

K: Look nine pence for all a teddy bear.

T: I can't hear you, well work it out with the pennies. I   310
     know what you did, you spent two pence there didn't
     you and that left you with eight pence and so the next
     time when your toy cost eight pence you thought you
     had nothing left, but it says start with ten pence every
     time doesn't it so you can work out again ten pence take 315
     . . . spend eight pence and work out how much you'll
     have left.

L: Put them down Gordon.

T: Oh you got the card with nothing on it did you.

L: Yes I got two times. Two times.   320

A: I got it there.

T: You had it as well. You're putting all your p's for pence
     round the wrong way, look these two are right and all
     these are wrong. Oh dear you have done these close
     together. Will you put that p round the right way. . . .   325
     You've got that round the wrong way, you've got them
     back to front, you've put p9. That's difficult isn't it.

G: A kitten – three pence.

T: But you're forgetting it's money you're spending. Read
     these to me ten pence take away one leaves nine . . . ten 330
     pence take away . . .

L: I've got nothing again.

T: Sorry . . . ten pence take away . . . you haven't put take
     away, there that's what I want to show you . . .

A: I'm going to buy a kitten three pence. I'm going to buy a 335
     little kitten.

T: Now the next one.

L: Ten pence.

T: What's that? Your p, that's going to be your p for nine
        pence.   340
A: What did you buy? I bought a kitten what did you buy?
        You didn't buy anything did you? I bought a kitten.
L: I tried to find . . . I tried to find a kitten.
A: Aeroplane.
L: I tried to find a kitten.   345
A: Oh I wanted one of them. I'm going to go on holiday
        soon . . . 'cos I've saved . . . oh dear my aeroplane
        broke, didn't it. I've got to buy another one. I am rich.
G: Two pence's not rich. It's not enough to buy bubble gum
        and a bazooka.   350
L: Super bazooka. C'mon Karen.

8 The achievement of mastery

In this chapter I am going to present a small episode from the mathematics work of a top infant class. The teacher had chosen to take a group of children whom she considered ready for work on place-value. For this teacher, consonant with the current discursive practices in which she is inserted, children are taken to 'discover the place-value concept'. This means that she set the work up in a particular way and produced a certain reading of what happened. I want to examine the effectivity of that reading, while also producing an alternative, a reading which renders visible aspects of signification which she cannot easily 'see'.

The current position on place-value is amply presented by Williams and Shuard (1976) in a section entitled appropriately 'the emergence of the place-value concept':

> From a variety of forms in which children experience our number
> system – the cubes and rods, recordings of sums of money and
> measuring, graphs, the abacus and symbols for numerals – these
> develop a capacity to read and write numbers with a confident
> recognition of their meaning.
>
> (Williams and Shuard 1976:163)

Although Williams and Shuard give a place to symbols, it is a secondary role produced out of a recording of a set of experiences, these being physical manipulation of objects. It is these which lead to the production of place-value as a concept or, as Williams and Shuard state it, a capacity.

The notion of experience and activity held by the teachers is one which presumes that there can exist an unmediated relationship between subject and object, between knower and known, between the subject and the physical world. While this is rather less sophisticated than the notion held by many psychologists, including Piaget, it shares with all such ideas a reduction of the importance of the role of the symbolic in understanding. This is apparent, for example, in the way in which language, and processes of signification in general, are regarded as neutral (subsidiary) parts of the process of conceptual development by both teachers in the classroom and in Piagetian theory.

For Piaget the role of signs, both linguistic and other, such as gesture, is one of 'representation'. Signification is not a part of the process of progressive abstraction from experience.

Correspondingly, for this teacher, the role of language was to represent concept formed through activity and experience. The teachers did not, of course, use the notion of signification as such; they restricted their concern to spoken and written language, and the writing of mathematical signs. The uses of language were seen as secondary in that they were not part of the process of understanding, which was their central concern, they were, instead, what was erected on the foundations of understanding. Thus the primary function of writing was seen as 'recording', to provide a record of activities which children has already performed. What the children wrote, then, was seen as a written description of those activities. Thus what appears as a calculation, e.g. $12 +$, is, in fact, presented to children as a *post hoc*

$$\frac{14}{26}$$

description of the action of taking twelve material objects, uniting them with a set of fourteen other objects, and counting the set which is the sum. The exercise of writing makes the children familiar with the writing connections, but the mathematical signs function as representations of objects and physical operations performed upon them. The children do not do calculations with the written signs. Only later, when the children have 'understood' the principles of the operation in concrete terms, are they given calculations to perform and represent with signs alone. But this is not assumed to help them understand anything. Such calculations can be mastered perfectly well by rote learning. It is the operations with material objects which provide the foundations for the written calculations.

I am going to examine a group of children, all aged six to seven years, being introduced by their teacher to the topic of place-value in a situation of normal classroom practice. The whole of the time spent working on place-value by these children during a three-week period produced approximately five-and-a-half hours of recordings, the sound tracks of which were entirely transcribed. In the class in which the recordings were made it was the teacher's routine to take a small group of children – those whom she considers to be ready for the topic in question – and to work with them for a short time, usually about fifteen minutes, before setting them tasks which they then carry out themselves, either alone, in partners, or as a group. In this case the teacher and the children started their session sitting around a table. The teacher had by her an easel, referred to as 'the board', to which she had pinned a large sheet of paper. She began by giving the children a large box of matches and a box of elastic bands, instructing them to make 'bundles of ten'. When they had made enough bundles the teacher asked them to take four bundles each and also four 'single ones'. Transcript E on p. 178 presents what occurred at this point, the beginning of their first session working with place-value.

In Transcript E I will show that some of the features of our number system, an appreciation of which is necessary for an understanding of place-value, are made to signify through the communication which takes place. One of the main points of the teacher's enterprise is to get the children to see the numbers expressed by two digit numerals not as a unified value, as they may be understood in the children's familiar use of them to represent a cardinal value when they have counted a set of things, but as a union of two separable values. To accomplish this the teacher hardly misses an opportunity to ensure that a number be expressed as a union of a number of tens and a number of ones. The first instance is at line 25 and thereafter it occurs throughout the corpus. We can distinguish three basic discursive strategies used by the teacher to ensure that a number is expressed in this way. They all consist of ways of formulating the expression of a number when the children have not themselves presented it as so many bundles, or tens, and so many ones – which they very seldom do. The simplest strategy is that in which the teacher, in response to a child's utterance, reformulates the expression. For example:

MICHAEL: . . . forty then.
TEACHER: just forty. Just four bundles of ten, right.

This is the strategy which occurs least frequently. Far more common are the other two in which the teacher initiates a collaborative reformulation of the expression of a number to which the children have referred either verbally, by using its name, or symbolically, using written numerals. The first of these takes the form of a question which elicits information about 'how many' bundles of ten, and single ones, make up a number. For example, see lines 95–102 on p. 181.

MICHAEL: Twelve.
TEACHER: Twelve yes (*she points to the '1' of the '12'*).
How many bundles of ten?
CHILDREN: One.
TEACHER: (*Pointing to the '2' of the '12'*) – and how many single ones?
CHILDREN: Two.
TEACHER: Two, right.

The final strategy of this kind consists of a prompt in which the teacher begins an utterance where she names one of the numerals of a number, using it to express a cardinal value, and indicates that the child should complete the utterance by providing the numerical category or set to which, in the context of the symbol and/or the matchsticks in question, she must be referring. For example, see lines 112–16 on p. 181.

TEACHER: Two and four (*she points to the '2' of Ahmed's '24'*).
Two bundles of . . . ?
CHILDREN: Ten.
TEACHER: (*Pointing to the '4' of '24'*) – and four . . . ?
SUE: Single ones.

Occasionally these strategies occur together, as in this example (lines 77–80):

ANNE: Five.
TEACHER: Five tens and how many single ones did you have to put out?
ANNE: None.

The teacher uses these strategies repeatedly. Transcript E (p. 178) provides a typical picture of the frequency with which these strategies occur when the teacher is talking to the children. In fact the whole corpus shows how she employs one or the other of these strategies or a combination of them. In view of this it is worth remarking on the fact that the children themselves only spontaneously refer to a number as composed of a number of tens and a number of ones when there is a specific communicative purpose in doing so. These strategies of reformulation are one of the methods by which the teacher re-presents certain features of our number system to the children. Her response to a child's reference to a number is discursively to reflect that same number back to the child in a different form: in a form which makes the number signify not as a unified value but as the union of two separable values. As she does this the teacher at the same time leads the children to see that value as being related to groupings in tens. She does this quite simply by uniformly using the numerals to refer to tens or ones, ensuring that the children do so, having the matchsticks made into bundles of ten in the first place to provide concrete referents for the numerals, and by deliberately not basing the value of numerals on anything other than ten. In addition, the teacher makes salient the fact that a numeral's value is related to its position. This is not made explicit in the same way as are the particular values of numerals, for the teacher does not say that numerals, or the same numerals, may have different values depending on their place, even though it is this which is considered by many to be what confuses children and makes place-value difficult for them. The point is displayed rather than explicitly stated. Nevertheless, it is clear that the teacher again makes the relation signify and that she does this discursively from the beginning.

Of course the point is partly made by the way the teacher ensures that a number is reformulated, for it is without exception that the numeral on the left refers to the tens bundles, while that on the right refers to the ones. But how is the relation established in the first place, so that the children can express the number in this way? The teacher establishes the relation through the conjunction of verbal and gestural pointing. Consider this example (lines 18–29, p. 179):

TEACHER: Seventy ...? (*As the teacher says this she writes '7'.*)
CHILDREN: Six.
TEACHER: ... six. (*As she writes the '6' to complete '76'.*) If we were talking about Anne's matchsticks what would that seven mean? (*The teacher points to the '7' of '76'.*) Think about Anne's matchsticks that she put out for us. Anne, what does seven mean – (*she points to the '7' again*) – when I'm talking about your matchsticks? What have you got seven of?
ANNE: Bundles.
TEACHER: Seven bundles of ...?
ANNE: Ten.

The function of pointing is to direct attention and here the teacher, by gesturally pointing to the '7' while verbally pointing to Anne's matchsticks and asking what *that* seven means, is directing attention to the relationship between '7' and the bundles. In the context of the participant's knowledge that the '76' was written to describe how many matchsticks Anne put out, the '7' represents the particular seven bundles which everyone can see in front of Anne. If fact, at this point, the first time it is used, this strategy does not elicit a response, and the teacher asks a simple question which Anne can answer. But it is important from the teacher's point of view that the '7' refers not simply to bundles of ten. The teacher prompts, and when Anne says, 'Ten', the relationship is made: that 7 refers to those particular bundles of matchsticks. After this (lines 37–42, on p. 179), the teacher goes on to display that the '6' expresses six when it refers to the single ones in the bundles.

The conjunction of verbal and gestural pointing is again a discursive strategy which the teacher uses repeatedly. By frequently pointing to bundles of ten as she points to the number on the left, and to single ones as she points to the numeral on the right, the teacher establishes that when two symbols are used to express a number the numerals are to be treated not as a unity, together denoting one value, but as two separate values: that on the left the tens, that on the right the ones. That is, she uses her own body to create a new relation of signification out of other signs. She unites signifier and signified.

The end of Transcript E (p. 182) marks the end of the teacher's explanation in the first session. For the rest of the session each child worked with the partners they had chosen at one of the tasks the teacher had rehearsed with them. The children in turn chose some matchsticks, made up of 'bundles' and 'single' ones, from their pile and presented them to their partner, who then wrote on their paper the number describing how many matchsticks in all had been 'put out' for them.

This was followed up by a variety of activities. For example, the children performed a similar task to that in the first session but instead of matchsticks they used money, giving each other amounts of money in single pence and ten pence pieces. They also played a board game where two teams threw dice and moved a small counter along a part of the board that was marked out in ones up to ten, and having reached ten in ones recorded this by moving a larger counter one place along the part of the board marked in tens up to one hundred. Following this the session from which the next extract is taken occurred. In this session the children had been performing a task in which they found the sum of two numbers. They each had forty-four matchsticks, four bundles and four single ones, and they were working in partners. Each partner 'put out' a number of matchsticks, then both children wrote down the two numbers in the form of a calculation, e.g. 14. The

$$\frac{14}{12}$$

teacher asked them to take only forty-four matchsticks each in order to avoid the possibility of, and any confusion which might have resulted from, the children producing a written sum which had ten or more in either the tens or ones place. Just prior to this the teacher asked the children to take another four matchsticks, so that each child then had forty-eight. With forty-eight matchsticks each the children may now have a sum with ten or more in the ones place. When this happens a two-digit number will describe how many ones, not as a unified value, but as one ten and a number of ones 'left over'. That ten may then be classed together with, or added to, the tens in the place of the sum. When dealing with actual matchsticks, as the teacher and children are doing in this extract, this may take the form of physically taking ten of the ones and putting an elastic band around them to make another bundle of ten. Here is an example of physically creating a new sign, in this case an iconic one: 'a bundle of ten'. It is this possibility, that when there are more than ten ones in a total they may be transformed into a ten and a number of ones left over, that is being made to signify by the teacher here:

TEACHER: Right Michael I think you need to turn your paper   1
           over, it's got rather full. You're alright. So everybody's
           got forty-eight matchsticks. Right Anne put out a
           number for me out of your forty-eight matchsticks and
           tell me what you're putting out.   5
ANNE: (*Putting out three bundles.*)
           Thirty.
TEACHER: Oh I'd like some ones as well please. So I'd like some
           tens and some single matchsticks.
ANNE: (*Adding eight single matchsticks to her three bundles.*)   10
           Thirty-eight.
TEACHER: Oh you're making it difficult, so I've got to write down
           three bundles of ten – (*as she writes '3' on the board*) –
           and eight – (*as she writes '8' to complete '38'*). Right
           Michael put out some for me.   15
MICHAEL: (*Putting out four bundles and two single ones.*) Forty-two.
TEACHER: Forty-two, right, four bundles of ten – (*as she writes '4'
           beneath the '3' of the '38'*) – and . . .
MICHAEL: Two.

TEACHER:	... two ... (*as she writes '2' beneath the '8' of the '38' to complete '42'*). Put your matchsticks together those two children. Thirty-eight Anne and forty-two Michael. Anne please put your thirty-eight over to Michael. (*Anne puts her thirty-eight matchsticks in a pile on top of Michael's.*)	20
		25
SUE:	Eighty. Eighty altogether.	
MICHAEL:	(*Counting all the matchsticks in the pile.*) Forty-two ...	
TEACHER:	Right now can you put them down in the middle so that we can see what's happened?	30
MICHAEL:	Seventy. Eighty it's eighty. Altogether it's eighty.	
TEACHER:	Now what's happened, where's Anne's thirty ...	
MICHAEL:	Eight. I had forty-two.	
TEACHER:	Thirty-eight. Now you had how many?	
MICHAEL:	Forty-two.	35
TEACHER:	Forty-two (*she takes the pile of matchsticks and spreads them out in the middle of the table*).	
MICHAEL:	I did.	
TEACHER:	What's happened? Right. Four, two (...).	
MICHAEL:	Got muddled up.	40
TEACHER:	Right, forty-two. How many tens have we got altogether? One, two, three, four, five, six, seven (*while counting, the teacher moves each bundle a few inches as she tags it with a number, stressing the final 'seven'*).	
		45
SUE:	Seven.	
TONY:	Seven.	
MICHAEL:	Seven.	
TEACHER:	Seven and how many single ones?	
ANNE:	I know.	50
AHMED:	Eight.	
ANNE:	Eighty.	
TEACHER:	One, two, three, four, five, six, seven, eight, nine, ten. (*As they all count, the teacher tags each matchstick with a number by moving it a few inches. They all stress the final 'ten'.*)	
		55
ANNE:	Eighty.	
TEACHER:	So if we wanted to we could get another elastic band	

	and make that into another bundle. We've got eight bundles of ten.	60
PUPIL:	That's eighty.	
TEACHER:	Eighty. Now just a minute. . . . Right, watch this one.	
MICHAEL:	Twenty-eight, twenty-eight.	65
TEACHER:	Twenty . . .?	
SUE:	Eight.	
TEACHER:	Right. So let me write that down, twenty-eight, twenty-eight. Right Karen I'm going to borrow some of yours. Oh sorry I forgot to show you the other number. The other number. The other number is going to be twenty-one, two, three, four, five . . .	70
MICHAEL:	Twenty-six.	
TEACHER:	Twenty-six.	
TONY:	Forty, forty.	75
SUE:	Forty, forty, fifty-four.	
TEACHER:	Now listen when you get a number like this it's going to be more than another ten isn't it? So put your forty there, count out the next bundle of ten, two, four, six, eight, ten, now how many tens have I got here?	80
CHILDREN:	Five.	
TEACHER:	Ten, twenty, thirty, forty, fifty.	
MICHAEL:	Fifty.	
TEACHER:	But I've still got another . . .?	
CHILDREN:	Four.	85
SUE:	I said fifty-four so I'm right.	
MICHAEL:	They begin with the same letter, fifty-four.	
TEACHER:	Fifty-four, so I had twenty-eight – (*as she writes '28' on the board*) – and twenty-six – (*as she writes '26' beneath the '28'*) – and adding them all together was?	90
MICHAEL:	Fifty-four.	
TEACHER:	Fifty . . .?	
MICHAEL:	Four.	
TEACHER:	Fifty-four – (*as she puts a line beneath the '26' and completes the sum as '54' thus 28*) –	95

$$\frac{26}{54}$$

Now you've all got enough matchsticks now to do things like that . . .

Here the teacher continues to use the discursive strategies we have analysed, to make significant the aspects of place-value already discussed. Here, however, she uses them additionally to establish the main point being made, that the single ones may be made into another bundle. The interesting feature of the transcript is not only that this point is made to signify discursively, but also that the questioning strategy of the teacher does not elicit a response when it might be expected to do so. At line 29, when the teacher has asked Anne and Michael to put their matchsticks together, making a pile containing seven bundles and ten ones, she indicates that something relevant, something they may notice, may have happened. She asks them to 'put them down in the middle so that we can see what's happened' (i.e. in the middle of the table where everyone can see them). At line 32, and again at line 39 she asks, 'What's happened?' The teacher is attempting to get the children to see that of the many things that have happened, among which, as Michael says, the two sets have, 'Got muddled up', one event is that enough ones have now been produced potentially to make another bundle. This is the relevant event in the context of the lesson on place-value. The children, however, do not see this. They seem throughout to be interested in the total sum (lines 11, 16, 26, 28, 31, etc.). At lines 41–5 the teacher demonstrates that the eighty is composed of seven bundles of ten and one ten, and in the face of the children's repeated focus on the cardinal value of the whole set, tells them, 'So if we wanted to we could get another elastic band and make that into another bundle. We've got eight bundles of ten' (lines 59–61). Again here, then, the creation of the difference with a system of signification of 'fifty' as a cardinal value and the sign 'five bundles of ten' is what the children have to be brought to 'see'.

Now the children might have noticed this themselves. After all, they could see the seven bundles and ten ones in front of them, the teacher was indicating that something relevant was going on, and it can be argued that they knew that something to do with tens and ones was relevant. Perhaps their attention was misdirected by what was more familiar to them and might appear to be the point of the exercise: finding the total sum; but it is difficult to see what else the teacher might have done to prime them to make the relevant 'discovery' for themselves. And even had they done so it is clear that the teacher would have led them to it discursively through her manipulation and counting of the array of matchsticks. In the end she tells them explicitly, and later she repeats the lesson, when her questioning strategy does not elicit a correct response this time (lines 77–80, p. 167):

TEACHER: Now listen when you get a number like this it's going to be more than another ten isn't it? So put your forty there, count out the next bundle of ten, two, four, six, eight, now how many tens have I got here?

CHILDREN: Five.

In all these examples of the children beginning place-value, the teacher, in a sense, *tells* the children what they are supposed to be experiencing and discovering. Occasionally the information is as explicit as at lines 77–80, but even when the teacher is not being forced to be so didactic she is providing the children with cues which reveal the properties of place-value which the objects they are manipulating are supposed to supply. This, however, is not part of the teacher's intention, and the phenomena which our analysis show are rendered invisible by the teacher's understanding of experience as central and by the way we tend to take talk and gesture for granted in interaction. In this sense, then, the children are brought to a reading of the values the teacher wants to get across. This means that since the teacher has set up the lesson in terms of the manipulation of objects, there is every reason to suppose that this is what she 'sees' and, concomitantly, what the children have to be brought to 'see' in their manipulation.

The teacher's intention in giving the children matchsticks to count and group – and represent with numerals in a place-value system – is that the relations of value between the numerals in that system will be apparent to the children because they will be presented concretely as relations between bundles and single matchsticks. On the contrary, it is the properties of the place-value systems which are used to make the matchsticks, and the grouping of them into bundles of ten, which signify in particular ways. If the teacher did not do this, there would be no reason for the children to give the grouping of matchsticks any significance. In the first place, the fact that our place-value system uses a base ten is an arbitrary cultural and historical fact: it is not necessary either culturally or psychologically. For certain purposes, and at other times in history, other bases have been used. In fact, the children read the grouping in tens as arbitrary, and the teacher has no justification for why we should use ten instead of any other number, as this extract shows:

TEACHER: Right I want you to . . . now, perhaps you can guess why I wanted you to put those matchsticks into bundles like that.

CHILDREN: No.

TEACHER: Well, do you think I chose the number particularly?

CHILDREN: No.

TEACHER: Do you think it could have been eleven or twelve in the bundles?

CHILDREN: Yes.

TEACHER: No, but you can count in tens and use one that's on the abacus don't we when we're counting.

The teacher cannot provide a justification for grouping in tens other than the one she does elliptically – that it happens to be the way we all agree to count – so there is no reason for using base ten other than that it is conventional (unless, of course, it is because we have ten fingers). From the very beginning, then, when the teacher chooses ten as the number in the groups, she is making the objects signify in a way which is consonant with convention. The children's activities are being determined by a convention, and not vice versa.

The power of a place-value system derives from the way in which symbols are used: from the systematic properties of a pattern which allows a finite number of numerals to be combined in such a way that any natural number may be represented by them. This power was a product of what Kline (1953) calls 'notation directed change'. It could be argued, therefore, that it arose, in other words, from changes not at the conceptual level of grouping, but in the way in which numbers are made to signify.

Despite the fact that the children in these examples spend most of their time handling and talking and writing about matchsticks, they are learning something about how to represent quantity. The children can, in fact, already do all the operations which can be seen as the kind of 'logico-mathematical' thought demanded by their lesson. They would have grouped any objects into any conveniently small number the teacher asked them to; and they would have decomposed any number into a number of tens and a number of ones before they started. What they have to understand is that the same work on paper may have a different value in terms of the quantity it represents, depending on the place the mark is put in relation to other marks, and that the possible values of those marks are all numbers of ones or tens.

The children's activity does not provide the experience from which they may abstract that understanding. In fact, the properties of the place-value system are used to help the children to understand their activity. The teacher is constantly, and often literally, pointing out that a numeral in a particular place represents a different pile. She manufactures a correspondence between the value of a numeral and a pile of matchsticks which the children can count, hoping that this correspondence will be obvious to the children. When it is not, she is forced to tell them explicitly as, for example, when she says:

> Three. (*She points to the '3' of the '34'.*) Look it tells you doesn't it? How many bundles of ten?

The message here is that, if we want to know how many bundles a child put out, we need not look at the bundles themselves, but at the signifier of a numeral in the tens column. The bundle has dropped to the level of signified and it is this numeral which is now the new signifier.

In these examples the teacher actually physically provides the force which unites signifier and signified. She links them with her own body, as in lines 20–2 of Transcript E, p. 179. Here, the teacher points to both the bundles and to the 7 of 76. She practises such relations of signification many times during the lesson, uniting spoken numeral and matchsticks, written numeral and matchsticks, and spoken and written numeral. By continuing to make these relations she actually takes the children towards the production of the place-value sign. The matchsticks, spoken numbers, and written numerals appear to act variously as signifiers and signifieds, thus producing complex signifying chains. Since mathematical discourse is written, it is necessary for the teacher to provide the relations of transformation from the spoken to written numerals. She points to a collection of bundles and relates it to a numeral in the tens place on the board. In the same way she relates single matches to a numeral in the ones place. Similarly, she links a spoken number to a written numeral in a particular place on the board (for example, Transcript E, lines 20–6). It can be argued that in this way the initial demonstration of the production of the sign in relation to place-value is effected by the teacher. The signifier, a numeral in 'place', cannot be made to link directly with a number of bundles and single matchsticks because 'place' as an element of the signifier does not represent bundles at all, but values; in this case the value of the place on the left transforms the ideogram into units of 1×10.

A case-study

I should like to illustrate the effects of the processes I have been analysing with an examination of the work of one particular child in the group learning place-value. Here the child makes certain advances

in his understanding, and also certain errors, which derive from his use
of written numerals as signifiers. The teacher's reaction to these errors
illustrates how, without a distinction between what the child can do
alone, and what he can do with help, and with a view that only
experience and activity foster understanding, the child is held back
from further progress in the curriculum when it is plausible to suggest
that a certain kind of help would encourage progress.

The child in question is Michael and the partner with whom he is
working is Tony. I will begin with an example of them performing a
task in the manner in which the teacher has instructed them. In this
example the children had forty-four matchsticks each, and they had
been asked to put out a number each, to put the two sets of matchsticks
together, to count them to find the total and, at the same time, record
their activities in the form of a calculation:

MICHAEL: My turn to put one out first innit?   1
TONY: Yes. Yes – (*Michael puts out two bundles*) – twenty.
MICHAEL: Three (he adds three single ones to the two bundles).
TONY: Twenty-three, and . . . (*Tony puts out one bundle*) . . .
MICHAEL: I put my number down first. Two, wait, wait two.   5
          Right?
TONY: Two three.
MICHAEL: And there's three. Which one . . .
TONY: Three goes round like that.
MICHAEL: Three. Twenty-three, now you write down your   10
          number. What's your number? Ten. So I put a one.
          One there?
TONY: Yeah a one. We'll have to sort this out won't we?
MICHAEL: Yeah and then put a line.
TONY: A line. Twenty-three I have to put the same as you I   15
          think.
MICHAEL: Now wait, put 'em together – (*Michael pushes his twenty-
          three and Tony's bundle into a pile*) – is thirty-three.
TONY: Thirty-three.
MICHAEL: Three and a three (. . .) there's your ten back – (*they   20
          have both written* 23) –
                         10
                         33

In this example the children do physically put the matchsticks together
(lines 17–18). It may be that the children count them to get the answer
of thirty-three. If this is the case, it is certainly not apparent on the

video tapes. The speed with which they do it suggests, however, that they do not have to count to get the answer. Certainly, it seems that Tony's facility with number bonds is such that he would not have to count. In this example what the children write is not the calculation. They are not manipulating written symbols according to an algorithm. As the teacher said to us, the children are 'recording'. They were not asked to perform the operation of addition with reference to the symbols on paper but to find the sum using the matchsticks, for which counting would be an effective procedure. Tony and Michael perform the task in this way several times. But they soon depart from the procedure of putting the matchsticks together:

TONY:	OK that's what I'm going to put out – (*Tony puts three bundles and one single one in front of him*).	1
MICHAEL:	What are you going to put out?	
TONY:	Thirty-one. (. . .)	
MICHAEL:	And then put – (*Michael puts three bundles in front of him*) . . .	5
TONY:	Thirty-one, you put thirty-one and three. Thirty-one. Thirty.	
MICHAEL:	Look I put thirty here, you put thirty-one out so if you put thirty-one out and I put thirty, put 'em together – (*As Michael says this he looks at what he has written on his paper and does not touch the matchsticks which remain in quite separate piles*) – 'scuse, and the answer is. Here y'are.	10

This is the first time that they depart from the procedure the teacher has told them to follow. The following example occurs a few minutes later:

TONY:	Two more of these and we'll show Miss.	1
MICHAEL:	Two more. OK.	
TONY:	(*He puts four bundles and two single ones in front of him*) – forty-two.	
MICHAEL:	I'll put twenty – (*puts two bundles in front of him*) – so I, I write my number down first.	5
TONY:	What is it? Twenty.	
MICHAEL:	Then you put your number down – forty-two. Wait, four and two.	
TONY:	Sixty-two, sixty-two.	10
MICHAEL:	That's what I make it as well.	
TONY:	Good then. One more. (*Again they don't physically put*	

> the matchsticks together and from lines 5–9 above,
> Michael does not take his eyes off the numbers he is writing
> on his paper.)   15

Here the two boys are departing from the procedure in different ways. Tony seems to use his facility with number bonds. He very quickly produces the sum while neither putting the matchsticks together nor, as Michael does, scrutinizing the numbers he has written.

Michael focused on the written numbers alone and calculated with them to find the sum. To do this he uses an algorithm which he is in the process of inventing. What this algorithm is becomes apparent in the following extract where he explains it to his teacher. It consists of adding the numbers in the tens column, then adding those in the ones column:

MICHAEL: Miss. May I tell you the easy way I found how to do it?   1
           (*Michael stands by the board and points to a sum written
           on it thus:* 20)
                20
                44
                ──
                64

           Look when you do one you put look – (*he points to the
           '20'*) – like if someone put out twenty you write down   5
           twenty, if someone put out forty-four (*pointing to the
           '44'*) you put out forty-four. You'll easy know how to
           put six down there (*pointing to the '6'*) 'cos you add up
           these two (*points to the '2' and the first '4' of the '44'*)
           and they make six (*pointing to the '6' again*) – so you   10
           put there and, and, and (*pointing to the '0'*) nought is
           nothing and four (*pointing to the second four of the '44'*)
           – so you put four there (*pointing to the '4' of the '64'*) –
           nought, nought doesn't make anything.
TEACHER: Yes, yes that's fine so long as you're always careful to   15
           get them in the right places – (*she gestures to the
           whole of the 'sum'*) – because, well, you're doing it
           with the matchsticks (*she points to a pile of
           matchsticks on the table*) aren't you, just to check that
           it's right. That's what you do you add up the four   20
           single ones (*pointing to the second '4' of the '44'*) – and
           none. (*She points to the '0'*) – two bundles of ten
           (*pointing to the '2'*) – and four bundles of ten
           (*pointing to the first '4' of the '44'*) is . . .?

MICHAEL: Sixty-four.   25
TEACHER: Six bundles of ten. OK . . .

No one had ever observed Michael using this strategy before to add two-digit numbers. The teacher said that she had not shown the children how to do it, Michael had never done it before in the classroom, and he said later that it was his 'easy way' and that his parents had not shown him. As he says to the teacher (line 1, p. 174), he 'found how to do it'.

Tony and Michael's shared interest in the task becomes that of finding the sum of the two numbers, which Michael refers to as 'the answer' (line 12, p. 173). Michael appears to focus on this aspect of the task even when (lines 25–6, above) the teacher's discursive strategies make other aspects salient.

Michael's elation is quite apparent. It seems to be the fact that the algorithm works, rather than simply getting the right answer, which gives Michael pleasure. Indeed, on most occasions Michael is told the answer by Tony, whose solution is of a different order and, in this situation, quicker. Michael, while often telling Tony to wait, is pleased when his method produces an answer which agrees with Tony's (e.g. p. 172, lines 4–6; p. 173, lines 6–11). An important feature of Michael's method is revealed in his explanation to the teacher (p. 174): he goes from left to right, adding up the tens column first. The teacher, however, adds the ones column first and does not comment on the fact that she and Michael begin with different columns. Being a good teacher she redefines the task to fit what Michael has done and replies using the discursive strategies analysed earlier to reflect back Michael's method in terms which make salient the values of the numbers in the different columns in relation to their denoting bundles of ones. Up to the final extract Michael and Tony have had forty-four matchsticks each and Michael's algorithm is perfectly suited to all the calculations that may arise using these numbers. But obviously it will have to be expanded if he is to deal with cases in which more than ten appears as the sum of one of the columns. For a time Michael's strategy works, as in the following examples:

MICHAEL: That's what I make it. . . . Do it in your head, say it in   1
          your head so we can concentrate. OK you put out
          separate (*Tony puts out three bundles*) – thirty. I'll put
          out twenty (*Michael puts out two bundles*) – and that's
          . . .   5

TONY: Thirty and twenty is fifty.
MICHAEL: We had eight more the next time, didn't we?
           Wait (...) wait, wait I've got thirty and twenty ...
TONY: Is fifty.
MICHAEL: ... Wait, is ... wait. Do it in your head, three ...   10
           (*again they do not physically put the matchsticks together*)
           ... hey I make it fifty. Shall I tell you how I do it?
TONY: How?
MICHAEL: Well look you see when you get a sum like this right,
           look, you write the two numbers down don't you –   15
           they're the tens and they're the ones. You put three
           ones down and I put two tens, you put three tens down
           and I put two tens. We didn't put any ones down any of
           us did we?
TONY: No.   20
MICHAEL: So, we've got this sum thirty and twenty haven't we?
           And altogether I add up this and that's three and two
           and that's what?
TONY: Five.
MICHAEL: Three, that's five so you write down five and there's no   25
           there so you put five and that's how you make it it's
           easy innit, see?
           (*During this explanation Michael points to the 'sum' on his
           paper as an example.*)

Then Michael is faced with a sum with more than nine in the 'ones'
column of his calculation and his procedure cannot work. The following example reports what happened when this occurred:

TONY: C'mon I'm leaving my forty-eight out.   1
MICHAEL: I put my forty-eight out. So forty-eight ... (*they each
           have four bundles of ten and eight single ones in front of
           them. They write down the 'sum'*) – wait. Eight and
           eight, what's eight and eight?   5
TONY: (*Counting on his fingers*) – nine, ten, eleven, twelve,
           thirteen, fourteen, fifteen, sixteen. Sixteen. Ninety
           ... wait a minute we can't do this one. I think we
           should put ours together forty ... (*Tony begins to take
           items from Michael's pile of forty-eight and to count them as*   10
           *he physically adds them to his own pile. Michael tries unsuc-
           cessfully to take his matches back and stop Tony*) ...
MICHAEL: Wait, wait I'm not ready yet, I'm not ready yet.

TONY: Forty, forty ... (*Tony puts the two sets of four bundles*
            together) ... so eighty-one, two, three, four, five, six,   15
            seven, eight, nine ... (*Tony 'counts on', naming the pile*
            of eight bundles as 'eighty', then adding the single ones to
            that pile one at a time, tagging each one as he does so.)
MICHAEL: What's it altogether?
TONY: Ninety, ninety-one, ninety-two, ninety-three, ninety-   20
            four, ninety-five, ninety-six.
MICHAEL: Wait.
TONY: Ninety-six.
MICHAEL: Wait.
TONY: ... one, two, three, four, ninety-six.   25
MICHAEL: Wait.
TONY: One, two, three, four.
MICHAEL: This makes up to eight – (*pointing to the two '4's written*
            in the calculation on his paper) – wait.
TONY: Here's your eight.   30
MICHAEL: Four and four's eight, I'll put an eight there. (*Michael*
            writes '8') – 48

$$\frac{48}{8}$$

            What's eight and eight, what's eight and eight?
TONY: One, two, three, four. Eight and eight is sixteen.
            Which is ninety-six.   35
MICHAEL: Oh I done it wrong, wait where's the rubber, where's
            the rubber? (*Michael erases the '8' he has written as the*
            sum of 4 + 4.)
TONY: Ninety-three, ninety-four, ninety-five. Ninety-six,
            ninety-seven, ninety-eight.   40
MICHAEL: Right, forty-eight and forty-eight is what?
TONY: Ninety-six.
MICHAEL: So I put a nine ... (*Michael writes '96'*).

Here the children put out all their matchsticks – forty-eight each –
and again use different solutions to find the sum. Tony, to whom the
answer is not so obvious when dealing with such large numbers, reverts
to putting the matchsticks together and counting them. Using this
method he very quickly finds the sum. Michael meanwhile tries to use
his method but this produces 48, and a two-digit number sixteen, to

$$\frac{48}{8}$$

put in a one-digit place. Faced with this, with Tony's certainty that the answer is ninety-six, and in the context of their knowledge that they should both arrive at the same answer, Michael defers to Tony, stops trying to make his algorithm work, and writes '96'. It might appear at this point that Michael has somehow 'failed', and in some senses he has. But his progress is instructive, nevertheless, and both its creative aspects and limitations deserve further comment. I will conclude this chapter with some comments on Michael's rationale.

Michael's rationale

It seems perfectly plausible that Michael had made some kind of discovery that he found very pleasurable. But what was the basis of his discovery? His pleasure seemed to be derived from his utilization of an effective procedure. It is this which the teacher found distressing. When shown the video tape after the lesson, she remarked:

> I'll have to take him back. He obviously hasn't got it. I'll have to take him back and give him more experience. . . . He shouldn't really be trying to do that yet.

Her distress seemed related to the fact that, because his procedure had failed, she felt that she had failed too. The fact that he had not had enough 'experience' of manipulation of the objects was felt to be at fault and for this she blamed herself. Yet complex relations of signification appear to be implicated in such examples as these. In Chapter 9 I shall attempt to explore how we might produce an analysis of pleasure which takes these features into account.

Transcript E

TEACHER: Right, now I want you and Anne to put out, away   1
from the others, a number for me. So many bundles
and so many ones, you choose how many you are
going to put out. . . . Right put them so that we can
all see clearly what number you're going to choose.   5
Right. Now are you going to put some of the bundles
with that? Are you? Right. You don't have to if you
don't want to. Now look at Anne's number, spread
out the bundles for us Anne so that we can see. (*Anne
has put on the table in front of her seven 'bundles' and six*   10
'single ones' thus.) Now Anne tell me what number –

	how many matchsticks you've put out there?	
	Altogether. How many have you put out on the table?	
ANNE:	Seventy-six.	
TEACHER:	Seventy-six. I'm going to put seventy-six on the	15
	board, you know how to write seventy-six don't you?	
MICHAEL:	Seven and six.	
TEACHER:	Seventy . . .? (*As the teacher says this she writes '7'.*)	
CHILDREN:	Six.	
TEACHER:	. . . six. (*As she writes the '6' to complete '76'.*) If we	20
	were talking about Anne's matchsticks what would	
	that seven mean? (*The teacher points to the '7' of '76'.*)	
	Think about Anne's matchsticks that she put out for	
	us. Anne, what does seven mean – (*she points to the '7'*	
	again) – when I'm talking about your matchsticks?	25
	What have you got seven of?	
ANNE:	Bundles.	
TEACHER:	Seven bundles of . . .?	
ANNE:	Ten.	
TEACHER:	. . . ten. If I had just written down Anne's number of	30
	matchsticks, er, number of bundles I would have had	
	to write . . .?	
MICHAEL:	Seven. (*Underneath the '76' the teacher writes '70'.*)	
TEACHER:	Wouldn't I? Because she would have seven bundles of	
	. . .?	35
KAREN:	Ten. That makes seventy.	
TEACHER:	And none – (*here the teacher covers up with her hand the*	
	'6' of the '76') – of the little single matchsticks but as	
	she's given us seven (*pointing to the '7' of the '76'*)	
	bundles and six (*pointing to the '6' of the '76'*) of the	40
	separate ones – single ones, we've got a number	
	seventy . . .?	
TONY:	Six.	
TEACHER:	. . . six. Right Tony you put out a number for us. (*In*	
	front of him on the table Tony puts out seven 'bundles'	45
	and eight 'single ones'.) Watch Tony so that you can	
	check (. . .). Yes Tony how many have you given us?	
TONY:	Seventy-eight.	
TEACHER:	Seventy-eight. Just a little more, just a few more than	
	Anne gave us.	50
KAREN:	Two.	

TEACHER: Two more. Seventy-eight. So how many bundles has
            he put out?
SUE: Seven.
ANNE: Yes seven.   55
TEACHER: Yes Sue and how many of the single matchsticks has
            he put out?
CHILDREN: Eight.
TEACHER: Eight. So I'll write that down. He had seven (*as she
            writes a '7' on the board*) bundles of ten and eight (*as*   60
            she writes an '8' to complete '78') single ones.
            Now. I'll give you something different. I'll write the
            number down and you put out the right number of
            matchsticks. Ready? Are you watching Karen? Thirty-
            four. Watch Karen and make sure she does it right.   65
            (*The teacher writes '34' on the board and Karen puts out*
            three 'bundles' and four 'singles'.)
ANNE: Yeah, she's done it right.
AHMED: No, that's four. Thirty-four.
TEACHER: How many bundles of ten?   70
TONY: Three.
TEACHER: (*Points to the '4' of '34'*) – and how many single ones?
CHILDREN: Four.
TEACHER: Right who hasn't had a turn? Ahmed? Put out this
            number for me. (*She writes '50' on the board. As Ahmed*   75
            puts out five 'bundles') – how many?
ANNE: Five.
TEACHER: Five tens and how many single ones did you have to
            put out?
ANNE: None.   80
TEACHER: None. Right. OK. Sue? (*The teacher writes '9' on the*
            board, and Sue puts out nine 'bundles') What's she put
            out? What number – how many's she put out?
TONY: Ninety.
TEACHER: Did I write ninety?   85
CHILDREN: No.
TEACHER: What number did I write out?
CHILDREN: Nine. (*Sue replaces the nine 'bundles' with nine 'single*
            ones'.)
TEACHER: Nine, changed your mind Sue have you? I though I   90
            might catch you out dear. Right. Who hasn't had a

turn? Michael. (*She writes '12' on the board.*) Are you
watching to see if he gets it right? (*Michael puts out
one 'bundle' and two 'single ones.*) Now.

MICHAEL: Twelve. 95

TEACHER: Twelve yes (*she points to the '1' of the '12'*) – how
many bundles of ten?

CHILDREN: One.

TEACHER: (*Pointing to the '2' of the '12'*) – and how many single
ones? 100

CHILDREN: Two.

TEACHER: Two, right.
Let's change the game. You write the number alright?
(*To Ahmed*) I want to borrow your matchsticks. You
can help . . . and use the board and you come out and 105
write the number. You're first Ahmed. (*Ahmed leaves
his seat and stands by the board as the teacher puts out two
'bundles' and four 'single ones'.*) Right, write that
number down please (*Ahmed writes '24'*).

ANNE: Actually I had to write another type of two. 110

TEACHER: No that's alright, twenty-four. we can all see that.
Good. Two and four (*she points to the '2' of Ahmed's
'24'*). Two bundles of ...?

CHILDREN: Ten.

TEACHER: (*Pointing to the '4' of the '24'*) – and four? 115

SUE: Single ones.

TEACHER: Single ones, right. Tony. (*She puts out four 'bundles'
and seven 'single ones' . . . Tony counts them and
writes '47' on the board.*) Forty-seven. Right, Anne.
(*The teacher puts out eight 'bundles', Anne looks at them* 120
and then writes '80' on the board) – how many?

ANNE: Eighty.

TEACHER: Eighty, yes, fine, er – who are we up to, Karen? (*The
teacher puts out seven 'bundles' as Karen comes round to
the board. Karen looks at the teacher's pile and writes* 125
'70'.) Well done. Is that right?

CHILDREN: Yes.

TEACHER: Seven bundles of ...? (*as she points to the '7' of Karen's
'70'*).

TONY: Seventy. 130

TEACHER: Seven bundles of ...?

CHILDREN: Ten.
TEACHER: And . . .?
CHILDREN: No singles.
TEACHER: No singles. Right, now I want you to play that game   135
            with a partner please.

9 Pleasure and the mastery of reason

In Chapter 8 I presented an interpretation of classroom data which attempted to show how the teacher was engaged, not in providing experiences of concrete objects, but in the production of signs. In this chapter I shall develop and extend this analysis to speculate about the production of signs, both in terms of teaching and of learning. I want to ask three basic questions:

1. What do we mean when we say that the teacher makes the relations of the number system signify?
2. How is the place-value sign produced?
3. How does this imply a learning process?

First of all, it is important to note that the notion of the sign is not coterminous with language. Semiotics, envisaged as the science of signs, includes signs as diverse as words and styles of dress. In this way it is possible to produce an analysis which does not make the separations made in developmental psychology, that is, between cognition, language, and context. However, as I have argued, it is not simply a case of adding them together. The new discourse reworks the terms and does not make these separations.

I will outline two terms which are important to my analysis – *metaphor* and *metonymy*. These terms were used by Jakobson and Halle (1956) to describe the basic semiotic processes. I shall also draw heavily on the work of the psychoanalyst, Jacques Lacan (1977), and the mathematician, Brian Rotman (1980). Jakobson and Halle used metaphor and metonymy to further exemplify the workings of a linguistic system, the syntagmatic and paradigmatic axes:

> The characteristic modes of binarily opposed polarities which between them underpin the two-fold process of selection and combination by which linguistic signs are formed: the given utterance (message) is a *combination* of constituent parts (sentences, words, phonemes, etc.) *selected* from the repository of all possible constituent parts of the code.
>
> (1956:7)

Metaphor is taken to describe the synchronic aspects of the code, its immediate, coexistent, and vertical relationships. Metonymy represents the diachronic axis – the sequential, successive, and linearly progressive relationships. For example, in the following sentence the placement of one word against another in the flow of the spoken utterance provides the metonymic axis, whereas the metaphoric axis is provided by the way in which various elements in the sequence can be replaced by others and yet held together by the same metonymic axis.

	The woman is writing		
synchronic/	man	singing	diachronic/
vertical/	child	speaking	horizontal/
metaphonic			metonymic

Although the above example relies upon a notion of the code, we can speculate that different discourses contain and rely upon form and content which are specific and recognizable, producing shifts in both the metaphoric and metonymic axes. I want, using this framework, to examine the peculiarities of school mathematical discourse. Formal statements in the discourse contain little or no metaphoric content. If we take the following example:

$$2 + 3 = 5$$

there is no metaphorical content in such a statement. The discourse operates in a way which is solely metonymic. However, if we begin to include features from non-mathematical discourses, metaphoric content begins to be introduced, and the statement is transformed in various ways. For example, even speaking the statement transforms it, because we could articulate it as:

two plus three equals five
or
two add three makes five

or some other combination of these or other terms. The metaphorical implications of *makes* and *equals*, for example, are quite different and certainly allow the speaker/hearer (implicitly) to link mathematical with other discourses – construction in the case of *makes*. We can change the statement in other ways, too, which modify the metaphoric and metonymic axes:

2 girls + 3 girls = 5 girls
or

two girls plus three girls equals five girls

However, if we modify it again to read:

girls plus girls equals girls

it no longer appears to be a statement admissible within mathematical discourse. In this sense, we can refer back to the gardening and cooking examples given in Chapter 5, where I argued that gardening and cooking could only become mathematics if certain transformations were accomplished. It is these transformations from non-mathematical to mathematical discourse which I am trying to specify. Both Jakobson and Halle (1956) and Rotman (1980) understand these as processes in natural language. Indeed, Rotman argues the relation as follows:

> The relation of mathematics to the world stems from its immersion in a natural language, from the fact that it draws its examples and models . . . many of its notions and procedures are ones described by language. For it is only to the extent that mathematics does this that it is applicable to, that is, impinges on the reality described by and inherent in language. So that whilst it is true that the mathematical sign '2' is an entity completely within the Code and interpretable through its internal relations with other signs in the Code, the applicability of all these signs – the usefulness of arithmetic – results from the relation of the signs '2' and 'two'.
>
> (1980:123)

However, describing universals of language as natural and by implication mathematical discourse as unnatural, invented, fails to engage with the social and constructed nature of other discourses and practices. I argued that gardening and cooking were discursive practices with their own rules of selection and combination. In this analysis no practice is non-discursive and therefore the task becomes not to specify the moves from natural language to some other code, but to specify the transformations from one discourse to another.

For the learner of mathematics, the effects of discursive transformations using *makes* or *equals* are likely to be different and to call up different discursive practices. *Makes* allows us to understand the equation $2 + 3 = 5$ as a process of production of 5, whereas *equals* points up the fairness of the distribution of both sides of the equation. The peculiarity of mathematical discourse is that, in its written form, it does not allow the entry of metaphoric content and may well be presumed to produce problems for learners, who have to suspend or repress this content in order to operate in mathematics. It is in this light that I want to make some further remarks about the place-value lesson.

Rotman argued that one of the aspects of mathematical discourse which was central was that the addressee of a mathematical statement was a non-subject:

> Mathematical addressees are theoretical and impersonal: mathematicians prohibit their codes from making any sorts of reference to the individual characteristic of the reader; or to his subjectivity or to his physical presence in the world. The addressee is merely the repository of conceptual shells that is necessary to decode mathematical signifiers. His psychology is transcendental: independent of cultural variation and the differences between one individual and another. Moreover, the subjectivity of the reader, what is signified by the 'I' of the non-mathematical discourse forms no part of the nature of the addressee.
>
> (1980:75)

This suggests that the so-called generalizability and context-free nature of mathematical discourse is achieved through the suppression of the metaphoric axis and therefore at some cost to the subject, since as object of this rational and rationalizing discourse, s/he is non-personal. The transcendental 'I' which Rotman refers to is the 'I' of developmental psychology, the 'I' which is natural, universal, and therefore independent of the very practices which I have discussed throughout the book. My central point, therefore, is that this so-called natural process of mastery entails considerable and complex suppression. That suppression is both painful and extremely powerful. That power is pleasurable. It is the power of the triumph of reason over emotion, the fictional power over the practices of everyday life. I shall argue that the power afforded by the mastery of this discourse is fictional, but that its effects are real and material. That is, when this fictional discourse is inscribed in the 'government of reason', the bourgeois and patriarchal rule by science, it is indeed inscribed with domination, the bid for a world freed from clouding emotions. The 'reasonable person', in Piaget's terms, is 'in love with ideas' and not bodies.

In the examples which I gave in the earlier chapters, the transformation of non-mathematics practices into mathematics appeared to be produced by means of a gradual series of shifts in relations of signification, such that the signifier/signified relations in one discursive practice shifted through the production of complex chains, ending with the insertion of the new signifier/signified pair as a relation within the new discursive practice.

However, in respect of school mathematics practices, the transformations can be understood as quite specific in their effects. That is, the multiplicity present in the significations in other practices is excluded by means of removing the external reference from the form of the statement itself. In the examples which I discussed, this appeared to be achieved through the maintenance of reference as an aspect of the signified, while at the same time displacing from the signifier, as in the examples in which a finger became an iconic signifier for a person or object, and then itself became a signified for a spoken numeral, later to be displaced by a written numeral as symbol. This had certain effects. It meant that the new statements became statements in which reference outside the string was absent or, we might say, suppressed, since it remained within the signifying chain itself which has led to the possibility of its production. However, this serves to suggest its constructed quality. This has been articulated by others, most particularly in those explanations which have stressed 'decontextualization' or 'disembedding', as in Donaldson's work (1978). However, although my reading stresses the removal of reference and therefore the production of a discourse which in principle can be read back on to anything, that is not the same as saying that it is 'without a context'. Principally, the discourse is produced within a specific set of practices and purposes which guarantee its applicability and its effects. These ensure the 'suppression' of its constructedness and the articulation of its generalizability as the basis of the nature of 'mind'. The power of such discourses, however, is precisely that they can form descriptions of, can be read back onto, *anything*. It is in this sense that they are apparently without context.

Yet it seems to me that decontextualization is an effect which renders this system of statements as statements of fact precisely because it claims a universal applicability – a rationality devoid of any content which can describe and therefore explain anything. Mathematics has, for centuries, held this position as queen of the sciences, when nature became the book written in the language of mathematics and when mathematics held out the dream of a possibility of perfect control in a perfectly rational and ordered universe. Rotman (1980) expresses this discourse as the product of desire:

The desire's object is a pure, timeless unchanging discourse, where assertions proved stay proved forever (and must somehow always have been true), where all the questions are determinate, and all the answers totally certain. In terms of the world, the desire is for a discourse that proxies the manipulation of physical reality achieving a perfect and total control of 'things', where no realizable process falls outside mathematics' reach. Where no counter-examples or exceptions or errors of prediction are possible.

(1980:129)

Rotman's use of the term desire focuses sharply upon the fantasy of a discourse and practice in which the world becomes what is wanted: regular, ordered, controllable. The imposition of this discourse onto the world therefore renders to the mathematician, scientist, psychologist, linguist, or whatever an incredibly powerful position. For s/he produces statements which are taken to be true. The result of a fantasy is lived as a fact. Let me pursue this a little further. What Rotman describes as the desire for a rational and controllable universe, which operates in ways which are logically ordered and predictable, is executed within those discursive practices which are regulated in this way. 'Reason's dream', as Rotman calls it, is seductive, for apparently it offers to its subject power over others, oneself, and the prediction and control of events. I attempted to demonstrate in previous chapters the way in which signifying chains were created from the old and the new discursive practices. In the case of the school mathematics examples which I gave, all aspects of multiple signification and external reference were absent from the relations of signification contained in the formal mathematical string. It is this which produced a discourse which could refer to 'anything'. The multiplicity and reference, therefore, are contained only for the speaker, within the signifying chains which produced the transformation in the first place. This also suggests that all aspects of value, emotionality, and desire contained within the signifying chain is also suppressed.

Am I justified in using the term 'suppressed'? I have argued that all such features are absent from a written mathematical string. I have also suggested that they are present for the speaker only in terms of a remaining *trace*, the signifying chains connecting the signifiers out of the discourse. In several of the examples I examined, children's mistakes appeared to be produced by the insertion of the signifiers within the wrong relations, the wrong practice. This suggests that the successful learner must remember to operate only within the confines of the discourse and not step outside it. Michel Pecheux (1982) uses the term 'forgetting' to refer to the way in which the speaker must, of necessity, forget the constructed nature of consciousness. It is this 'forgetting' which I am arguing is central to the production of the transcendental, bourgeois subject, who is the object of naturalizing and universalizing bourgeois discourse. The term, of course, has other resonances too. For Freud, forgetting is an act of the unconscious. The concept of the unconscious is central to my notion that the achievement of mastery is a fiction, itself invested in fantasy. To understand this as a subjective as well as a social phenomenon is what I want to address now. Freud argued that repression was necessary for the subject to engage in intellectual life, but this was not achieved without some cost. This is a very different approach from one which understands the achievement of formal reasoning as produced through a freeing of the subject in a secure environment where everything is permissible. However, such a view might be important in supporting the notion of reason as the pinnacle of human thinking.

There are, however, some interesting metaphors contained in mathematicians' and others' views of mathematical reasoning. Bertrand Russell argued that mathematics possessed not only truth, but supreme beauty. When 'ideas rose in clouds' for Poincaré, the link between the heavens and mathematics was evident. The idea of mathematics having beauty is present in many accounts and Piaget, too, was clearly 'attracted to the idea'. He wrote early in his career that 'the love of beautiful bodies elevates itself to the love of beautiful souls and from there to the very idea of beauty' (1920:57). The 'idea of beauty' was an idea of the beauty of mathematics and logic. Such sentiments are commonplace in the discourses of early mathematics education; for example, Harold Fletcher, the author of the much used *Mathematics for Schools*, wrote that 'children will derive pleasure from the purity and order which they discover' (1970:16). If mathematics provides a dream of an ordered and pure universe, rational and unsullied by the passions (where beauty becomes an idea), what kind of pleasure is the pleasure afforded by mathematics? The idea of an intrinsic pleasure in order is one which encapsulates some of the hope enshrined in the child-centred pedagogy's dream of the possibility of a rational schooling (Corran and Walkerdine 1981; Walkerdine 1984).

The Schools Council wrote in 1965, following Whitehead, that 'every child should experience the joy of discovery' and that this would lead to 'children's enjoyment of mathematics and their increasing con-

fidence in their powers' (214). These powers – mental powers – are, I
would suggest, powers of control of a rationally ordered universe. They
are also, as I have argued elsewhere, powers of 'self-control' (Walkerdine and Lucey, in press). The two go together. If one kind of pleasure,
and one kind of fantasy, is to replace another, what is this pleasure and
this fantasy, this dream of power, control, order, omnipotence. It must
of necessity lead both to the suppression of all that exists outside the
rational, the logically ordered discourse and, at the same time, create
the world to be ordered in the image of that fantasy, that indeed the
world becomes the 'mathematics text'. Many have argued that, in
everyday practices, problems are not solved by formal reasoning.
Donaldson (1978) quotes important work by Mary Henle in this respect. However, there is no doubt that the imposition of the discourse
upon practices means that any practice can become the object of logical
and/or mathematical modes of thought.

I shall argue that 'Reason's Dream' is invested in fantasy: a fantasy of
an omnipotent power over a calculable universe. This is a fantasy
central to the bourgeois order. Freud formulated a theory of defence
mechanisms and argued that the unconscious, the analysis of dreams,
was paramount. He suggested that the manifest content of a dream held
in place chains of associations, such that the latent content was co-
vered over. The originary moment for Freud in understanding unconscious fantasy was the infant's loss of its mother's breast. He argued that
the infant might 'hallucinate' the breast and thereby gain a sense of
wish-fulfilment. This idea of wishes or demands and the impossibility of
total satisfaction was crucial to Freud's approach. The 'original' wish is
transposed and transformed through a series of condensations and dis-
placements – to be revealed only in dreams, slips of the tongue, and so
forth. Since satisfaction is altogether impossible, the infant must
embark on 'filling the gap', of mastering, and dealing with, the loss.
One of Freud's most famous examples of how this might be achieved is
of a child playing with a cotton reel, saying 'fort' (gone) and 'da' (here)
as it is rolled towards and away from him.

This scene has remarkable similarities with Piaget's theory of object
permanence. Here, the child drops an object out of its pram. But, for
Piaget, the infant's 'discovery' of permanence – that the object continues to exist when no longer visible – is treated as both intellectual
and real. This is very different from a possible reading of Freud's
account. For Freud, this mastery is always a fantasy. Intellectual mastery controls the loss and is always at a cost to the subject. For Piaget,

this fundamental aspect has completely disappeared from the account. Mastery becomes real and not a fiction. There is no suppression.

This fantasy of wish-fulfilment, which Freud describes, is key to the idea that wishes can be fulfilled – a fantasy of omnipotence – that the mother can be brought in at will, like the cotton reel, masking the child's terrible dependency and powerlessness. Jacques Lacan (1977) modified Freud's account in several ways which are crucial to this story. He utilized structural linguistics to argue that the concepts of condensation and displacement could be mapped onto the linguistic terms of metaphor and metonymy. Chains of associations became chains of signifiers. He achieved this by inverting Saussure's fraction to assert the primacy of signifier over signified, viz.:

$$\frac{\text{signifier}}{\text{signified}}$$

His argument was that since the originary moment, the real could never be captured except in fantasy, and that fantasies were created in language, there was only any point in examining chains as ever more complex linkages of signifiers. Indeed, I have argued throughout the book that signifier replaces signifier, creating complex chains in the move from one discourse to another. Thom (1981) discusses the analysis of a dream by Laplanche and Leclaire where they demonstrate the phonological shifts in the condensation and displacement. Here, the calling out of 'Lili, j'ai soif' (Lili, I'm thirsty) shifts to the childish word for milk, 'lolo'. Laplanche and Leclaire make the link to the absent breast quite clear. Thom suggests that the primacy of the signifier is important because the signified 'eludes us, slips away from us' (13). The paper by Lieven, to which I referred in Chapter 4, also makes it clear that Eve's production of time adverbials coincided with her desire to take her baby sister's place, to have her bottle and, by association, the breast.

For Lacan it is the signifying order which makes it possible to know the real. Thus the chains of associations become chains of signifiers. Word-meaning in this analysis is replete with fantasy, pain, loss, pleasure, mastery. Here is no set of semantic primitives, but complex relations of desire. The moment of magical wish-fulfilment, where the child imagines it controls the mother, is described by Lacan as the 'Imaginary Order'. He contrasts this with the 'Symbolic Order', in which mastery is indeed the achievement of the Ratio, the Cogito, the transcendental ego. The 'subject of language' for Lacan, as for Pecheux, is a subject who forgets. The cost of the production of the transcendental subject is the fantasy of symbolic mastery. Since this fantasy involves the idea that the Symbolic Order is the Law, and a patriarchal law at that, the Law is the logos, logocentric, phallic. It involves the fantasy of possession of the Word, the Phallus (not the penis, but the phallus as signifier and sign only within the fantasy of the Symbolic Order). Consequently, women's relation to that order must always be seen as problematic.

Urwin (1984) utilizes Lacan's account to examine how children first come to operate in actual social practices. Using his concept of the mirror, in which the infant first comes to recognize itself as a unity (a transcendental 'I'), she argues that it is positioning in practices which allows children to generate meanings, which embody fantasies of power. In Chapter 2 I argued that the meaning of 'more', for example, involved the regulation of children's consumption. The parent thus regulates through discourse. But in discourse, and in fantasy, children can apparently regulate in return. They can play at regulating the mother who regulates them. This may be illusory, but it paves the way for the child's taking a position, of 'growing up' (Walkerdine and Lucey, in press). Here, Urwin is able to make a link between a Lacanian formulation and the idea of positioning in discursive practices. It necessitates a move away from Lacan's structural linguistics towards post-structuralism.

Lacan makes reference to arguments from structural anthropology to suggest that the basis of the phallus resides in the Law of exogamy, the exchange of women by men, to which Lévi-Strauss referred (1969). However, Lacan later realized some of the limitations to this universalism and revised his view to some extent (see Mitchell and Rose 1982). He later suggested that the 'phallus is a fraud' (Lacan 1977) and that certainty is impossible, since it is produced out of the threat of castration. Lacan places so much stress on the Law of exogamy because of the work on the incest taboo and the threat of castration imposed on the boy for desiring his mother. Becoming the Law, the phallus, control, is the way out of such desire. Lacan depends on two discourses: structural linguistics and structural anthropology.

Structural linguistics depends upon a concept of a linguistic system, understood according to precisely that universal mathematization which Lacan himself designates a fraudulence of certainty. I have tried to argue that structural linguistics depend upon an idea of language which, like that of cognition, divorces it from the practices of production.

These practices are historically-specific. They produce relations of signification out of particular positions and relations, in times and places.
I have thus criticized the idea of a timeless universalism, be it of
meaning, syntax, or cognition. While structural linguistics has been
revolutionary in its assertion of the fundamental arbitrariness of the
signifier/signified relation, and therefore, supporting an idea of *creation*
of systems of signification, not a simple representation of the real,
nevertheless, it asserts the possibility of a universal system, a knowledge
of an essential human, the fraudulent certainty. If signification is produced within practices, then the idea of universals, powerful as it is,
reduces and essentializes the very processes I have been trying to
discuss, namely that meaning and form are produced in mobile and
shifting discursive practices. Universals reduce that multiplicity and
shiftingness to relations within a finite and axiomatic system. As in
Chomsky, form is reduced to formula, to an empty string, a device in
the brain. Nowhere can we find signification itself, then, constructed in
practices. Such a reduction is key to the possibility of a powerful,
descriptive, and explanatory discourse. But it distorts in the very truth
it produces. It is the very historicity of such a concept of linguistics to
which I wish to gesture. I argue that the very *idea* of a system of
linguistic universals itself can be deconstructed and the productive
power of its truth revealed and demonstrated. In this way I shall also
briefly seek to re-question issues of power and value which have been
important in socio-linguistics, but which have remained trapped within
a view of universals as 'langue' and everything else as 'parole'. I want to
question and rework some of those notions, especially the production of
universals as normative, and difference therefore as pathological. I
suggest that what is taken to be universal is itself the imposition of a
particular truth and in this view class and gender are central.

Relatedly, critiques of the concept of exogamy, especially the work of
Elizabeth Cowie (1978), have argued that it supposes the very system
of exchange which it is intended to explain. Cowie argues that the
category 'woman' is produced as a sign within mobile and shifting
practices. That is, the sign 'woman' in exogamy is not exchanged but
produced in exchange of actual women. Thus the relations are
constituted in the practices themselves. However, as in my analysis of
discursive practices and the production of meaning, she argues that it is
not the case of a 'real' of women, who, as signifieds, are distorted in the
practices of exchange that represent them, but that rather, the sign is
created in the practices. The sign is thus mobile and not a fixed

representation. The point, therefore, is not truly or falsely to represent women but to demonstrate how woman as sign is produced as a relation within the practices themselves. 'Woman' does not designate real women but is produced out of a fusion of the material and the discursive, the positioning of women in actual practices. It follows also that there is no fixed or coherent identity of a real woman or real child, with or without power, but that power too relates to positions and therefore to the truth created in practices. Urwin has, as we have seen, taken this argument further in relation to child language, by examining the production of power and positionings within practices. The power offered by the entry into language is the potential control over the object of desire, the mother. Children, in this analysis, do not 'acquire language', but are subjected within discursive practices. Central to these are relations of fantasy, power, and desire.

Wish-fulfilment and mastery

It seems to me that we witness, in the examples discussed in earlier chapters, two kinds of pleasure, covering over pain and loss in different ways. I want to refer back to the two examples of infant school practice: the shopping game in Chapter 7 and the place-value work, discussed in Chapter 8. The two examples come from the same classroom. The 'shopping' group comprised children whom the teacher classified as relatively 'slow', while the 'place-value' group were the 'fastest'. Throughout the sequence transcribed from the shopping game the children appear to derive considerable pleasure from the distinction between the game and 'real shopping', particularly in respect of the low prices, which allow them to engage in a fantasy of people who could buy expensive items, go on a luxury holiday, and so forth. This group is composed of several girls and one boy. It is the girls who 'get into' the fantasy while it is the boy, Gordon, who reminds them that '2p's not rich'. They act out the fantasy by putting on 'airs and graces', changing voices, performing appropriate actions. The same phenomenon was apparent during their playing at shops, which I observed but did not video tape, and during one of the other activities, a ten-pin bowling game, where they appear to derive great enjoyment from pretending to 'go bowling'. In other words, it is their positioning within a practice which produces the possibility of the fantasy and of pleasure. This produces particular effects. They have a good time, certainly, but they do not get a lot of mathematics done. The focus of their fantasy upon the external reference called up by the practice prohibits the possibility of their deriving enjoyment from the power of mathematical discourse.

This forms a contrast to the place-value group, for whom this kind of fantasy is totally absent from the recorded sequences, even though they, too, play games. Yet Michael and Tony appear to derive considerable pleasure from the power of the methods they are using. Indeed, Michael's pleasure becomes apparently a desire to display his method and his powers by explaining, both to the teacher and to Tony, his 'easy way'. When Michael's method fails, at the end of the sequence, he becomes mute and sullen for the rest of the lesson, and sucks his thumb. The failure of his powers appears to have produced an opposite repression into infantile behaviour.

There are many other examples of play throughout the various corpuses of transcripts. There is no instance of play with objects, for example, which is not at the same time the production of a fantasy and the insertion into an imaginary discursive practice. In this respect, examples of 'object play' and 'fantasy play' become a sterile dichotomy. Corran and Walkerdine gave the example of four-year-old Jason, playing with toy vehicles and blocks which he constructed into a complex imaginary web:

J: Look, it's lost its lights. LOOK. He shouldn't be driving backwards should he? (*He starts moving a pair of vehicles backwards.*)
GC: No, he won't be able to see where he's going if he goes backwards.
J: He's trying to get out, he is. He can see in his mirror, he can. Daddy can see where he's going in the mirror. . . . Look, he's trying to get out but he can't. The gates are locked all over the place.

(1981:48)

Here, Jason transforms the blocks from a road for vehicles to drive along into gates to get out of. He takes several different positions within the fantasy: he controls the 'he' who is driving, he identifies with Daddy who can reverse while looking in his mirror, and he makes cars do forbidden things. This is both an example of object play and a fantasy which inserts Jason into a car-driving practice.

Urwin (1984) has examined many instances of 'pretend play' among considerably younger children. However, in several exchanges, Urwin examines the relationship between a fantasy positioning within a discursive practice and an identification with a powerful adult. This allows the child to fantasize about both the positioning and the power inscribed within it. In this case, as with the example of Jason, the object is Daddy:

Jack. 1.2.0.   Video recording in a standard play setting

Jack's mother has been asked to read a book for five minutes and to ignore the baby's overtures as far as possible. While his mother is not attending to him, Jack picks up a round baby mirror. Holding it in two hands, he looks at himself and says 'baby'. He moves the mirror from side to side, and says 'brrm, brrm'. He then lowers the mirror, looks round and reaches out for a toy truck, some way away from him. He pushes it along the ground going 'brrm, brrm', repeating this several times, with exuberance.

'Brrm, brrm' has been in Jack's vocabulary for some weeks, associated with pushing things along, with toy cars and with pointing out real cars in the street. The connection between holding the mirror and saying 'brrm, brrm' is either mediated by the action of steering, the roundness of the mirror, the way he is sitting, or a mixture of these. According to his mother, Jack has very recently been allowed to sit in the driver's seat of the car, so long as she is beside him, when the family has been out together and the father has stopped the car in order, say, to go into a shop. Up to this point, then, driving has always been associated with taking the place of the father.

(314–15)

Let us explore the distinction between the fantasies engaged in the shopping and place-value groups. It seems very important that the two groups were engaging in their mathematics in different ways. That is, the group who were working with the 'shopping game' could position themselves as subjects, in fantasy, as shoppers who could buy what they were normally unable to buy; they could become 'rich'. This fantasy was made possible by the distinction of prices and the game – that is, 'unreal' pricing – that *difference* allows or permits the fantasy to operate through the articulation or 'play' of its contrasting terms.

The children could therefore enter it. However, in so entering, they are positioned in fantasy, as what they are not – 'rich'. It exists for them as other – the place from which it is possible to do and be what they want. They can buy goods which they could never normally do and yet which are constantly held up to them. 'Being rich' – being and having material possessions and a lifestyle to match – is a fantasy presented to them in which they are inserted in a vast array of popular cultural forms and practices. Such fantasies set up the possibility that the person both 'wants' such things and yet is deprived of them. Like the girl who, in her domestic play, bought 'chicken, bacon, and steak', these children can, in fantasy, enter and imaginary world from which they are, by virtue of their class position, denied. This world in fantasy is held out as the resolution of dreams – of being in control of one's destiny, by having the material wealth of one's dreams, and 'being a rich person'. Such fantasies have the material effects of magical wish-fulfilment. They support an order in which 'wishes could come true'.

For Lacan, the Imaginary order is the place in which, in fantasy, desires can be met, 'wishes come true' as it were. The point of origina-tion is the mother–child dyad in which the infant must, of necessity, deal with the absence of the object of satisfaction – the breast, the mother. The gap is filled by fantasies. Later, the insertion of the child in actual practices facilitates active manipulation and provides, for the child, a site of power over the 'lost object', 'the object of desire'. In the infant's imagination, satisfaction is possible, but only there. However, in fantasy the infant can 'possess' the mother – satisfaction is possible.

The children in the shopping game could, then, using Lacan's read-ing, be understood as being framed within the Imaginary. They take, in fantasy, a position which gives them wish-fulfilment – they 'become rich' – the circle is closed. This fantasy is enticing and pleasurable. But let me pursue what certain effects might be. The children are posi-tioned differently from their inscription in actual shopping practices. In actual shopping, to become a subject demands both engagement with the practices and the relations of signification, and the relation between goods and money. Power within that practice is competence as a shopper. However, satisfaction is as illusory as it is attainable. Goods which can be purchased sit alongside those which cannot. Money does not flow limitlessly but is produced through the subject's inscription within other practices, in this case the labour relation. The young children of 4 in the Tizard corpus (see p. 13) existed within such practices. They learnt that money was scarce, goods expensive, and that money was produced in exchange for work. Those relations were present in the very multiplicity of the signifiers which marked the relations of the practices. The one I examined particularly was *more* (see Chapter 2). It is possible to suggest, therefore, that desire is inscribed in the very signifier *more* as it exists as a relation within such practices. Moreover the meaning, as the work of Varnava-Skouras (1981) suggested, may well be different depending upon one's position within the 'labour market' or those practices in which productive labour is produced. The Other therefore – the 'other positions' of power over purchasing, commodities, scarcity, wealth – is already present in the relations of signification themselves. In this shopping game the children can occupy in fantasy those other positions. But such fantasy does not make them wealthy. Indeed, it appears to prohibit their 'mastery' of the relations of subtraction, which are the pedagogic goal of the task.

Their pleasure is double-edged. While they fantasize about being rich they cannot 'master' subtraction. They are held in a position of relative powerlessness in the practices of school mathematics. They are 'slow learners'. But what, then, is the lesson they are slow at learning? Money is produced in exchange for labour power. In some ways, the position of these children seems somewhat akin to the anti-school 'lads' described by Paul Willis in *Learning to Labour* (1978). Here the boys' anti-school position, related especially to taking a position of adult males (rather than school 'children') meant that they were powerless in school: they never learnt anything and were therefore at the bottom of the heap in the labour market. These children, then, are slow to learn the lessons of education – positioning, status, power. While they fantasize about it, they are kept from prowess in the only practices which 'may' (and I use this signifier advisedly in 1988) produce a changed position.

My research is not intended to prove or approve the value of the education system, but rather suggest how subject-positions and double binds might be produced within it. Their inscription as subjects within everyday practices is not, therefore, produced by a rationality in which formal decisions can be made (*à la* Donaldson) but is cross-cut, in the very relations of signification themselves, by desire. Absence, lack, loss, prohibition are present. And the subject's experience of that practice, and therefore of the practices in which 'numeracy' is produced, must be relations of desire. They are not formal systems, but lived relations of power and powerlessness, of wanting, having, being; they are continually open and shifting, not closed axiomatic systems like mathematics. Numeracy is not mathematics skills applied – here mathematics becomes relations in which numeracy practices are produced and suppressed.

However, Lacan's account suggests that the subject's incorporation into symbolic systems provides another and different fantasy. What Lacan refers to as 'the Symbolic' is the order of 'language' in which desire is not just filled in fantasy, it is controlled. In order to pursue this difference further, I want to refer back to the differences which I explored between the non-mathematical practices and the production of a school mathematical discourse. In formal mathematical discourse all external reference, the multiple signification of other signifiers, was displaced, remaining only as 'traces' in the signifying chain itself. In this lay the discourse's power, as it could then be utilized to refer to *anything*.

The 'meanings' inscribed in such signifiers inheres both in the metonymic relation within the string itself and the power and value accorded to the discourse which claims for itself a universal validity. However, everything else is excluded, including the addresser and addressee – there is no 'I' and 'you' in a mathematical string. There is no grammatical subject or object. For Lacan it is the pronouns I, you, he/she/it which position the speaking subject 'in language' and thereby fix an identity. It is in all these senses that I have wanted to suggest that much is suppressed in order to reach the mathematical string itself.

But, more than this, I have argued that mathematical discourse is also the object of a fantasy – a fantasy of omnipotent power and control of the universe. It is therefore a discourse in which, in the relations of signification themselves, anything can be included, anything can potentially be read in this discourse – it thus provides power over anything. The pleasure inscribed in it is unlike that of the shopping game. It does not insert the subject into a fantasy of wish-fulfilment, of being somebody else within, or a different relation in, the same practice, but rather provides a fantasy of mastery. The pleasure afforded is a different pleasure – a pleasure of control – the 'somebody else' that the mastery of mathematics makes possible is somebody who is certain, gets right answers, has closure rather than being ceaselessly caught in the web of desire. Desire is mastered. Control over and self-control become as one. I am therefore suggesting that the learner of mathematics is not caught in the play of desire in the Imaginary, but believes himself to have control of it. It is none the less pleasurable. It is extremely powerful and it involves the manipulation of a universally applicable symbolic system – a fantasy of playing God, 'the Divine mathematician', the fantasy inscribed in the Cogito, the Ratio. If desire is controlled it is not fulfilled, or satisfied. Its Other, therefore, the loss, the object desired, exists waiting in the wings, in the external reference suppressed in the discourse. The Other of mathematics is uncertainty, irrationality, out of control, madness, and so on. To follow Lacan's argument, then, the symbolic is not constituted out of certainty, but produces certainty out of a terror, control or be controlled, master the *loss*. The Imaginary was created to fill the gap of that loss, the Symbolic to control it. Such a system produces a very powerful body of truth, against a terrifying Other which it must 'know'. That Other constantly threatens those claims and stands outside it. For Lacan, as for Freud, that Other is Woman. For Lacan, femininity is not a natural phenomenon, in which reason, a masculine attribute, attests to the natural complementarity of the sexes. Rather, reason, as mathematics, becomes a fantasy of masculinity in which masculinity has to be constantly *proved*, as does woman's exclusion from it. The proof of masculine superiority and female failure has constantly to be remade and desperately reasserted (Walkerdine 1985b). The proof of 'real understanding' comes to stand as a signifier of the real, the claim to know, which woman can rarely possess. Real understanding as a signifier within the discursive practices of modern education comes to operate against a set of differences, exclusions, from which it is marked.

'Real understanding' becomes a fantasy which has to be proved to exist and which is constantly under threat. I shall argue that sexuality and class are central to the sets of exclusions and inclusions which are produced. In this analysis, mastery of mathematics is not the end point of a naturally achieved maturation, or a developmental sequence which is universally human, as in all theories of cognitive development. Rather, it is a specific and powerfully created discourse in which power and control are inscribed in its very form. For Lacan, such mastery is a possession and, indeed, possessive metaphors abound within the psychological discourse. We are said to 'have achieved' formal operations, to 'have' a concept. Such possessions mark out the possessor as in possession of a truth, a knowledge of the universe. The point, therefore, is to suggest *not* that such a claim to truth and to possession is a certainty but rather that it is produced out of a desire and lived through a fantasy, though one which has immense and real effects. It cannot be an ahistorical truth about the human animal. The argument is that the naturalized, universal subject is not natural at all, but the effect of complex discursive practices which create the possibility of meaning, form, position. Although materiality is central, there is no simple 'I' who sees or does not see the world as it really is. Materiality is always made to signify.

These examples provide for us a quite different sense of the highly emotionally charged aspects of the production of meaning and the entry into mathematical discourse, that so-cognitive of endeavours. It allows us to specify in principle the unconscious aspects which are present in the fantasies to be achieved. The fantasy of the rational subject, of cognitive mastery as independence, becomes a fantasy circulating in the discursive practices of education. Only certain pleasures are sanctioned, only certain routes produce autonomy. But the unsanctioned pleasures and fantasies rupture the smooth surface of the discourse. Many children talk not of the safe and sanitized pleasures of discovery, but those invested in winning, beating others (Corran and Walkerdine 1981). Here, power is visible, terrifying, and fleeting. Here is the pleasure of beating and the pain of being beaten, but it is a long way from the dream of reason. I have tried to demonstrate the fantasy involved in that dream, the dream of the educators and the mathematicians, playing at God. Reason's dream is a fantasy of equality, an attempt to create 'normal subjects' while failing to tackle fundamental oppressions and exploitations. The pathologized counter-discourses are testimony to that failure. The romantic liberalism of love, equality, and freedom is not so easily achieved. In the final chapter I shall consider how fictional identities are created in the classroom, how fantasy is made to operate as fact.

10 The practices of reason

At the beginning of the book, I argued that post-structuralism offered a way beyond universalizing notions and beyond the science/ideology distinction. Foucault uses the term *veridicality* to refer to the creation of truth. What he means by this is that scientific discourses create objects which they claim are true. As in child development, the claim is to be describing a real child, who exists. Here, the real is not something which cannot be known because of the complexities of ideology but becomes, rather, something like the 'real image' in computer graphics, which never existed in the first place. 'Veridicality' marks the idea that what is claimed as real is the biggest fiction of all. My claim is that 'the child' is an object of pedagogic and psychological discourses. It does not exist and yet is proved to be real every day in classrooms and laboratories the world over. How is this achieved?

I shall argue that the central concepts in the child-centred pedagogy and early mathematics education may themselves be regarded as signifiers, that is, aspects of discourse. That discourse claims to tell the truth about the universal properties of 'the child' which 'has concepts'. Just as I argued in Chapter 3 that the experiment could be read as a discursive practice in which power was produced by the discourse through which *experimenter* and *subject* were positioned and then a reading of the subject produced, so a similar argument may be made about the classroom as a place where *teacher* and *child* are produced as signs. It can be argued further that what is crucial about this analysis is that *language* and *cognition* become similarly amenable to the analysis. In this view, the attempts within psychology and mathematics, for example, may be seen as aspects of the attempt to construct a rationally ordered and controllable universe. I have argued that such an attempt is deeply bound up with the modern form of bourgeois government and the emergence of the modern state. It is also deeply involved with the attempt to describe and therefore regulate 'woman', 'the child', 'the working class', 'blacks', and 'the mad' (Walkerdine 1984, 1985a, 1986a, 1986b; Walkerdine and Lucey, in press).

The purpose of examining the conceptualizations which form the bedrock of modern practices is to draw out the terms that are key to the regime of truth which is constituted in and by the practices. My claim is that the discursive practices themselves, in producing the terms of the pedagogy, and therefore the parameters of practice, produce what it means to be a subject, to be subjected, within these practices. In the same way that I have analysed other discursive practices, it can be stated that the terms in the discourse such as *experience, discovery, stage,* etc. are signifiers which take their meaning from their position and function within the discourse itself: they enter as a relation. However, my main point was that there was no simple relation of representation between signifier and signified. The signifier *experience,* therefore, does not represent an unproblematic signified – which it either truly represents or distorts. Rather, the discourse itself is a point of production and creation. In Chapter 9 I made reference to analyses of the signifier 'woman' as a relation within discursive practices. In the same way we can treat these terms as signifiers too. However, in the examples of the production of meaning within other practices, it was the fusion of signifier and signified which formed the sign. When I say, then, that *experience* is created as a sign within the practice, or *the child* is produced as a subject, what I am talking about is the production of signs. If language does not represent reality, but rather the regulation of a practice itself produces a particular constellation and organization of the material and discursive, then it can be argued that something is produced.

The signifier *more* cited in Chapter 2 entered into a specific relation in the domestic practices regulating consumption. That is, it did not serve to represent a specific set of actions on objects. Rather, it was used within specific practices in which certain objects and actions were talked about. *More* or *less* did not form a contrastive pair, it was rather *more* and *no more*, while quantity relations in similar practices were inscribed in these practices using terms such as *a lot* and *a little*. It therefore became impossible to talk of a simple competence, or ability, but rather a complex set of relations of signification where signs produced were specific to the practices themselves and often had multiple signification within the relations of regulation. The practices, therefore, provide not a point of description of the real but a point of production, of creation of *signs*. 'The child' as a sign within the child-centred pedagogy is not simply a description of a pre-existing child. The practices themselves, in their regulation, produce what it *means* to be a child: what behaviours, words, etc. are used and those are regulated by means of an apparatus of classification, and a grading of responses. 'The child' becomes a creation and yet at the same time provides room for a reading of pathology. There are no behaviours which exist outside the practices which exist for producing them, not at any rate in this particular sequence, constellation and with these particular effects. The discursive practice becomes a complex sign system in which signs are produced, and read, and have truth effects.

The truth of children is produced in classrooms. 'The child' is not coterminous with actual children, just as Cowie (1978) argued that the signifier 'woman' is not coterminous with actual women, but central to the argument is the specification of that relation. If children become subjects through their insertion into a complex network of practices, there are no children who stand outside their orbit. My argument has been precisely that 'language' and 'cognitive development' are not descriptions of a real which takes place outside practices: all language, all signs, concepts, and so forth are produced as and by relations in specific practices. These practices therefore produce and read children as 'the child'.

I will use the concept of *positioning* to examine further what happens when such readings are produced and how children become *normal* and *pathological*, fast and slow, rote-learning and displaying real understanding, and so forth. In other words the practices provide systems of signs which are at once systems of classification, regulation, and normalization. These produce systematic differences which are then used as classifications of children in the class. It is the meaning of *difference*, which is a central feature in the production of any sign system in terms of the relations with other signs within the discourse. Similarity, that is, those signs which are linked within the discourse, also pile or heap together to provide *evidence* of a related classification. Thus *activity*, *doing*, *experience*, *readiness*, and so forth operate in relations of similarity, while *rote-learning* and *real understanding* are signs of contrastive opposition, of difference.

I shall attempt to demonstrate that these signs are produced, and that often one sign may be taken as an indicator of the presence of another (similarity). Thus, for example, *activity* heralds a sign system, a complex discursive practice, whose terms and limits may be specified. Within this, then, children become embodiments of 'the child', precisely because that is how the practice is set up: they are normal or pathological, and so forth. Their behaviour, therefore, is an aspect of a position, a multi-faceted subjectivity, such that 'the child' describes only their insertion into this, as one of many practices. But the behaviours do not precede the practice precisely because their specificity is produced in these practices. This is why the discourses of developmental psychology can themselves be understood as not simply providing a distortion of a real object, but may be read as evidence of *real understanding*, while *passivity* may be read as coterminous with, or similar to, *rote-learning, rule-following*.

Let me develop further certain distinctions which I feel are key to the analysis I am trying to undertake:

Child Teacher

Object Environment

Play Work

'The child' is constituted as the bedrock of the practices. The Plowden Report remarks on its first page that 'underlying all educational questions is the nature of the child himself' (DES 1967:1).

The child, then, has a nature which is basic, a baseline below which nothing can enter. The child is active, enquiring, discovering. It can be discerned by its nature, described, detailed, classified. Mathematics becomes cognitive development. Cognitive development becomes a description of the child. This exists as a regime of truth, a system of classification in which what counts as a properly developing child may be recognized, and in which certain behaviours are required and produced. By this I mean that the practices operate with a set of techniques, activities designed along certain principles. Thus everything in the pedagogy itself necessitates the production, reading, and evaluation of certain behaviours.

These produce the practices in which 'the child' becomes a sign to be read and in which a normal is differentiated from a pathological child. 'The child' develops through active manipulation of 'objects' in an 'environment'. Here all of the practices become objects existing in a biologized environment. The Plowden Report is full of illustrations, all of which describe the school, the classroom as an 'environment'. This sets up another aspect of the readings which are to be made, which I have explored elsewhere (Walkerdine 1984). 'The child' is a unique individual, developing at his/her own pace in an environment. In this way, the classroom therefore becomes the site of such development. However many children there are in a classroom, each is an individual – there is no sense of 'a class'. Indeed, it will be remembered that 'the class' forms a signifier in contrastive opposition to 'the child'. In this way, examining both the texts and practices themselves, it is possible to produce a reading of the pedagogy. There is no pre-existing object, 'the real child' which the discourses and practices fail to represent or describe adequately. If they are points of production, they have positive and not simply negative effects. In this sense they are our 'raw material', the 'real' of a child is not something which can be known outside those practices in which its subjectivity is constituted. The signified only forms a sign out of fusion with the signifier. The signifier exists as a relation within a discourse. The material can only be known as a relation within a discursive practice. To say, therefore, that 'the child' is a signifier means that it must be united with a signified. Particular children are subjected (that is, the practices regulate what they do) and they also therefore present behaviours to be read, as normal or pathological.

I have begun to explore what this might mean elsewhere (Walkerdine 1984), but here let me take the analysis a little further, using the distinctions *work* and *play*, *rote-learning/rule-following*, and *real understanding*. *Work* forms a relation in the 'old discourse'. In the new, children learn through doing, activity, and *play*. For example, the whole of the scheme *Early Mathematical Experiences* is founded upon play as a device for mathematics learning:

> To fulfil the aim of the EME project, many teachers pooled their experiences and ideas, helping in the collection and revision of materials for the booklets. Their suggestions and experiences were co-ordinated by a small project team who also spent time observing teachers and their assistants at work with young children. It was found that there were many different methods of presenting activities and learning situations to the children, but these could be grouped loosely into four main categories:
>
> 1. Children playing freely with as many activities and materials as possible, without adult intervention.
> 2. Children playing with materials which have been deliberately provided by teachers to encourage the acquisition of certain concepts, but still without adult intervention.
> 3. Children playing with materials of their own choice with the active participation of an adult.
> 4. Children playing with materials which have been selected by a teacher who was leading and guiding them towards the acquisition of certain facts.
>
> (Matthews and Matthews:1978)

Work forms an opposition of this. Work is bad because it relates to sitting in rows, regurgitating 'facts to be stored' not 'concepts to be acquired' through active exploration of the environment. Work, then, forms a metaphoric relation with rote-learning and rule-following. Each describes a practice, a mode of learning which is opposite and antithetical to the 'joy of discovery'. Play is fun. There are also other aspects of work which could be further elaborated – for example, it leads to resistance. Children regulated in this way do not become self-regulating (Walkerdine 1984, 1985a). But *work* is also a category to be outlawed by a system of education set up in opposition to child labour. It constitutes a category which frees 'the child' to be something distinct, playful, not an adult, outside the field of productive labour, innocent, natural. Related, therefore, is a series of values, fantasies, fears, desires which are incorporated into the discursive practices. These are multiple significations, connecting, weaving in and out of different discursive practices. It follows that *work*, as constituted as an opposite of *play*, can be recognized as a difference, as everything which does not signify play. It is also recognized as a danger-point, a point to be avoided. It is pathologized. It is learning by the wrong means. It is not 'natural' to 'the child'. If any child is observed 'doing work' this is likely to be understood as a problem. Hence the distinction between 'rote-learning' and 'real understanding', and the fear of the teacher in Chapter 8 that Michael's strategy appeared to offer no evidence of 'real understanding'.

First, what happens when a child produces high attainment as well as producing behaviour to be read as *work*? If play is the discourse of the school, through what discourse do children read their performance? If 'real understanding' is coterminous with the fantasy of possession of total power and control, how is it distinguished and what is the relation of this to 'getting the right answer', 'being certain', etc. How does *possession* of *real understanding* provide a fantasy, a chimera which has to be constantly and continually provided to exist out of a terror that looking around every corner is its Other, rote-learning, work? Why is there such pressure, remorseless and unrelenting, to 'prove' that real understanding causes real attainment, and moreover that certain children have 'it' and that others just so surely do not, despite high attainment? What is invested?

I have made the point elsewhere, in relation to judgements of girls' performance (Walkerdine 1985b) that one of the features of the apparatuses and technologies of the social, the modern production of truth through science, is that *proof* and practices for the production of evidence, as in my own work, are central to the production of a truth. The certainty of 'real understanding' is ceaselessly proved in practices, even though the evidence is often ambiguous. Here I want not so much to dwell on the evidence itself, as to question the motivation to provide proof, in particular of the opposition of work and play, rote and real. The particular aspect of this which I have examined in some detail relates to gender (see also Walden and Walkerdine 1985).

Now if the power of control over the universe invested in mathematical discourse is a fantasy, I am not setting out to demonstrate the *real* of the proof that girls *really can* do maths or boys actually do not have real understanding. Rather, it is how those categories are produced as signs that I am interested in and how they 'catch up' the subjects, position them, and in positioning create a truth. For is not girls' bid for 'understanding' the greatest threat of all to a universal power or a truth that is invested in a fantasy of control of 'woman'? Teachers will often go to great lengths to demonstrate that boys have real understanding. By the metaphoric chain created, *activity* is frequently read as a sign of understanding. Understanding, then, is evidenced by the presence of some attributes and the absence of others. Activity – playing, utilization of objects (Lego, for example), rule-breaking (rather than following) – can encompass naughtiness to the point of displays of hostility and conflict towards the teacher. All of these and more are taken to be evidence. Conversely, good behaviour in girls – working hard, helpfulness, neat and careful work – are all read as danger signs of a lack. The counter-evidence – hard work in boys and understanding in girls – is also produced as evidence, but when it is, other positions come into play (see Walkerdine 1985b).

Evidence of real understanding, therefore, depends first upon a set of practices in which real understanding is the goal of an explicit framework of the 'activities' set up, as in all of the examples given in this book. Second, readings are made possible that the correct accomplishment is the result of understanding, and failure produced through a lack of requisite experience, readiness, concepts. Third, the likelihood of favouring one explanation of success over another depends upon other characteristics which define a real learner (Walkerdine 1985b, 1986c). Fourth, complex investment of desire would seem to be implicated in proving the presence or absence of certain qualities. I shall only refer here to evidence which is, in fact, presented elsewhere. Despite their relatively good performance in the early years (Walden and Walkerdine 1982; Walkerdine, Walden, and Owen 1987) there are massive attempts to attribute girls' success to rule-following and rote-learning. Conversely, boys frequently do not achieve terribly well and yet evidence of failure itself is produced as evidence in support of understanding.

Later, in secondary school, this is carried to such elaborate lengths that in one comprehensive school in which we worked (Walden and Walkerdine 1985) boys were frequently entered for 'O' level despite their poor attainment in 'mock' examinations while girls were excluded despite their good performance. Let us examine further what such girls and boys do in the classroom and how their teachers' readings are produced. In the early years, as I have suggested, certain aspects are taken as evidence of understanding. In secondary school this is taken further. Naughtiness becomes more specific. While conflict and rule-challenging provide proof of masculinity, only that directed at the overthrow of the discourse itself, the teacher's right to 'mastery', provides the evidence of possession of 'it', understanding of the logos. Thus competing claims to masculinity are set up – pro and anti school – which to a certain extent contradict each other (see Willis 1978). However, it is specifically overt challenges to the teachers' authority, power over the knowledge, which are validated and hailed by teachers as evidence of real understanding or 'brains', 'brilliance', and so forth. The children who display such behaviour are overtly attacking. The behaviour is most obvious in class lessons. The challenging is difficult for it threatens the teacher's control and yet simultaneously provides the desired evidence. The destruction of the Other through rational argument is the shaky price paid (Walkerdine 1985b).

Possession of the Phallus is simultaneously its public ownership and overthrowing of the Other. The children who succeed without such displays, in school, are *never* given the accolade 'brilliant'. Their success is caused by 'hard work'. That is, such children present behaviour which is threatening, since it provides none of the signs which suggest activity, such as overt challenges, and yet, which produces successful work. It presents 'danger-signs' – the right result in the wrong way. Such behaviour must act as a continuous threat to the 'proof' of 'real understanding'.

Within the practice, the teachers' power is constituted in relation to the management of the classroom and of the knowledge itself, the double-meaning captured in the term 'discipline', which Foucault (1979a) has made much of. One of the central features of the logico-mathematical discourse is the production of formal logic, modes of making a case, constructing an argument: rational argument. This requires the reduction of the discourse of the kind I have described elsewhere in relation to mathematics: everything except the central form of the string, with its empty and metonymic signifiers, is suppressed. An argument therefore has as its component apparently the ultimate in rationality, conducted by equal partners – power produced through the winning mode of argument: the mastery of its form. Yet, as I have tried to elaborate, it is replete with conflict, the destruction of the Other is both feared and desired. It is a necessary component, but one which is removed from the form and content of the discourse itself. It is a contest for control, a struggle for power. In these accounts of the production of rational argument relating to home and early education, a central component to the production of the 'capacity' for rational argument is the mode of control of conflict (Walkerdine and Lucey, in press).

The old methods of rigid, hierarchical organization and overt discipline were to give way to a more invisible form of power in which overt conflict between teacher – or parent – and child becomes displaced onto rational argument, in which a central trope is the 'illusion of control' (Newson and Newson 1976). More and more the practices centre on the rendering invisible of the power relation, and of offering to the child within the practice an elaborate fantasy of omnipotence, mastery, control. The Newsons state this as engineering disciplinary conflicts such that the child believes itself to have 'chosen' the solution, rather than its external imposition. Conflict becomes 'feelings'. The child is so positioned within the practice as to have not 'seen' power, and believes itself the originator, controller of its actions, its choice. It is a powerful illusion, an illusion of choice and control over one's destiny taken to be centrally implicated in producing the possibility of 'rational argument'. This becomes a further displacement such that power is invested in the 'winning' of the argument. The child is rationally ordered and can rationally order in return. There is no 'authority' outside the mastery of the form of the discourse itself. This is vital. For it is central to the modern pedagogic practices of 'disciplining' and means that regulation can be accomplished by rational argument. The teacher's power, then, is invested in that mastery. It is a denial of hierarchy, of policing, of government, except through mastery. Challenging the claim to know is thereby central. However, it seems to me that it requires certain key features. First, the learner must recognize, or join in, the illusion of choice and control. Second, the learner must feel secure in making a challenge to authority which is also replete with conflict. S/he must therefore not be afraid, but rather welcome such a challenge. The first and second criteria form a central part of modern discursive practices: the illusion of choice, of security and safety, are key features of what is taken to be correct classroom life.

The positioning of pupils' readings of the practices, the construction of their identities, was not the object of this book. That it is profoundly gendered and divided by class and race is clear. The bourgeois universal subject turns out to be very specific indeed! (For a fuller discussion of data relating to these issues see Walkerdine and Lucey, in press, and Walkerdine (ed.) *Girls and Mathematics*, forthcoming.)

Some concluding remarks

Arithmetic was the fundamental tool of the Industrial Revolution. Its makers saw it as a series of sums of addition and subtraction. The difference is lost between buying in the cheapest market place and selling in the dearest, between investment and return. For Jeremy Bentham and his followers, the most consistent champion of this type of rationality, even morals and politics came under these simple calculations.

(Hobsbawm 1968:69)

The avalanche of numbers after 1820 revealed an astonishing regularity in the statistics of crime, suicide, workers' sickness, epidemics, biological facts. Mathematicians attempted an analysis of such phenomena. Poisson invented the term 'law of large numbers' in 1835 as the name of a mathematical fact, that irregularities in mass phenomena would fade out if enough data were collected. Although the term 'law of large numbers' is a standard probability in mathematics, Poisson's first usage was the analysis of jury trials.

(Hacking 1981:20)

Nothing could seem more apolitical, more cognitive, perhaps more boring, than analysing children's learning of mathematics. But, as I have tried to demonstrate, the calculating mind and calculating the child are as one. It is my contention that the modern order is founded upon a rational, scientific, and calculating form of government, a government which claims to describe and control nature, according to natural laws. Thus mathematics can be understood as absolutely central to the production of this order. Not only did psychology, linguistics, and child development lay claims to calibrate and describe the real child in minute detail, but they also claimed mathematics as fundamental.

Although the history of childhood offers us ample exemplars of the creation of 'the child' (eg Aries 1973; Hoskin, n.d.; Rose 1985), I have been interested in the rational cognitivism that has so recently been invested in children. Teaching children to read and write proved not to be enough to stamp out rebellion. The liberal order of choice and free will had to be created by inventing a natural childhood which could be produced and regulated in the most invisible of ways. Mathematics became reason.

Not only did mathematics become reasoning and cognitive development, but language became the universals of language development; form and meaning as universals. There is no space here to examine the production of standard languages and their place in the creation of modern government (but see Cohen 1979; Balibar 1974; Hoskin, n.d.; Rose 1985). However, it was here that meanings were prised out of practices and made to operate according to natural laws.

In this book, I have tried to tell a story which attempts to rethink how we might understand linguistic and cognitive development and their relation to pedagogic practices – in this case the learning of mathematics. That story is at once material and discursive and about signifying practices. Moreover, I have sought to demonstrate that we cannot understand such an account outside of the fantasies described in the search for total control. This suggests that issues of pleasure, desire, and anxiety are important aspects of the production of a discourse which involves the suppression and repression of aspects of signification which are central to non-mathematical practices. I want finally to point to a number of ways in which the kind of analysis I have begun might be developed.

The majority of work within developmental psychology and psycholinguistics takes 'language' to be a transhistorical, bounded linguistic system of structural linguistics. However, it is important to examine the attempts to demonstrate that signification is socially and historically specific. Much modern semiotic work, for example in literary and cultural studies, owes its foundation to the work of Roland Barthes (1972), and there have been some recent attempts to incorporate this understanding into developmental psycho-linguistics (for example, Sinha, in press). In addition to this, the work of the Russian linguist Volosinov (1973) and the related literary work of Bahktin (1981) provide important points for exploration of the relation between the material and the discursive. But, in addition to this, there is work which suggests clearly that what we now understand as 'natural language' is an historically produced phenomenon. Specifically, it is argued that the codification of language is part of attempts towards rational government, and especially the political necessity of producing a governable nation out of disparate groups. While it would be important to chart those shifts, for the purposes of theories about young children it is vital to understand that what is now unproblematically regarded as the study of the 'acquisition of natural language' is the examination of an historically and socially specific set of practices. It can be argued that 'natural language' is imposed on young children and, moreover, related to the emergence of mass schooling and mass literacy (Hoskin n.d.; Rose 1985). If this is the case, 'the natural' and the normal become categories which are discursively produced and cover a pathologization, which is evident in the debates, from linguistic deprivation to sociolinguistics (see Walkerdine 1986b). It is significant that in this debate – class and race specific as it is – it is mothers who are held responsible for the emergence of the 'natural'.

To understand this state of affairs we must examine the emergence of modern family forms and specifically the rise of the bourgeoisie and proletariat in the nineteenth century. Yet the debates about children's development at home and school often unproblematically assume not only the presence of mothers, but compare mothering practices across class and race, and moreover attempt to define the mother's effectiveness as a pedagogue (Tizard and Hughes 1984). Yet when did the mother become a pedagogue? To understand this we must also chart a history of the emergence of a particular definition of mothers' responsibilities for the rearing of children related to a system of compulsory schooling until sixteen (Riley 1982; Urwin 1985). Such practices are quite unlike the aristocratic practices of leaving children to servants (Steedman 1985).

Such details may seem peripheral to those engaged in the study of development, but they are vital if we are to begin to understand the historically and politically specific production of 'the truth' about children. Moreover, it is only by taking apart these truths that we can construct the possibility of a different account. Indeed, not only is such a history important for the study of 'language', it is also necessary in relation to 'Reason'. The history of practices of calculation and the emergence of forms of government in the nineteenth century relating to calculations of the population are very important for our story (Cline-Cohen 1982; Hacking 1981). 'Political Arithmetic' was an attempt to use arithmetic techniques to calculate those aspects of the population which could then be amenable to scientific forms of government. Foucault (1979a) has documented the emergence of a whole ensemble of technologies of administration premised on such sciences. It is my contention, following this, that practices of schooling now began to produce a new professional class – an educated bourgeoisie who could calculate and reason scientifically – and a proletariat who would be reasonable in order to be governed. If we examine modern schooling practices, the emergence of 'brilliance' as 'reason', and the necessity for the correction of pathology as the lack of autonomy, self-control, and regulation, this story begins to have some substance. If this is so, it puts the study of cognitive development and the relation of development to schooling in quite another light.

I have argued elsewhere (Walkerdine 1984) that in the child-centred pedagogy, discipline shifted from visible to invisible (Bernstein 1975), overt to covert regulation. At first, power was visible, vested in the presence of the authority of the teacher, but within child-centred pedagogy power became diffuse and subversive. The 'free' child was more highly observed, regulated, and monitored than ever before (Rose 1985). Yet this child was not to recognize the criteria for regulation. Power then became the overthrow of the Other in rational argument – the teacher's claim to know. I submit that such power is essential to the new profession of reasoners and that the fantasy inherent in 'Reason's Dream', an idealized and calculable universe, is part and parcel of the dream of rational government. The dream, therefore, is not just a wild and crazy dream of playing God, but a fantasy invested in current attempts to govern through bourgeois democracy. Its concomitant is the rise in the 'caring professions' to render the governed governable.

Compare this fantasy of power, then, with the pleasure of wish-fulfilment – of endless food and wealth, as with the children in the shopping game, or the pleasure in 'being top' and 'beating' (with its sadomasochistic connotations) of the children doing their work in Chapter 9. Such pleasures, fantasies, and powers are the fantasies of the oppressed in a system which denies them wealth and power. Only the reasoners, then, achieve the accolade. Yet the mathematics educators, with their belief in the natural intrinsic motivation of 'order and purity', can only pathologize those whose fantasies are located elsewhere. But where else can we look, how else can we understand this, except as a socially- and politically-specific question in an unequal and divisive social order? I suggest that those concerned with a critical position in developmental psychology must engage with such questions, for they are crucial for a practice which does not simply seek to describe the status quo as natural, but works towards the possibility of transformation. Psychologists can no longer stand on the sidelines with a belief that natural child development is either politically neutral or politically progressive.

The fantasies of plenty and of power cover over the gap left by pain and anxiety. In the examples I gave of lexical development (see Chapter 2) the regulation of the domestic economy was central to understanding the comprehension and production of terms concerned with quantity (more) and money, for example. It is here that several issues not developed in this volume become pertinent. It is women as mothers who are largely held responsible for the regulation of the domestic economy. It would not be surprising, therefore, to find difficulties between a mother attempting to manage all-too-scarce resources and a daughter who blamed her for not being good enough. The mother is not the source of power or deprivation, but is positioned in this way and may seem so to young girls (and the memories of grown women so replete with images of bad mothering) (Walkerdine and Lucey, in press).

But if mothers are *positioned* as responsible for resources and for pedagogy, what is experienced as *caused* by them is to be located in the social, historical, and political positioning of them there in the first place. By examining the effects of poverty and wealth, mental and manual labour upon domestic regulation, we can begin to understand how girls and boys themselves become positioned (and develop anxieties and pleasures) through the fusion of signifier and signified within the practices themselves.

Much is to be gained by an analysis of the specificity of signification in the production of particular subjectivities. When we approach the crossing of boundaries from one practice to another, home to school, the anxieties and pleasures produced by being a 'big' or 'sensible' girl seem directly related to whether the girl is so positioned in school. This means, apart from anything else, that there can no longer be a unitary category 'the child', let alone 'girl', or 'boy'. If class and race, poverty and wealth, mental and manual labour produce differently regulated practices, then it is important to examine a multiplicity of subjectivities produced in such conditions.

I would argue that every aspect of lexical development, for example, is amenable to such an analysis and moreover can be related to domestic, school, and work practice. It would also be important to examine how women become positioned as quasi-mothers within the caring professions and how, within teaching, this renders them opposite to, and yet responsible for, the reasoning children they are supposed to produce. In this position they become the Other of the professional reasoners. They are the bourgeois professional nurturers who are there to correct faulty nurturing on the part of proletarian mothers.

All of these ideas form the basis of other possible stories. They are stories which remain to be told, narratives yet to be constructed. The stories are at once historical, social, linguistic, and psychological. And they cannot be separated from a politics which demands their telling. If we are to remove ourselves from the pinnacle of omnipotence on which we as psychologists sit, all-seeing, making scientific pronouncements upon the nature of the child, then must we not also begin to leave off our cloak of respectability? The scientist's story is invested in a fantasy of what it is desired to prove and therefore what must be kept in check. In many places psychologists are struggling to tell other stories – stories of women, of blacks – stories of marginality which refuse to celebrate the child but will no longer be silent.

References

Adlam, D., Henriques, J., Rose, N., Salfield, A., Venn, C., and Walkerdine, V. (1977) 'Psychology, ideology and the human subject', *Ideology and Consciousness*, 1.

Althusser, L. (1971) *Lenin and Philosophy and Other Essays*, New York and London: Monthly Review Press.

Aries, P. (1973) *Centuries of Childhood*, Harmondsworth: Penguin.

Bahktin, M. M. (1981) *The Dialogic Imagination*, Austin, Texas: University of Texas Press.

Balibar, R. (1974) *Les Français fictifs*, Paris: Hachette.

Barnes, D. (1969) *Language, the Learner and the School*, Harmondsworth: Penguin.

Barthes, R. (1972) *Mythologies*, London: Paladin.

Bernstein, B. (1975) *Class, codes, and control*, vol. 1, London: Routledge & Kegan Paul.

Beveridge, M. (ed.) (1982) *Children Thinking Through Language*, London: Edward Arnold.

Bierwisch, M. (1970) 'Semantics', in J. Lyons (ed.) *New Horizons in Linguistics*, Harmondsworth, Penguin.

Brown, R. (1973) *A First Language: the early stages*, Cambridge, Mass.: Harvard University Press.

Bruner, J. S. (1975) 'From communication to language: a psychological perspective', *Cognition* 3:255–87.

Burgin, V., Donald, J., and Kaplan, C. (eds) (1986) *Formations of Fantasy*, London: Methuen.

Clark, E. (1973) 'What's in a word? On the child's acquisition of semantics in his first language', in T. E. Moore (ed.) *Cognitive Development in the Acquisition of Language*, New York: Academic Press.

Cline-Cohen, P. (1982) *A Calculating People: the spread of numeracy in early America*, Chicago: University of Chicago Press.

Coghill, V. (1978) *Infant School Reasoning*, Teachers' Research Group, unpublished mimeo.

Cohen, M. (1979) *Sensible Words*, Baltimore, Maryland: Johns Hopkins University Press.

Cole, M. (1981) *Mind, Society and Development*, San Diego, California: Center for Information Processing, mimeo.

Cole, M. and Scribner, S. (1974) *Culture and Thought: a psychological perspective*, London: Wiley.

Cole, M. and Traupmann, K. (1979) 'Learning from a Learning Disabled Child', Minnesota Symposium of Child Development, unpub.

Corran, G. and Walkerdine, V. (1981) 'Cognitive development: a mathematical experience?' paper presented at The British Psychological Society Conference

Corran, G. and Walkerdine, V. (1982) *The Practice of Reason: investigations into the teaching and learning of mathematics in the early years of schooling*, University of London Institute of Education, mimeo.

Cowie, E. (1978) 'Woman as sign', *m/f* 1:49–64.

DES (Department of Education and Science) (1967) *Children and their Primary Schools* (The Plowden Report), London: HMSO.

Dienes, Z. P. (1960) *Building Up Mathematics*, London: Hutchinson.

Donaldson, M. (1978) *Children's Minds*, London: Fontana.

Donaldson, M. and Wales, R. J. (1970) 'On the acquisition of some relational terms', in J. R. Hayes (ed.) *Communication and the Development of Language*, London: Wiley.

Estes, K. W. (1976) 'Non-verbal discrimination of more and fewer elements by children', *Journal of Experimental Child Psychology* 21:393–405.

Fletcher, H. (1970) *Mathematics for Schools*, London: Addison-Wesley.

Foucault, M. (1979a) *Discipline and Punish*, Harmondsworth: Penguin.

Foucault, M. (1979b) 'On governmentality', *Ideology and Consciousness* 6: 5–21.

Freud, S. (1920) *Beyond the Pleasure Principle* (standard edition, vol. XVIII), London: Hogarth Press.

Freud, S. (1937) 'Analysis terminable and interminable', *Complete Psychological Works of Sigmund Freud* (standard edition, vol. XVIII), London: Hogarth Press.

Gelman, R., and Gallistel, C. R. (1978) *The Child's Understanding of Number*, Cambridge, Mass.: Harvard University Press.

Glucksberg, S., Hay, A., and Danks, J. (1976) 'Words in utterance contexts: your children do not confuse the meaning of "same" and "different"', *Child Development*, 47, 737–41.

Grieve, R., Hoogenrad, R., and Murray, D. (1977) 'On the young child's use of lexis and syntax in understanding locative instructions', *Cognition* 5:235–50.

Gruber, H. and Voneche, J. J. (1977) *The Essential Piaget*, London: Routledge & Kegan Paul.

Hacking, I. (1981) 'How should we do the history of statistics?' *Ideology and Consciousness* 8:15–26.

Hayes, J. R. (ed.) (1970) *Communication and the Development of Language*, London: Wiley.

Henriques, J., Hollway, W., Urwin, C., Venn, C., and Walkerdine, V. (1984) *Changing the Subject: Psychology, social regulation and subjectivity*, London: Methuen.

Hirst, P. Q. (1976) 'Althusser and the theory of ideology', *Economy and Society* 5(4):385–412.

Hobsbawm, E. (1968) *Industry and Empire*, Harmondsworth: Penguin.

Holland, V. M. and Palermo, D. S. (1975) 'On learning "less": language and cognitive development', *Child Development* 46:437–43.

Hood, L., McDermott, R., and Cole, M. (1978) '"Let's try to make it a good day": some not so simple ways', paper presented at the Centre for Psycho-Social Studies Conference.

Hoskin, K. (n.d.) *Cobwebs to Catch Flies: writing (and) the child*, University of Warwick, mimeo.

Howe, C. (1981) *Acquiring Language in a Conversational Context*, London: Academic Press.

Howson, A. G. (1978) 'Changes in mathematical education since the late 1950s', *Educational Studies in Mathematics 9*.

Hughes, M. (1981) 'Can pre-school children add and subtract?', British Journal of Educational Psychology 1 (3):207–19.

Hughes, M. and Grieve, R. (1980) 'On asking children bizarre questions', *First Language* 1:149–60.

Jakobson, R. and Halle, M. (1956) *Fundamentals of Language*, The Hague: Mouton.

Karmiloff-Smith, E. A. (1977) 'More about the same: children's understanding of post-articles', *Journal of Child Language* 4:377–94.

Kavanaugh, R. B. (1976) 'On the synonymity of "more" and "less": comments on a methodology', *Child Development* 47:885–7.

Kline, M. (1953) *Mathematics in Western Culture*, Harmondsworth: Penguin.

Laboratory for Comparative Human Cognition (1980) *Culture and Cognitive Development*, mimeo.

Labov, W. (1969) 'The logic of non-standard English', *Georgetown Monographs on Language and Linguistics* 22:1–31.

Lacan, J. (1977) *Ecrits: a selection*, London: Tavistock.

Lee, D.M. (1962) *A Background to Mathematical Development*, London: Oldbourne.

Lévi-Strauss, C. (1969) *The Elementary Structures of Kinship*, London: Eyre & Spottiswoode.

Lieven, E. (1978) 'Conversations between mothers and young children: individual differences and their possible implications for the study of language development', in N. Waterson and C. Snow (eds) *The Development of Communication*, London: Wiley.

Lieven, E. (1982) 'Contexts, process and progress in young children's speech', in M. Beveridge (ed.) *Children Thinking Through Language*, London: Edward Arnold.

Lock, A. (1978) *Action, Gesture and Symbol*, London: Academic Press.

McCabe, C. (ed.) (1981) *The Talking Cure: essays in psychoanalysis and language*, London: Macmillan.

MacLure, M. and French, P. (1981) 'A comparison of talk at home and at school', in G. Wells (ed.), *Learning Through Interaction*, Cambridge: Cambridge University Press.

Maier, E. (1980) 'Folk mathematics', *Mathematics Teaching* 93.

Mathematical Association (1956) *The Teaching of Mathematics in Primary Schools*, London.

Matthews, G. and Matthews, J. (1978) *Early Mathematical Experiences*, London: Schools Council/Addison-Wesley.

220 The Mastery of Reason

Mitchell, J. and Rose, J. (eds) (1982) *Jacques Lacan and the Ecole Freudienne: feminine sexuality*, London: Routledge & Kegan Paul.

Newson, J. and Newson, E. (1976) *Seven Years Old in an Urban Community*, Harmondsworth: Penguin.

Olson, D. (1977) 'From utterance to text: the bias of language in speech and writing', *Harvard Educational Review* 47:251–81.

Paz, O. (1985) *The Labyrinth of Solitude*, Harmondsworth: Penguin.

Pecheux, M. (1982) *Language, Semantics and Ideology*, London: Macmillan.

Piaget, J. (1920) 'Psycho-analysis and its relation with child psychology', in H. Gruber and J. J. Voneche (1977) *The Essential Piaget*, London: Routledge & Kegan Paul.

Piaget, J. (1926) *Language and Thought of the Child*, London: Routledge & Kegan Paul.

Piaget, J. (1952) *The Child's Conception of Number*, London: Routledge & Kegan Paul.

Riley, D. (1982) *War In The Nursery*, London: Virago.

Rose, J. (1985) 'Peter Pan, language and the state', in C. Steedman, C. Urwin, and V. Walkerdine (eds) *Language, Gender and Childhood*, London: Routledge & Kegan Paul.

Rose, J. and Blank, M. (1974) 'The potency of context in children's cognition: an illustration through conservation', *Child Development* 45:499–502.

Rotman, B. (1980) *Mathematics: an essay in semiotics*, University of Bristol, mimeo.

Russell, B. (1964) *Principles of mathematics* (2nd edn), New York: Norton.

Samuel, R. (1983) *People's History and Socialist Theory*, London: Routledge & Kegan Paul.

Saussure, F. de (1974) *Course in General Linguistics*, London: Fontana.

Schools Council (1965) *Mathematics in Primary Schools*, London.

Scribner, S. and Cole, M. (1981) *The Psychology of Literacy*, Cambridge, Mass.: Harvard University Press.

Sewell, B. (1981) The use of Mathematics by adults in daily life, Leicester: Enquiry Officer's Report, Advisory Council for Adult and Continuing Education.

Sinha, C. (1980) 'Functionalism, semiotics and language acquisition', British Psychological Society Developmental Section Conference, Edinburgh.

Sinha, C. (in press) *Language and Representation: a socio-naturalistic approach to human development*, Brighton: Harvester Press.

Sinha, C. and Carabine, B. (1980) 'Interactions between lexis and discourse in conversation and comprehension tasks', *Journal of Child Language* 8:109–29.

Sinha, C. and Walkerdine, V. (1978) 'Conversation: a problem in language, culture and thought', in N. Waterson and C. Snow (eds) *The Development of Communication*, London: Wiley.

Snow, C. (1977) 'The development of conversation between mothers and babies', *Journal of Child Language* 4:1–22.

Steedman, C. (1980) *The Tidy House*, London: Virago.

Steedman, C. (1985) 'The mother made conscious', *History Workshop Journal* 20:151–63.

Steedman, C., Urwin, C., and Walkerdine, V. (eds) (1985) *Language, Gender and Childhood*, London: Routledge & Kegan Paul.

Thom, M. (1981) 'The unconscious structured like a language', in C. McCabe (ed.) *The Talking Cure: essays in psychoanalysis and language*, London: Macmillan.

Tizard, B. and Hughes, M. (1984) *Young Children Learning*, London: Fontana.

Trehub, S. E. and Abramovitch, R. (1978) 'Less is not more: further observations on non-linguistic strategies', *Journal of Experimental Child Psychology* 25:160–7.

Urwin, C. (1982) 'The contribution of non-visual communication systems and language to knowing oneself', in M. Beveridge (ed.) *Children Thinking Through Language*, London: Edward Arnold.

Urwin, C. (1984) 'Power relations and the emergence of language', in J. Henriques et al., *Changing the Subject*, London: Methuen.

Urwin, C. (1985) 'Constructing motherhood: the persuasion of normal development', in C. Steedman, C. Urwin, and V. Walkerdine, *Language, Gender and Childhood*, London: Routledge & Kegan Paul.

Varnava-Skouras, G. (1981) 'Children's ideologies, forces in the reproduction and transformation of societies: a cross-cultural study', *Final Report to the SSRC*, London: Institute of Education.

Volosinov, V. N. (1973) *Marxism and the Philosophy of Language*, New York: Seminar Press.

Vygotsky, L. S. (1962) *Thought and Language*, Cambridge, Mass.: MIT Press.

Vygotsky, L. S. (1978) *Mind in Society*, Cambridge, Mass.: Harvard University Press.

Walden, R. and Walkerdine, V. (1982) *Girls and Mathematics: the early years*, Bedford Way Papers 8, University of London Institute of Education.

Walden, R. and Walkerdine, V. (1985) *Girls and Mathematics: from primary to secondary schooling*, Bedford Way Papers 26, University of London Institute of Education.

Walkerdine, V. (1975) 'Spatial and Temporal Relations in the Linguistic and Cognitive Development of Young Children', unpublished Ph.D. thesis, University of Bristol.

Walkerdine, V. (1981) 'Sex, power and pedagogy', *Screen Education* 38: 14–25.

Walkerdine, V. (1982) 'From context to text: a psycho-semiotic account of abstract thought', in M. Beveridge (ed.) *Children Thinking Through Language*, London: Edward Arnold.

Walkerdine, V. (1984) 'Developmental psychology and the child-centred pedagogy', in J. Henriques et al., *Changing the Subject*, London: Methuen.

Walkerdine, V. (1985a) 'On the regulation of speaking and silence', in C. Steedman, C. Urwin, and V. Walkerdine (eds) *Language, Gender and Childhood*, London: Routledge & Kegan Paul.

Walkerdine, V. (1985b) 'Science and the female mind: the burden of proof', *Psych-Critique* 1 (1).

Walkerdine, V. (1986a) *Surveillance, Subjectivity and Struggle: lessons from pedagogic and domestic practices*, Minneapolis: University of Minnesota Press.

Walkerdine, V. (1986b) 'Video replay: families, films and fantasy', in V.

Burgin, J. Donald, and C. Kaplan (eds) *Formations of Fantasy*, London: Methuen.

Walkerdine, V. (1986c) 'Post-structuralist theory in everyday social practices: the family and the school', in S. Wilkinson (ed.) *Feminist Social Psychology*, Milton Keynes: Open University Press.

Walkerdine, V. (ed.) (forthcoming) *Girls and Mathematics: new thoughts on an old question*, London: Virago.

Walkerdine, V. and Corran, G. (1981) 'Experience and discourse in early mathematics learning', Piaget and the Helping Professions Conference, Los Angeles.

Walkerdine, V. and Lucey, H. (in press) *Democracy in the Kitchen? the regulation of mothers and the socialization of daughters*, London: Virago.

Walkerdine, V., Walden, R., and Owen, C. (1987) 'Some methodological issues in the interpretation of data relating to girls' performance in mathematics', *Equal Opportunities Research Bulletin* 10.

Walkerdine, V. and Watson, D. (forthcoming) *Young Girls and Popular Culture* (working title).

Waterson, N. and Snow, C. (eds) (1978) *The Development of Communication*, London: Wiley.

Wells, G. (ed.) (1982) *Learning Through Interaction*, Cambridge: Cambridge University Press.

Wilden, A. (1980) *System and Structure* (2nd edn), London: Tavistock.

Williams, E. M. and Shuard, H. (1976) *Primary Mathematics Today*, Harlow: Longman.

Willis, P. (1978) *Learning to Labour*, London: Saxon House.

Index